LOOKING
INTO
MIND

Paul Damiani (rear) and Anthony Damiani

LOOKING INTO MIND

How to Recognize Who You Are and How You Know

Conversations with
ANTHONY DAMIANI

PUBLISHED FOR THE PAUL BRUNTON PHILOSOPHIC FOUNDATION BY
Larson Publications

International Standard Book Number: 0–943914–50–7
Library of Congress Catalog Card Number: 90–61197

Published for the
Paul Brunton Philosophic Foundation by
Larson Publications
4936 Route 414
Burdett, New York 14818

94 93
10 9 8 7 6 5 4 3 2

Photo page ii courtesy of Jan Hallén

Contents

Dedicated to

Richard S. "Red" Witter

1928–1993

About This Book

Looking into Mind is an edited transcription of a series of informative and inspiring conversations about discovering, consciously developing, and living by the deepest intelligence of one's own mind. It will be especially valuable for anyone with a self-reliant nature and a yearning for a nobler and more satisfying experience of the self, the world, and their relationship.

In 1983, Swedish author and translator Anna Prim Bornstein invited American philosopher Anthony Damiani to speak with a group of her friends about the opportunities and problems of independent truth-seeking. Anthony accepted her invitation and traveled to Sweden with his son Paul for a three-week visit. During his time there, he led an intensive series of lively discussions over a period of ten days.

These conversations focus on what Anthony considered the most indispensable elements of any approach to truth about reality: getting a direct experience of the core of one's own mind, seeing how it transforms one's own being into thoughts, and understanding the implications of that continuous experience. He considered this experience and understanding essential to establishing an authentically spiritual perspective and providing an unshakeable foundation for moral action, human virtue, and spiritual aspiration. He saw meditation and a proper understanding of the mind's role in constructing one's everyday environment as the most valuable tools for anyone seeking deeper contact with their own inner reality, especially those without regular access to a fully qualified spiritual teacher. And his main purpose was to put his Swedish friends on their own feet as quickly as possible.

From the practical side, these conversations show how to use meditation as a means to experience the mind directly, free of any imagery whatsoever. From the intellectual side, they give a compelling and accessible analysis of our everyday experience, suggesting that the environment we experience is intimately related to how we think and what we think about. Anthony presents this combined approach as the most direct route to reliable spiritual independence and immediate knowledge of one's own soul. In addition, he provides a wealth of practical information about the day-to-day process of claiming one's full humanity.

Though Anthony's work extends considerably beyond the scope of the material presented here, these conversations are an excellent introduction to several of his key ideas and his way of bringing them to life. His custom was to gather together, as a focus for discussion, a selection of writings that approached the same idea from different directions. Then he would guide the discussion in such a way as to develop a progressively deeper understanding of the central idea. He never lectured, choosing instead the Socratic approach of stimulating people to recognize the importance of the questions raised and to think about them together with him. He dealt with units of meaning, not with formal classifications, often "feeling" more than "thinking" his way into and through the ideas with the hope of awakening one's intuition. He was much more concerned that such discussions be "fertile" than "final," arousing one's own impulse to understand and get a more profound personal experience of the ideas. But he insisted on continually returning the discussion to the main points he hoped to bring to life, approaching points one step at a time and shelving more advanced issues until fundamental ones were understood.

In these particular conversations, Anthony draws extensively on writings from personal notebooks that Paul Brunton had reserved for posthumous publication. He made this selection for two reasons. First, many of the Swedish people he was speaking with had studied Paul Brunton's earlier works. Second, he felt that these notes were the most accessible and stimulating resources available for the topics he chose to focus on. His son Paul read notes that Anthony had marked out, then Anthony developed their meanings through discussion. We have not differentiated among the Swedish speakers, who are denoted as "S" in the text. Most of the notes referenced have since been published in *The Notebooks of Paul Brunton* series. In that sixteen-volume series, one or more of Paul Brunton's twenty-eight major "categories" (his main themes) appears in each volume.

The published notes are cited in the present book by volume number, category number, chapter number, and entry number. For example, V13, 21:2.146 means Volume 13 in the *Notebooks* series, category 21, chapter 2, entry number 146. A small number of the notes quoted here were not included in the published series, and are identified as "unpublished."

The conversations themselves are self-explanatory. Unfamiliar terms are sufficiently explained in the course of the discussion. Chapter titles are somewhat arbitrary, given that the discussion revolves primarily around two major themes; they were devised merely to give an indication of the main themes discussed there. For readers who would like more detail on specific topics, we have provided a list of supplementary readings at the end of the book.

About Anthony Damiani

For hundreds of us who met him in the 1960s and 1970s, Anthony Damiani (1922–1984) was a man of many facets, any one of which would have made him remarkable. But first and foremost he was a *man*—a vital, passionate, kind, and dynamic human being who revered life by living sincerely. He saw the meanings embedded in each person's experience as lines of a primordial scripture that one is born to embrace and understand—with and as one's whole being. His genius lay in piercing the secular veneer, uncovering these meanings, and awakening the heart to an awareness of the sacred song at their core. This was a process of giving birth to truth, not as a conceptual exercise but as an act of love, an exquisite expression of the proper relation between a soul and its source.

Anthony's mental energies were volcanic, as though surging upward from the very core of what compelled his attention. His burning desire to experience, understand, and express the undeniable significances of being human led him through a variety of life-experiences and specialized fields of study. When he discussed spiritual philosophy, he often seemed incandescent with enthusiasm about the value of what he had discovered and could share. But he had little regard for pretension either in himself or in others. While his generous spirit always encouraged us to be ourselves and supported each of us wholeheartedly in times of inner or outer personal difficulty, his penetrating gaze or mischievous humor soon deflated us when we became too puffed up about anything we thought we had learned. On first impression, he was the very antithesis of the conventional image of a spiritual teacher.

* * * * *

Anthony Damiani was born in 1922 into an Italian immigrant family on the Lower East Side of Manhattan, and grew up in

Brooklyn. As a child and young man, he suffered the fate of many a potentially deep thinker: his long silences were interpreted by teachers as indicating a learning deficiency and he was often placed among "slow learners" in his classes. Even then, he could not settle for surface appearances, pat answers to questions that were themselves too shallow, and read Plato secretly. His artistic nature first expressed itself in drawings and paintings that showed extraordinary sensitivity and perceptiveness.

Anthony spoke of two particular events from his youth that awakened him to the possibility of a higher life. One was when he first heard Schubert's *Quintet in C.* He said, "Once I heard that piece, I *knew* there was a heaven." The piece awakened in him a lifelong passion for inspired music and kindled a serious aspiration to become a classical pianist. The second came when he was watching a newsreel from India at a Brooklyn movie house. In the background of the main scene, he saw a yogi meditating on the sun. The image burned into his mind, and from that time forward learning the art of meditation became one of his main preoccupations.

He married his childhood sweetheart, and together they started a family which eventually included six sons. Though they had little money, he often spoke fondly in later life of how happy they were in their first Brooklyn flat. They had few domestic furnishings, having chosen instead to spend most of their earnings on inspiring books and a highly diversified collection of fine music.

Anthony held a variety of jobs, often two at a time. They included working as a waiter, then as a maitre d'hotel, spending nine years as a longshoreman on the New York docks, and managing a major New York City bookstore. He also took many classes in philosophy at Brooklyn College, CCNY, and the New School for Social Research, though he chose not to earn an academic degree. As his family grew in size, it became increasingly difficult for him to find the time and quiet to continue his self-directed studies in philosophy and mysticism while earning enough money to support the family. His solution was to start working nights as a token seller in a relatively slow section of the New York subway system; there he was able to pass the night immersed in the thoughts of Plotinus, Buddha, Shankara, Patanjali and many other great sages—and earn money at the same time.

Possibly the most important single event in Anthony's development was when he met the British philosopher Paul Brunton. From the day of their first meeting, Anthony felt that he had found his destined teacher. He was profoundly inspired by Paul Brunton's ability to integrate mystical philosophy and modern science into an approach to self-realization especially suited for the modern mind, and to express his findings in clear English. The breadth and depth of Paul Brunton's research, application, and personal achievement catalyzed Anthony's own desire for a comprehensive updating and philosophic synthesis of the wisdom—practical and spiritual—of both East and West.

But Paul Brunton took no students formally, describing himself as "a writer and researcher, with some experience in these matters . . . that is all." Anthony often had to be content with limited outer contact, making himself of service when appropriate, and acting primarily on the inspiration he drew from within himself from Paul Brunton's example and occasional explicit instructions. Nonetheless, a unique and very special relationship developed through the years between these two genuinely remarkable men as Anthony learned that the best way to venerate one's spiritual teacher is to work sincerely at becoming one's own best self. In his "retirement," Paul Brunton praised Anthony highly and often recommended him to people seeking help with their studies and personal development.

Shortly after meeting Paul Brunton, Anthony resolved to give up his study of the piano and focus his aspirations on meditation and philosophic studies. Listening to inspired music remained, however, an essential part of his inner development. Because music was for him more transparent than words as a vehicle of spiritual discovery, he often discovered his next guiding intuition through a piece of music, and integrated it deeply into his feelings before trying to approach it in an intellectual way. This practice was of such value to him that it later became an integral part of his teaching method.

The next major contribution to Anthony's development came through a detailed study of the great Neoplatonic sage Plotinus. In Plotinus' *Enneads*, Anthony found what he considered the most comprehensive extant statement of the metaphysical aspects of perennial philosophy, a teaching that complemented his understanding of Paul Brunton's writings and held out the promise of answering his remaining questions. His studies in Plotinus and related Platonic teachings continued for the rest of his life and formed the foundation of his own most important creative work.

In 1963, the Damiani family moved out of New York City to the

Finger Lakes region of upstate New York. One moving van contained their domestic possessions. Another was filled with books on philosophy and mysticism. Throughout his years of working in bookstores, Anthony had always taken first choice on any new or rare esoteric books. His collection was astonishing not only for its intrinsic breadth and quality, but also for the extensive underscoring and marginalia that testified to his thousands of hours of intensive study.

Upstate, Anthony took a night job as a toll-taker on the New York Thruway, a job that like his subway work allowed time to study. In 1967, he suffered a severe heart attack and experienced death. He said later that during those moments when he thought he was leaving life behind, his heart overflowed with love and tenderness for all living things. Though he had previously envisaged his new home as primarily a hermitage for retreat and study, harvesting the fruits of contemplation in relative solitude soon became unthinkable.

Later that year, he rented a small storefront in Ithaca, New York, and filled its shelves primarily with his own books. He kept his night job on the Thruway and spent most of his days in the store. This store, with a statue of the Buddha in the window, attracted inquisitive students and some teachers from Ithaca College and Cornell University, as well as many other people who just happened to be passing through town. The man inside soon legitimized and catalyzed our deepest spiritual urges.

In those days, Anthony was a dynamo. He slept only a few hours between getting off his night job at seven in the morning and leaving for the store shortly after noon. At first, only a steady trickle of people came to buy or borrow books and then returned to discuss them with Anthony. Soon, the number of us eager to discuss spiritual issues or learn the art of meditation with him grew large enough that informal evening classes began in the back room of the store. Anthony often wore his toll-taker's uniform while giving these classes, so that he could rush out at the last minute to drive fifty miles to make his 11:00 night shift on the Thruway. Within two years, his animated classes on Jung's psychology, Hinduism, Buddhism, Christian Scholasticism, Platonism, Paul Brunton's writings, and an exciting new approach to a genuinely spiritual astrology had attracted more people than the store could hold.

In 1972, Anthony and his wife Ella May donated five acres of their family land to what became the Wisdom's Goldenrod Center for

Philosophic Studies, and we built its first building ourselves. Through the next seven years, we built three more buildings as our needs grew organically, including an extensive library. The library was dedicated in 1979 by His Holiness the XIVth Dalai Lama of Tibet, who spent three days with the Wisdom's Goldenrod community on his first U.S. tour. The Dalai Lama praised Anthony's activities at Wisdom's Goldenrod as an excellent balance of the spiritual and the practical, and he spoke of Anthony himself as "a truly great man."

Throughout all the developments that took place after he opened the bookstore, Anthony took great pains to present himself as a fellow student, not a teacher, and he always taught without salary or payment of any kind. But after the Dalai Lama's visit, it became obvious even to Anthony that he had become, even if unwittingly, a spiritual teacher.

* * * * *

Anthony Damiani died in October, 1984. He left behind a variety of materials that merit publication, including numerous essays, a nearly completed book on philosophical symbolism, and a wide selection of recorded classes on how various spiritual issues are treated in different philosophical and religious traditions. The points he declined to pursue in detail in the Swedish discussions are developed in forthcoming material being prepared for publication here at Wisdom's Goldenrod. We chose the conversations in this book as the most widely accessible introduction to his work.

Special thanks from each of us go to the Damiani family, not only for their help in preparing this book and for granting us the rights to publish it, but much more importantly for sharing Anthony and themselves with us through all these years. Together we send this book into the world with the hope of sharing Anthony's inspiration toward individual integrity and global philosophic understanding. "If people who claim to be interested in spirituality can't find a harmony and make peace among themselves," he used to ask, "how will the politicians ever make peace?"

Editors
Wisdom's Goldenrod Ltd.
Valois, New York
May 1990

LOOKING INTO MIND

ONE
Opening the Door to Mind

Anthony: The best thing we can do during the short time I am here is to concentrate on mentalism and meditation. These are the two leading things. If I can get across to you the sublime value of meditation and the perspective that a proper understanding of mentalism can provide you, it will be like opening the door. You know, "Open Sesame." It's the door that opens you up to everything, and from there on you can be on your own. You can get to know your own soul intimately.

So mentalism is the theoretical side and meditation is the practical side. The two of them together will put your feet on the ground. From then on the infinite journey begins.

S: Could you start by saying something about meditation?

Anthony: Yes. Meditation is a difficult thing. There are different stages in meditation. For most people to be able to keep their mind occupied with one trend of thought continuously is very difficult, and that is why some people find meditation very boring. First of all, you have to be concentrated on some abstract theme. It could be the name of God, or it could be a quality of God, or it could be some quality of the mind. It could be any of these abstract themes, but then to think very concentratedly on it for a period of half an hour is very strenuous.

Most people can only get concentrated on things that they are interested in, whether it is some sport, some amusement, some business, or something of that nature. Then they can be preoccupied for a half hour, thinking about it. Like when a businessman is occupied with some business matter, he can think about it for a half hour, an hour, but it is a whole different story when you have to think about some abstract theme. And if your heart is not in it, meditation is very difficult.

But assuming your heart is in it, that you want to get behind the darkness you live in, then you have to find some theme that will arouse your interest and hold it for a period of time. You can't think about a doorknob for a half hour. You have to find something that is inwardly compelling and interesting enough. That's the first requisite. You have to find something of that nature. If you tell a person, "You are looking for your soul and these are just exercises to get you to train your mind so that you can employ it in that direction," they are still going to have the problem of "How can I develop the concentration to do that?"

Some people can get very interested in a question like "Who am I?" because nobody knows who they are. When I say you don't know who you are, I mean that besides your name you know only a few personal historical things. None of us really knows who we are. Some people, if you tell them, "Sit down and ask yourself who you are and keep thinking about that without stopping," they can do it. They can follow that up. They can keep asking themselves, "Who am I?" and try to find out. Close the eyes, get still, try to breathe very quietly and get very concentrated. Just keep thinking about that one thing over and over again. You have to get so concentrated and absorbed in it that you forget the physical world. You forget the physical body. That is like being absorbed. It is like the state of an artist, when he is so inspired that he forgets everything except what he is doing.

I don't know that there is an easy way to meditate. But assuming that a person is interested and says, "I have to find out who I am, I have got to know," then that person will succeed. But if he doesn't have a real, profound interest he is not going to do it. It won't last. He will try for a few times, but after a while he will give it up. That is one of the basic difficulties.

There are others who want to find God. You still have the same problem. You'll have to go through this process of interiorizing your attention and then focusing it on some idea in your mind. You get so wrapped up in the idea, so absorbed by the idea that you forget everything else. You live for a while, maybe just for a few moments, in the world of the idea, in the mental, not in the physical. It can take years to do. If you want to play a Beethoven sonata you start practicing the piano and maybe after twenty years you'll get there. Meditation is harder, because you can see the Beethoven sonata written down. You enjoy it. You sit down, you practice every day.

If you want to be an engineer you sit down and you work hard and you study and you'll be an engineer. You get help. Teachers will come around. You go to school. But with meditation nobody is going to help you. And the worst thing is that you are even going to try to defeat yourself. Nobody really wants to meditate unless they are already convinced in some sense that the life they live is unreal, that the world they are living in is a big lie, that they are being fooled every moment in time. We get up every morning and are happy another day has started. We go about like little busy mice, getting things and buying things and storing things. It goes on and on: "I don't think you ought to meditate." But then again there is a problem. We are all going to die and everybody is afraid to die. Maybe *that* might wake us up. We know we are going to die, and we are going to die without finding out who we were, what we came here for, what it was all about. *That* might help a person to meditate.

When you are twenty you think you are immortal. When you are thirty you start having doubts. When you are forty you'll know for sure. So very often older people, when they reach a certain age, begin to realize this and they do start meditating. You could call it praying, too. There is a similarity. Sometimes when people have an encounter with death they get interested in prayer, meditation. Unless a person has some encounter with his mortality he is not going to do anything. He is going to go on living day by day thinking that every day is going to come for sure.

You see, I am trying to discourage you people from meditating, so that maybe you can convince me that we should meditate. There is no real secret in it although we can speak about it as a secret. The whole secret is simply concentration. That is the whole secret of meditation. I suppose everybody at some time or another has experienced concentration, when their mind was very focused. It's like a magnifying glass—you get a magnifying glass and focus it and then it burns a paper. At some time or other everybody must have had the experience where their mind was very sharp, very alert, very concentrated. They could apply it to almost any problem and they would be able to solve that problem. That's really the secret of meditation, to be able to develop a very concentrated mind. And it becomes a very powerful mind, too. But like I said it requires tremendous interest and fascination with the subject itself—the mind. What is the mind? Who am I?

There was a writer, Stefan Zweig, who went to the studio where Auguste Rodin used to make his sculptures. He watched him work and saw the way Rodin was completely oblivious of everything except his work. He said, "In those few moments I found out more about meditation than in all the books that I have read about it." Rodin had this tremendous power to get so concentrated that nothing existed but what he was doing and he was completely absorbed in it. He made the sculpture *The Thinker*. After Zweig saw Rodin, he recognized what concentration was and saw what it meant to be in an absorbed, rapt, meditative state. For most people who sit down to meditate, it is a question of how long will it be before they fall asleep. That is usually the problem.

When a person sits down to meditate, he must have in mind precisely what he is going to do and then he has to stick to it. Once you sit down it is too late to decide what you are going to do. I sometimes tell people, "Memorize something that you like very much—you know, one of the great philosophers, a statement or a paragraph or page, whatever." But it has to be something that is compelling, is interesting, mysterious, and attracts your attention. You memorize that and then you sit down. You say it to yourself. You concentrate your attention on it and you try to squeeze out, extract all the meaning that it has. Sometimes you could do it in a few days, sometimes it takes a couple of weeks. That would be the easy way to start. That is one way of doing it.

Then there is another way. A person could say a *mantra* to himself. In early Christianity they used the prayer called the Lord Jesus prayer: "Lord Jesus Christ, Son of God, have mercy on me, a poor sinner. Amen." They'd say that over and over again. And they would get their mind very concentrated. They would say it so often that the repetition after a while goes on by itself. The mind gets very, very quiet, it gets so quiet you can hear it, because it gets very still. These people claim that just by repeating and concentrating on the mantra you can get so concentrated that your mind gets taken away from you and you get into the absolute quiet. You can't say it mechanically, or it won't work. You have to put a lot of feeling into it: "Lord Jesus Christ, Son of God, have mercy on me, a poor sinner. Amen." This method is used in the Byzantine and the Greek and

Eastern Orthodox Church. The Hindus claim the same thing, and so do the Tibetan Buddhists. They say, take a mantra like *Aum mani padme hum.* Say it, keep saying it, repeat it, get your mind concentrated on it, and after a while your mind gets very, very quiet. You have fewer and fewer thoughts. But if you say it mechanically, then again, the same problem comes up.

There are other ways. You can sit and look at the tip of your nose with your eyes and just keep looking at it without the eyes wavering. Or you could take the picture of someone that you respect and look up to, an idealized portrait of Jesus or of a sage, someone that you look up to. You keep looking at his image. You very intensely concentrate on his image. It will be very difficult for thoughts to come in if you are concentrating on the image. You get so concentrated on the image that you could see—I am talking about what takes months—you can see his image whether your eyes are open or closed. He is right there in front of you. You have achieved concentration. You can close your eyes and you can see his image right before you. You can get so concentrated that there is what is called mental union with your own mind. You achieve a state of union with your own mind. These are all different ways.

I have explained to many people these different ways over a period of years and it always comes down to this: "I can't do it." "Well, why can't you do it?" "Because when I sit down I get tired. I get sleepy. I get angry. I get frustrated." "Well, no one can stop you from getting angry. You have to do that." "I don't have the will." "Well, no one can give you the will. You have to do that. Nobody can do this for you." You know what I am talking about? Nobody could do this for you. It isn't possible for a man to come over and inspire you so that for a couple of years you work hard at it. That is out of the question. Sometimes you could find a great man like PB [Paul Brunton]. You read a little bit of his writings every day and that keeps your enthusiasm going. But the fundamental fact is that human inertia, human stupidity will simply stop you dead within a couple of weeks. So that is the basic problem most people have.

I discouraged you all? Good. I used to have a lot of illusions when I was young that you sit down and you meditate and in a couple of years you are going to get enlightened. And you go around with a big aura around your head. It never works out like that. Every day was a fight. Every day for years and years and years. It is the most difficult thing that a person could do. And then, on top of that, you have to bring certain changes into your life. You have to try to live a more ethical life, to live the things you believe. And today who wants to do these things? Why bother? There are more interesting things to do. In my case, I would rather sit and study and read, see? That would take me away from meditation. But if somebody likes to play tennis he will rather go and play tennis.

So there are always those things that you have to deal with. And then we have certain idiosyncrasies, certain complexes. They seem to be hidden, but they are really not. You sit down to meditate and if you are a young man thoughts of a woman will come up all the time. And vice versa, if you are a young woman thoughts of a man will come up. That is always a problem. When you are left alone with your mind it throws up all these desires, wishes, tendencies that you have. It keeps throwing them up. So you have to deal with that. You sure you want to meditate? Then you have to get the room dark, you have to keep the light out so you don't evoke images.

Now, are you sure you want to meditate? I know for a fact that usually a man has to be pushed into a corner, kicked in the belly, hit over the head. He has to be bleeding. He has to be in pain. And then he says, "That's enough, I am going to meditate from now on or else." He has to actually be pushed into that condition. Most people are like that. We don't go to these things because we have heard about them from others. We go to them because there is no place else to go. Sooner or later you've got to get bored with the world. The glamour falls away. It becomes an uninteresting place. You see the repetition of human stupidity—folly and greed go on and on and on and there is no cure. There is no solution out there. The only solution is to find some peace within yourself. But to get to that is very difficult, very painful. Most people find that there is something for them in the world. The world has a certain glamour. They must go out there and do something. I am not saying that we shouldn't do our share, whatever our share is. We all have to do our share in the world. But above and beyond that, it takes up all our time, all our energy. Our preoccupation with it is endless. Until these things are understood, thrashed out in your mind and looked into, I think you'll find that meditation is very difficult. But let us say that you finally decide that it doesn't make sense to go on living the way you are, because there is something in us that is more than an animal. Everyone sooner or later begins to ask questions: "Why am I living? What am I doing here?"

So why don't I leave it to you to ask questions?

S: Could there be any danger in meditation?

Anthony: If a person has a neurotic disposition it can get exaggerated in meditation. If a person tends to be passive he can be subjected to forces that he doesn't understand. He or she can become mediumistic. It is much more likely to happen to a woman than to a man, because a woman can be passive much more easily than a man can. If a person doesn't have certain ethical considerations in mind . . . for instance, if you think of someone in meditation and you wish the person harm of some kind, that could be very dangerous. Things of that nature—there are a few. But one of the things we have to try to remember is that we all have our shortcomings and it is very hard, almost impossible, to eradicate them all at once. So what most people suggest is that you meditate and in the meantime you try to improve your character as you go along. Otherwise there is always the danger that the peculiar neuroses or the emotional unbalance or the preoccupation with unhealthy issues may get exaggerated if you practice meditation.

S: What did you mean by being passive during meditation?

Anthony: Well, very often when people sit down to meditate their attention is very nebulous, as though they were in the womb again. Whereas if you are concentrating, if you are attentive to what you are doing, you won't be passive. In other words, your mind is being controlled and directed by you. But if you are passive, you sit down and you let your mind get very relaxed and let any thought come in or go out indiscriminately.

There is another kind of passivity which is different. That happens when a person gets very very intensely concentrated, and he can feel something coming into him that wants to . . . bring him in. Then he has to be passive. But this is a different kind of passivity. This isn't a womblike passivity. This is an alertness. You know this is happening. You watch it very carefully. You surrender. But you are alert and it brings you into the heart.

What I am trying to talk about as a problem is the general inability for a person to be attentive to what he is doing. If you practice the piano or another instrument, you have to be extremely alert. Let us say you are playing a piece of music. You have to be alert. You have to read the notes. You have to use the fingers to hit the right notes. You have to be totally present. If for one second you're not, you can't do the next measure. That is being alert, that is being attentive. The other way is being passive, not being able to concentrate. Not being there as to what is going on.

S: Even if you are concentrated and alert couldn't you be confronted with an astral world?

Anthony: Then you are not paying attention. You are not paying attention. Look, make out I am a young man twenty-five years old and I love a woman. Now I can see only this woman, I can't see anybody else. When you are paying attention to what you are doing you are concentrating on a certain thought or idea. The astral world can't come in. It is only because your attention falters that you get into trouble. The same thing happens when you are playing a piece of music: the moment your attention falters you stop, you stop right where you are.

S: Is the point of concentration the watching?

Anthony: Yes. Suppose you get a picture or image, but you are watching and you know it is only a thought. The whole trick lies in attention. As a matter of fact, that is the meaning of meditation: attention, attention, attention.

S: What happens if you lose your attention . . . I mean you were being quite concentrated and then you lose it?

Anthony: You bring it right back again. In other words, you are concentrating on something. A second later you are thinking about something else. You bring the attention back and do it again. And you keep doing that over and over, because your mind won't stay put. Your mind will always go somewhere else. It is like a crazy monkey. So you are concentrating on one thought. "Lord Jesus Christ, Son of God, have . . . did I pay my rent?" You take the mind, "No, stop right here, back to this."

S: But what is the difference between studying and meditating? Studying also requires concentration. You have to pay attention.

Anthony: They come very close together. Sometimes when you study very intensely you can experience a certain joy in understanding. That could happen in studies and reflection. But the difference is that in meditation you eventually want to cut off the world completely—

any sound, any sight, any touch, any contact. In meditation you eventually want to cut it all off.

Let me put it this way. It's possible while you are dreaming to wake up in the dream without disturbing yourself and experience everything as though it were an idea. When you are studying you can't do that because you are usually aware of the page or the printed book or the light flickering. But in meditation the idea is to get completely into the mental world. So you have to break off everything else. That is the purpose: in meditation you are supposed to get to that position where there is only the world of ideas.

S: *Do you mean to be conscious that you are dreaming?*

Anthony: Yes, you are conscious that you are dreaming and you experience the world as idea, the dream world as idea. Then the next possibility may be that you experience the very world that you live in as an idea. But one at a time. Meditation is to lead you into the mind itself. Because all that you know, all that you can experience, all that you think you are, anything that you can bring up is always *within your mind.* There isn't anything else for you but your mind. And you have to experience that for yourself.

There is a lot of technical information about the different stages of meditation. For example, when you get to the third level it becomes pure contemplation. But I don't want to go into that right now.

S: *You have been talking about different ways of meditation. Do the different ways have different effects? Can a certain kind of meditation capture your power of attention not only while you are meditating but also in everyday life?*

Anthony: If you do any meditation it will show up in your everyday life. Inevitably it must, because you have acquired the faculty to stay attentive. Attention is like an acetylene torch. With an acetylene torch you can cut steel, and with attention—concentration—you can penetrate into the most difficult problems and come up with an understanding. But without the ability to concentrate you wouldn't be able to. In the everyday world, there are businessmen who are capable of tremendous concentration, but only on things of their world, on business matters. If you take them out of that into something abstract they can't do it, whereas here it can be the reverse. When a person has learned to concentrate inwardly, abstractly, it inevitably must flow out into the personality, so that when he is doing things in the ordinary world he can bring that ability to concentrate to bear on everyday problems. But very often what happens, too, is that if a person gets very, very concentrated he doesn't like to go back into the world, he likes to stay inside. It is nice there, it is comfortable. It is very quiet and peaceful. So he doesn't want to go back into the world. Sometimes people go through stages for years where they are happy just inwardly. They don't want to get caught up into the world. But that's not right. They are supposed to also develop outwardly.

To study the more advanced philosophy you have to have tremendous powers of concentration. So fundamentally then it comes to this: when you really get interested in yourself, you are going to learn to meditate and until then you wait.

Shall we sit for a half hour or forty minutes, an hour?

TWO
How Do You Know Anything?

Anthony: How do you know anything?

S: By experience.

Anthony: You have to tell me more, because that's just another way of saying experience is equivalent to knowing. If you say by experience, I would ask you, what do you mean by experience? How do you know this thing or this person?

S: By knowledge.

Anthony: You are telling me *what* it is you know. I am asking *how* is it you know. How do you know something?

S: Through your senses. You see that thing.

Anthony: What do you mean when you say you see the thing?

S: You get the picture through your eyes.

Anthony: An image is formed in the retina in the eye. Is that what you mean?

S: Yes, very physical.

Anthony: In the retina it is upside down and a little tiny image, but that is not what you see. In other words, if you were to look into the retina of a person's eye and he was looking at a tree, the tree in the retina would be upside down. It is only a tiny little image, whereas the tree is a hundred feet high. What you see is the tree that is a hundred feet high. You don't see the tiny little image in the retina in the eye.

S: The eye is one thing and then you can feel the tree with your hands. That gives you another sensation.

Anthony: But if you go feel the tree, then what you are talking about is nerve fibers that are stimulated and then the stimulation travels all the way through different nerves to the brain . . . and then what happens? Then you feel the tree?

S: You get some sort of sensation which comes from the concrete world, and when you hear the wind blow through the leaves, that is another sensation. I am not saying that is the real thing. But when we say experience, that is what we experience every day.

Anthony: I think what you are telling me is that there is a world outside and there is a reflection of that world outside in you. Isn't that what you are saying?

The problem is something like this. Let us take any of the senses—the eye, for instance. You are looking at an object: there is an image formed on the retina and that travels through the optic nerve up to the occipital lobe, where it sets up a galvanic disturbance. Now that is the process of physiological sensation. But is that the same as knowing? I mean, do you know anything? Isn't it only when the *mind* knows that you know something? In other words, a dead man with his eyes open wouldn't know anything. There is an image formed on the retina, but he doesn't *know* anything. So again I ask you, what do you mean when you say, "I know something."

For 150 years, they have been speaking about this process. They describe in considerable detail how this whole process of sense-knowledge takes place. And the scientist, the physiologist, has pointed out that the retina is receptive of an image. Now the strange thing is that it is not this image, it's only an electrical disturbance of the optic nerve that goes to the brain. It's not the picture of the cup. When it reaches the occipital lobe, *then* you know the cup. But the word "then" is the one I am trying to understand. What do they mean, "then" I know the cup? How did a physiological process become a mental event? They haven't answered it and they won't. It's impossible to answer the question in that fashion. They can't understand how a physiological process becomes a mental event or an idea in the mind.

So if you think about it very intensely you'll see that the problem of knowledge is still a difficult problem that each one has to understand. If what I am saying is true, then you are a mystery to yourself. Wouldn't that be so? Because if we can't understand how knowledge arises, all we can say is that we know we have knowledge. I see a cup,

I see a tree, I see you; and the physiological process doesn't explain how an idea arises in my mind because I can show you that if you go step by step there is one step where you have the so-called material event and the next step where you supposedly have the mental idea. And you didn't show me how you got from one to the other. Now, if this is true, then you are a mystery to yourself. You don't know who you are. All that you know are these images that are constantly in front of you and you say, "The world is out there, I am here; and inside, some mysterious place inside, the world is reflected within me." This is the common view even among twentieth-century scientists. And everyone you speak to has this illusion. They think that the world is out there, my mind is inside, and the world is mirrored in my mind.

Let's try something else. Imagine you are dreaming and you appear in your dream and you look at a tree and you say, "I see a tree." Now who is seeing the tree? The dream character or you who are having the dream?

S: I can't answer, it must be the "I" in me.

Anthony: The I in you? So you are suspicious that when you are looking at a dream, the dream person who says "I see the tree" doesn't see anything. He is just a dream person and the tree is a dream tree. And when the dream person says "I see a dream tree" that dream person doesn't see anything. The person who is having the dream sees the tree.

S: Aren't the dream person and the dreamer the same person?

Anthony: Are they the same person? I hope not, because I wouldn't want to be some of the things I've dreamed. Let me ask you this. Who sees the dream? Obviously you are having the dream, you are the one who is seeing it. Isn't that so? You are looking at the dream, you see the dream. You get up in the morning and you tell somebody, "I had a dream last night." Again—your eyes were closed—how did you see the dream?

S: In the imagination.

Anthony: You didn't use your eyes, then, to see the dream? You mean you saw the dream without your eyes, and when there were some odors in the dream you smelled them without your nose?

S: How can you smell something in a dream without the sense of smell?

Anthony: That is what we are trying to find out. Where is the sense of smell, where is the sense of sight? Where is the sense of hearing?

Suppose that in this dream, someone brought you a beautiful bouquet of roses and you smelled them. You are telling me that you smelled them with your imagination, just like you see the dream with your imagination. So in other words, despite all these different senses that you were telling me were the origin of knowledge, you are telling me now, "No, I see my dream sheerly with my mind. When I go to sleep and I dream, I don't open my eyes and look at my dreams. I see the dream directly. I perceive the dream without the use or the intermediary of my eyes, and I smell what is in the dream without the use of my nose."

Now if that is so, then what is the means by which we know what is going on in the dream? You said your imagination. Yes, we could say the imagination. You could say that your mind knows without the use of these senses. It sees, it tastes, smells, without the use of these senses.

So again the question arises, "But how does this happen? How does the mind know anything?" Again, we ask the question, "How do I know anything?" It isn't that the answer "experience" is wrong. It is just that we are being very specific. We want to know precisely, so that we have no illusions about it. And we find out that when we try to understand what the scientist or the physiologist is talking about, their analysis does not work. They really cannot explain how perception arises. They say "then," "after," "somehow" the molecular activity in the brain is replaced by an idea, a thought, and *then* you see the object. And we pointed out that you can't proceed in that whole analysis to the point where consciousness arises. It just doesn't flow. There is a break in the logic which you cannot surmount. You cannot cross over from a so-called material world to a mental world. You have a process in physiology and then you have a process in consciousness. And they have been saying for over a hundred years, "Don't worry, we'll solve it. We'll solve it." And philosophers have been telling them, "Don't worry, you'll never solve it that way."

This is a problem that is very, very ancient. It has been thought out by great thinkers who I think know what they are talking about.

But the scientists at this point have not solved it, although they claim that they will eventually do so. It cannot be solved that way. And the question that any thinking person will ask himself instead of getting into irrelevant matters, the question that sooner or later any intelligent person will ask himself is "How do I know anything?" If I cannot answer this question my whole life may be nothing but a sheer illusion and I go on living like a puppet thinking that all this is real. You know, in a dream you eat strawberry cream pie and it tastes very good, very real, and you wake up and you say, "But it was only a dream!" And it is very possible that you may wake up from this life and see that it is only a dream, that there is no real world out there unless you are there. So do you follow the point here? You must first try to understand how it is possible for knowledge to arise, and if you cannot understand how knowledge arises then you are in difficulties.

Did it ever upset you that you could see a dream without the use of your eyes, that your mind is an organ of thinking which can perceive without the use of any intermediary apparatus?

S: What bothers me really is not that I cannot know if a tree is a tree. What really bothers me is that I cannot know anything for certain in my thoughts and feelings. I feel something very strongly and the next day I understand, oh, it was nonsense. That feeling didn't tell me anything real. It told me a lie.

Anthony: We'll get to that later. This is more basic.

S: What is more basic, the tree?

Anthony: I mean the perception of the everyday world. Because I have to perceive the chair so I could sit on it. I have to see my food so I can eat it. First we start with the empirical perception. And if it doesn't bother you, go home. [laughter] Don't stick around. When I was a teenager I couldn't go to sleep when I found out that I didn't know how I knew anything. As a matter of fact, I felt threatened for a few weeks. I felt darkness everywhere.

So we are like people living in a dream and we don't want to wake up. We are sleepwalkers.

S: If this world is an illusion, when will you know? When will you wake up? How do you ever know?

S: When you die, don't you wake up then?

Anthony: I won't know that until I die. In the meantime I have to go on living.

S: Also with a question. You go on living with a question?

Anthony: Yes, could you live with a question for a while?

S: I have to.

Anthony: Now you could do something about it or you could just let it hang there waiting for someone to give you an explanation. But if you don't work it out, it won't be *your* understanding. You know, it's like if I am sick the doctor comes over and writes a prescription and says, "Take the medicine and you'll get better." So I get the medicine, but then I tell the doctor, "You take it." That won't work. It has to be mine. And everyone sooner or later, some way or another, has to wake up and say, "I have to find this out for myself, because what someone else knows doesn't count." That is a situation we are all in. This is not something that they could manufacture in a factory and sell to you. This you have to get by yourself. Now most people are not interested. They go to church on Sunday and that is enough. They don't want to know any more. They figure they have done their duty.

This is one of the problems that philosophers are interested in—they want to know how they know. So they go through this enquiry and this reflection into the meaning of knowledge and what makes knowledge possible. And they have to start there. Because if we don't start there we might be assuming that we have such a thing as knowledge and it might be a lie. Maybe we have no knowledge. You know, like people in a dream—they dream that they have knowledge. They say, "I know this and I know that." They don't know anything. When they wake up they say, "How stupid I was."

S: To enquire, look into yourself—it might be a way to make your dream more enjoyable. That would be all right, wouldn't it?

Anthony: Sure. But you'd still be dreaming. And you would never know what was real. Do you remember many years ago people used to think that the world was flat? And there were some people who disagreed. They said, "No it is not flat, it is round." And they offered different proofs. They said, "If you look at the mast of a ship as it comes towards you, you see more and more of it and that shows that the ship is on a curve." Through many processes of reasoning they came to the conclusion that the world was round. And then some people set out and proved it by taking a ship around the world. So what they did was to reason the thing out and then apply a test to the reason, and if they succeeded then they knew that they were on the right track. In other words, applying their reason to the situation brought an understanding of what was going on.

In the same way, people used to say that the sun rises. Every high school boy today knows that the sun doesn't rise. It is the earth spinning. And yet every morning you look there and you see the sun go up. So on one hand your senses are telling you that the sun rises and on the other hand your reason points out to you that the sun doesn't rise and you can prove it. In a case like that, you realize that it is through reasoning that you can come to some understanding of what is going on. You have to use your reasoning powers. In other words, do you think it is possible by reasoning very intelligently on the experience that you are presented with to come to an understanding of how you know?

We would have to take as given the world that we perceive. My eyes see colors, my nose smells . . . but given this phenomenal aggregate, then I have to reason on it. The scientist tells me that what I see comes from out there, goes into my eye, makes an image in the retina of my eye, travels up the optic nerve, and *then* I become conscious of the thing out there. I could point out, through reason, that he has a process which is correct up to the point where you have a molecular activity in the brain and *then* you have a thought. Here you have on one hand motion in the brain cells, the neurons firing, and then on the other you have consciousness. But these are two utterly distinct different kinds of things. And reason would say, "How did thought arise from motion? What are you talking about?" Only through the use of reason can I criticize the scientist when he says that. So reason is going to be the means that we have to use to get to understand something about how we know. We won't worry about who we are yet.

So, we have to use the process of reasoning to try to understand something about how knowledge arises. Would you rather spend your time—and it may take a long time—using your reason to try to find out how you know, or using it to fix your plumbing or paint your room? What would you rather do with your reason? What do you think most people do with their ability to think and to reason? Do you think they would spend it on this kind of a subject? They call it abstract, but I don't think it is abstract. I think it is the most concrete thing in the world. When I want to know how I know, I think that is more concrete than the brick wall I am faced with. Do you see what I am talking about? Because I say I know a brick wall. How do I know the brick wall? It is hard, it has a certain color, a certain size, dimension. I perceive all these sensible qualities about it and that is how I know a brick wall. But when I say "I see," I have already brought into question what I don't understand—how I can see anything—because we just pointed out that the popular description of the process of seeing stops dead somewhere along the line and then the thought arises.

So which is more concrete? Which is more practical—the willingness to sit down and try to understand this process of knowledge, or fixing the concrete brick wall? This is a problem that arises because for most people knowing is unimportant: "Let me put up the chimney. I'm not going to worry about how I know it exists."

S: *If we are dream persons sitting here, then how could we think or realize anything? Whatever we will figure out will only be a dream. So we must find out who is the dreamer if we are to realize anything.*

Anthony: To find out who the dreamer is, you would have to bet on the assurance that knowledge could deliver. So we are back to the question of knowledge. Unless I know how I know and unless that "knowledge" is valid, there is no sense saying I know who I am, because I would only be reflecting the primeval ignorance that I started out with. So the question of knowledge always comes first. When I want to know who I am, I give my name, my social security number, where I was born, this, that . . . but all these events are sensible things that I got through my senses. And we just pointed out that we have no assurance that this is knowledge because along the way something happens which shows that this is not the way we know. In other words, we are locked into our own thinking, within our own thoughts; and unless we can find out how thoughts operate, how they work, we will always be caught in them. So that is really the problem.

Do you remember the story of Archimedes? It is one that I like a lot. A king told someone to make him a ring, all gold. So the artisan came back and gave him a gold ring. Now the king was suspicious that the artisan had mixed in a little brass. So he told Archimedes, "I want you to find out without destroying the ring if it is all gold." So the poor scientist was given an order and he had to figure out how to do it. And he thought about it a lot, kept thinking, and he couldn't figure out how to find out if that ring had brass in it. One night he was very quiet from thinking. He made a hot bath and as he got into the bath he saw the water rise—"Eureka!" He figured out that objects of the same size will always displace the same amount of water, but they will weigh more or less depending on what they're made of. In other words, every metal has a specific gravity, so by determining the volume and weight of the ring, he could tell if it was pure gold or mixed. So he found out something through the use of reason. He jumped out of the bathtub without his clothes saying: "I got it, I got it, I got the answer."

But Archimedes, of course, was a great mathematician—capable of tremendous concentration of reasoning, even thinking without any images. As a matter of fact, he was capable of such concentration that when the Romans captured Syracuse and they told him to stand at attention, he was so deep into thought that he didn't hear them. And one of the Roman soldiers speared him to death. He is one of my favorite examples of people who are capable of getting immersed in such profound thought that the world disappears for them. They are lost in their thought, literally and actually. The world ceases to be for them.

So evidently Archimedes was of the opinion that if he wanted to find out something he had to turn within himself and through profound effort at reasoning come to an understanding of what that particular problem was and work it out. And you can find other examples. Remember August Kekulé, the man who discovered the benzene ring? He thought about that problem for a long time. Then one night he was dreaming and he saw the elements of the formula as if they were dancing in a circle. They were having a dance and he realized that he had to arrange the formula into a circular diagram. That was how he discovered the benzene ring. He got the idea from within himself.

So again and again, any time a person wants to think something through, he has to really immerse himself very deeply and get to the bottom of it through concentrating inwardly. The mind has to be focused to a point, and he has to keep that point on the problem until he finds out the solution. Now you are going to have to make the same kind of effort if you want to understand mentalism—how the entire world that you perceive comes from your mind and is the experience of your mind by your mind. How can the mind have an idea, externalize this idea—an idea that could be the whole world—and perceive it out there?

S: How?

Anthony: You will have to go through that whole process of reasoning and I am not about to do that. But if you read *The Hidden Teaching Beyond Yoga* and go all the way through up to the second chapter of *The Wisdom of the Overself*, PB presents you with that whole logical chain of reasoning, and you have to go through that. You have to understand very carefully every step of the process. I don't think I could do that. It would require a couple of pots of coffee and staying up all night, you know, smoking a pack of cigarettes. I am not going to do that. You are going to have to do that.

S: So what you're talking about now is that you really create the world from inside yourself before you perceive it?

Anthony: Before you see the brick wall there, you have to think it. It isn't that there is the brick wall out there—that first you see it and then you think it. It is the other way around. You think the world into existence and then you see it. But you put it *out there*, just like in a dream you put the world out there and then you see it. In the very thinking, the world is concomitant with the thinking. And you start wondering how it all came to be. "Oh, I see, I see through my eyes," you say in the dream, "and I smell with my nose." But the one who is *having* the dream says, "Nonsense. You neither see nor smell—I am the one who sees and smells."

Take, for instance, how do you know your body? Through your senses?

S: To think the world into existence must mean that you think the body into existence too.

Anthony: Of course. Because your body is part of the world.

S: But don't the thoughts and the world come at the same time? You say the thought comes first, then the world?

Anthony: By that I mean *logically* first. I don't mean in time. It isn't that the first moment you have thinking and the second moment you have the appearance of a world. I mean that in terms of principle, thinking is prior to that which is being manifested. But there is no time when this is happening, because time is something *within* thought. Time is something that exists within the thought of the world—that is, within the World-Idea.

S: So you create time at the same time as you create your body and the world?

Anthony: Yes. If we assume, and we are only assuming because we haven't thought this out, that the World-Idea is being constantly brought forth from moment to moment, then obviously time only exists within the creation and not outside the creation. Outside the creation there is no time. You have to have creation in order to speak about time.

All this is just a preliminary in the sense of trying to understand how we know anything. This is no confrontation with the problem. It is a very, very involved problem and it will require tremendous amounts of energy and persistence to work it out for yourself. So unless you *realize* that it's a problem, then I really don't like to discuss it. For most people it is not a problem. They are too busy about their job, raising their family. I am not saying these things are wrong. They are important. I raised a family too. I had a job. I do all these things. They are important. But sometimes something happens to a person and he says: "No. They are not important. What is important is—what am I living for? That is important." And then of course they think he is crazy. They take him to a psychiatrist and try to get him cured. And the psychiatrist doesn't know what *he* is living for either.

So usually that has to become a very important problem in order for a person to get interested in philosophy. You have to remember—philosophy is very big, it is a huge subject and this is only one aspect of it. Because there is so much to trying to understand ourselves, knowledge, why we are here, what the meaning of existence is. And each person has not only to work out these general problems in philosophy, he also has to work out the meaning of his personal life—which is not the same as someone else's life, no matter how close that other person is. Everyone has to work out the particular meanings that are in his life.

So philosophy is a very big subject. It's a grand subject. It's a grand learning and would require your best effort. To make a commitment is difficult. In the old days, they wouldn't teach you philosophy until you were at least forty years old. The Jesuits wouldn't make you undertake any of these things until you were forty. Plato pointed out that you start to study philosophy when you are forty, at least. Most of us wait longer than that.

So why don't we read a few quotes from PB? We will read one quote at a time. I'll try to find the easy ones. And we'll talk about them in a random way. You could ask questions and I could try to explain as we go along. Maybe some things will come out that are worthwhile, maybe not. This man has written a number of books. But in the last twenty years of his life he was constantly writing, not publishing anything. He was getting together what I consider the greatest, the most thorough exposition of philosophy that I have ever come across. And this is only a very small section, this is on mentalism. He writes very straightforward English, it's not convoluted. But the ideas are difficult.

> Mind is not something which can be touched and handled, as surgeons and students touch and handle the brain. *(unpublished)*

Anthony: That's relatively easy. Mind isn't a material thing. It has no smell, no shape, no form, no color. It's intangible, it's invisible, it's formless. That is what he is saying here. And he is not identifying it with the brain. The brain is something you could touch. You go to the butcher's shop and buy three pounds of brain. But if you go to the butcher's shop and ask for three pounds of mind, you can't get it.

> By the light of mind, man is able to know, think, reflect, and feel. *(V13, 21:2.146)*

Anthony: I think what he is saying is that when you think, it's by the mind that you know that you're thinking. When you feel something, it is by the light of the mind that you know. Here is a good example. Pain is absolutely mental. Isn't that so? We have to try to see what he means, "By the light of the mind you can reflect, you can think, you can feel."

S: The mind comes first and then the rest follows. The mind comes first before you can do anything.

Anthony: Elaborate a little bit.

S: Well, the other sentence said that the mind is different from the brain. Obviously we have a brain, but in order to understand anything we must have the mind operating. So the mind must be on a higher level than the brain in order to have experiences, to have the sense impressions and so on. So, from there you can go back to the elaboration of "how do I know anything?" Obviously the brain is involved—through the brain and the nervous system sending the sensation, it gives me the idea that I'm experiencing something.

Anthony: Could we make it simpler, more direct? Let me put it this way: the most immediate experience you have is that of your own mind. The most immediate experience you have all the time is your own mind.

When you say, for instance, "That wall is hard," you have to actually think the hardness into existence. You say, "Well I don't know that I am doing that!" But the fact remains that you *have* to think it. If you don't think of something, there won't be anything there. You are always thinking.

What I am trying to say is that the immediacy of your experience is of the mind's functions. If you got that, you've got it. Because that is our immediate environment. We live in the mind. We *are* the mind. We experience ourselves functioning. But we lose sight of that, and we're preoccupied with what it did, rather than what it *is*. So PB says that it is because of the mind—and *only* because the mind is there—that we can know that there's thinking, know that there's feeling, know that there's willing or any of these things. If you subtract the mind, there's no knowing of anything.

I am avoiding the academic issues. I am trying to see if I could spear you with an intuition. Did you ever have the experience, for instance, of being very tired, you've worked and you're traveling on the road? You pull over and stop. You get a motel room. You're so tired, you flop into bed and you fall asleep. You wake up, and for a moment you don't know where you are. But you know *that* you are. It just lasts a minute and then, "Oh, I remember." But in that moment that you don't know anything, nonetheless you know that you are. That's the immediacy of the experience of the mind.

You see, you can't think about the mind, you can't make an image, a symbol, a picture, a word. They are all phony. You can't grab the mind in any way. There is no way you can say, "Well I'll catch it when it goes by." Because you *are* the mind. So it is not something out there. You are the mind. You are *that* first, and then you could have a thought. If there is no mind there is no thought, there is no feeling, there are none of these. The mind has to be there. We first have to recognize that the mind is the primal existence. Then we can speak about the mind having thoughts, the mind having feelings. So mind is your immediate being.

S: Could you make an analogy with electricity, that you will never know electricity in itself, only its manifestations?

Anthony: Yes. You could know the mind in the sense that you *are* the mind. You can't know it as an object. When you say you know the chair, the chair is out there, you are here, and there is a distinction between the object and the *knowing* of the object. But with the mind you can't do that. You can't turn it into an object. You can't make an object of your I. Like if I say I don't exist, I would be lying immediately, because I am asserting that I am—I have to be there in order to say I am not. Alright? So the mind is of that nature: formless, intangible, no size, no shape, no color.

S: Yes, but if this table is mind, mind has shape and color.

Anthony: But this isn't mind. This is a thought in mind.

S: Aha, everything is a thought in the mind. But a thought must be mind also.

Anthony: It is a manifestation of mind, yes. But it isn't mind. Because then I can go to the butcher shop and buy mind.

Let's go back to when you are having a dream. You say that the dream is a manifestation of your mind. It is a thought in your mind. If I were to say that that thought is mind then I would be confusing the two, because then everything is mind and I'd be talking about nothing. So we make the distinction: on one hand you have the mind dreaming and on the other what it dreams about is content, the appearance or the manifestation of the mind or a thought of the mind. Now the mind could have many thoughts, one after the other. There is no end to the thoughts it could have. Every thought is a manifestation of the mind. It takes place, it arises, within the mind and it dissolves back in the mind. But the mind isn't any one of those thoughts.

The point here is that in a sense you *are* this mind and you have to try to experience this mind directly, that is, without any thoughts, without any activity. That means you have to *become* that mind, even if it is only for a moment, to experience your real self, what you really are.

All the time most of us experience only the thoughts, and we think we are these thoughts. "I am Maria so and so, age so and so, live here . . ." But these are thoughts that the mind has, so Maria has not experienced herself the way she is virginally, without any images, without any thoughts. And the only way you can have that experience is by being that. For instance, suppose I use the word "anger" and you say, "I don't know what anger is," so I go over and I hit you and you get angry. Now you know what anger is. I didn't turn to the dictionary and read you the definition, but I put you through the experience of being angry and now you know what anger is. In the same way, if I could provoke you into a situation where you could *be* the mind just for a moment, then you would know what you are. The next moment, thoughts would come again and you could see that there is a difference between what you really are and what you now think you are. So we make these distinctions.

S: *But there are distinctions between this thought and that thought, so it is not wrong to say that this is a lamp. It is a thought, but it is still a lamp.*

Anthony: Sure. Each thought will have its own nature, its own specificity. But the point I'm making is that if you have the experience of this mind that you really are, you would have the experience of your own soul. You are soul. That is the way he put it, because that is what you are. But when you get preoccupied with the thoughts that the mind has or that the soul has, then you lose that identification and you keep thinking of yourself as ABC, etc.—all these different things. So if we get back . . .

> By the light of mind, man is able to know, think, reflect, and feel. *(V13, 21:2.146)*

Anthony: The *I am* that you really are—the mind that you really are—makes it possible for you to know thoughts, for you to know feelings, for you to know things. Without the mind you can't know these things. When a person suffers intense pain he knows he is experiencing mind as it is. Pain is intensely mental. Everybody is a mentalist when it comes to pain. Everybody. Because then they know that they are experiencing something which is direct, immediate. There is no intermediary between you and the pain.

Here is a funny one, this is amusing.

> Chuang Tzu wrote: "Confucius and you are both dreams, and I who say you are dreams—I am but a dream myself." *(V13, 21:4.228)*

Anthony: If you change the word to "thought" it would be thc same thing. "Confucius and you are both thoughts and I who say you are a thought, I am but a thought myself."

> Consciousness presents its own products to itself, fabricating an entire world in the process. Mind makes and sees the picture. *(V13, 21:2.41)*

Anthony: "Consciousness"—you could use the word "mind." Go back to the dream analogy. That would help you. It is your mind that makes images and it is your mind that sees the images it makes. Remember we said that when she sees in a dream she sees without any eyes, ears, nose, anything. She sees the dream directly. You, too, when you have a dream you see the dream directly. You don't get up in the middle of the night and put your glasses on to look at your dream.

S: But my mind needs my body.

Anthony: Your mind *thinks* your body. It doesn't need it. It can get along without it. No, it's not flying anywhere. It needs you physically? Not really. It can get along without you. It puts you to bed every night, doesn't it, and says, "Go to sleep."

Did you follow that? I am just going to try to get one or two points across tonight. It is very important because if you can understand that, you can understand that you perceive the world first and then your senses make you aware of it. When you are looking at a dream and you are perceiving the dream, the important point is that without the use of the eyes, ears, nose, skin you are perceiving the dream. And when you think about that it'll shock you. Just think for a moment. You are in bed, you are sleeping. Make out you are going to bed tonight and you are going to have a dream. You say to yourself, I am going to watch this very carefully, this man is crazy. And you'll see that you see your dream without the use of your eyes.

S: Yes, I believe that.

Anthony: I can testify to it. It is not a question of belief. This is personal experience. Well then that suggests that you perceive the world also without the use of your senses. You are perceiving a thought without the use of your senses.

Just imagine that you see Maria in a dream and you are looking at her. You say she should have washed her ears. And then you say, "But I'm seeing the dream and I'm not using any eyes. My eyes are closed. I am sleeping."

The body can't see anything. That is the whole point. You are trying to get to the fact that there is a knowing agent in you that operates without the use of these senses. But you have to make these things reflectively clear to your understanding. So I try to find examples without going into philosophic discussions. It would be very very difficult to try to do something like that. I mean most of us who have studied people like Berkeley and Hume, Immanuel Kant, Schopenhauer and Hegel know that you spend many many years before you get these things clear in your mind. But sometimes it is possible, just by the right kind of picture, to give a person the idea and then he doesn't have to go through all that. Because once you get a sure intuition, from then on you know. If you can get it from an analogy like the dream where you see that the mind can perceive without the use of any senses, then it won't be difficult for you to understand telepathy, telementation, telekinesis, any of these things, because the mind can communicate directly with another mind. It doesn't need to pick up the telephone. But like we said, to understand the nature of mind is really a very involved, long process. We could start off on this beginning level and get a feel for it. And after a while we begin to realize that, sure, that's where all knowledge is coming from—from within my mind, my soul. But the word "soul" today is not legitimate.

> The theory that we perceive the outer world through a sensing process which results in a picture arising in the brain, or on the brain's surface as it does on the eye's surface, still leaves unexplained how we are able to perceive this picture itself. The brain cannot see it for it cannot see colours—only the eye can do that. Nor can the brain feel it, for then it would have to touch it, which will be impossible in the case of large pictures of outer objects larger than itself. Nor can the picture look at, feel, or experience itself. The gap in this theory cannot be crossed. Only by reversing this theory and acknowledging that our awareness of the world really comes to us from within, that by a trick of the mind it only *seems* to come from without, can the true and correct explanation be found. *(V13, 21:1.139)*

Anthony: We have been talking about that. It is a trick that the mind has. You are looking at the dream and you say the dream is out there and I am here, and you're looking at it and you say it's outside. But when you wake up you realize it was never outside. It was inside. Is that right? Is the dream-image inside you? When you are dreaming, it seems to be outside of you; but when you wake up you say, "But it was in me." But "in me" would make you very, very formless. In other words, if you see a whole city it is all within your mind or if you see the tip of a little pin it is in your mind.

S: Yes, but my mind is not in the head.

Anthony: Well, wouldn't your head be in your mind? That's true, you can't put the mind in the head. You *can* put the head in the mind. But when you say "in the mind," what is the mind, a box? And you could put things in it? So, then you are getting a feeling that this mind is not something that you could grab, touch, smell, taste. You can't do that with the mind. But without the mind you can't taste, touch, smell. Let's read the first part of that again, because this is what we have been discussing.

> The theory that we perceive the outer world through a sensing process which results in a picture arising in the brain, or on the brain's surface as it does on the eye's surface, still leaves unexplained how we are able to perceive this picture itself.

Anthony: In other words, when the picture is on the retina of the eye, you still haven't explained how you see. You left out the explanation.

Little by little it will get more difficult, but we are starting off by trying to get a feeling for this intangible, invisible presence which is our mind, which the ancients called the soul. That is why they said you can't lose your soul, you can't burn it, you can't cut it. They knew about these things and they spoke about it in these very strange ways. But today "soul" has come to mean something which is utterly ridiculous.

> In the process of sense-perception, registering impressions of the world are somehow transformed into mental states, that is, ideas. The world itself we never perceive, but only ideas. *(V13, 21:1.24)*

Anthony: What would he mean when he says we perceive only ideas? Let's talk about that. Suppose we take this red box here, and we say we perceive this box. If you analyze the statement that I perceive this box that would mean that I feel it, it has a certain smooth feeling to it, I can see the color of it through my eyes, I can taste it if I bite it . . . So if we analyze the perception itself, what do we get? We get an idea. Red is an idea. The feeling of smoothness is an idea. The analysis in its entirety can give you only ideas. Now if you took away the ideas, the idea of red, the idea of smoothness, the idea of hardness, if you took all those ideas away, what would you have left? So if you go through an analysis of what you experience when you say "I perceive that object" and you analyze every aspect of that perception you'll say, well, these are simply ideas. Because that is all you experience, ideas. Red is an idea. Red is not a thing, it is an idea.

Paul: In scientific terminology redness is an interpretation. Different creatures with different sense functions aren't going to have the same spectrum of colors and visible forms that we have. Those are anthropomorphic interpretations of an object. Smoothness is dependent on the tactile sensitivity of your sense organ. Every quality is an anthropomorphic idea. It is coming from yourself, it is human. There is no quality that belongs to the object.

S: But you need your senses to experience it.

Anthony: Yes, we're not denying that. We are simply pointing out that what you experience is an idea, a bundle of ideas. You could call them sensations, but that doesn't change the fact that they are mental. So you experience a bundle of sensations and you refer to this bundle of sensations as a thing. But if you analyze each one of the sensations then you realize that you are analyzing your ideas about what this thing is. You never could find the thing in itself. You only come to these sensations that you have which you call the thing. So if you really analyze your experience, you will come up with the fact that all you are talking about is these sensations that you experience—which are nothing but ideas. You try that. Try it by yourself. If you analyze everything, you'll see that fundamentally and ultimately that is all you experience. In other words, the entire world is an experience, in your mind, of an idea. You could say, "Well that idea has been there a hundred years." That doesn't matter. We'll get to the analysis of time later on.

S: But the peculiar thing is that it appears to be outside.

Anthony: Yes, that is what is strange. Just like when you have a dream. It appears outside. Whereas sometimes in mystical development a person experiences himself as the Witness-I and then the world is inside him and he is not in the world, but the world is within him. Just like if it were possible for you to awaken while you were dreaming, you would experience the dream within you, not outside of you. But you have to be awake without disturbing the dream. And sometimes that happens in the case of these experiences where a person realizes the whole world is within him. Not inside the chest, but inside the mind.

> The mind can have dealings only with kindred objects formed from its own substance, that is, with thoughts, ideas. Therefore when it knows material objects they must really be ideas. *(V13, 21:2.161)*

Anthony: In a dream it's easier to recognize. When you wake up you see that what you experienced in the dream was an idea. That is, all you experienced was ideas—when you wake up!—but when you are dreaming you can't say that. Because that fire that you are warming your hands by in the dream makes you feel warm all over. You feel that the fire is out there and you are warming yourself by it. But when you wake up you realize that they were just ideas. There was no fire there. That was just an idea in your mind, and that you were getting warm was another idea. So when you analyze dreams you can see that you always experience a world of ideas. When you are in the dream you can't say to yourself, "Well this is just an idea," unless you are an adept at yoga. When you're in the dream you actually experience the warmth of the fire.

Now in the same way, you are in the sensible world. You say that tree is an idea. Yes, it is an idea. When you really reflectively understand, then you know it is an idea. But for most of us that tree is out there, I am over here, in between there is distance, and to me that tree is just as real as I am. You don't say, "That is just an idea in my mind." You have to be *reflectively* aware that that is an idea, just like this body is an idea, that the two are ideas. But you don't have that experience in ordinary wakeful consciousness except at certain moments, like for instance if you experience a serious grief or bereavement. If someone that you love very much dies, for a few minutes you experience the world, the whole thing, as a dream. It is not real, it has a kind of unreality about it. But that will last for a few minutes, then it goes and then you are back.

Sometimes when you meditate you get a feeling of utter peace, quiet. You open your eyes and gradually you come back. That feeling that the world is a dream is still there, very strong. It takes a little time and then gradually you begin to go back into the world. You can also have an experience that the world is an idea in your wakeful consciousness, while you are awake. But this is not going to come easily, it is going to require effort. It is going to require the ability to keep the mind quiet.

> Every presented thing which is seen, smelled, heard, felt, or tasted, no less than every representative thought, idea, name, or image, is entirely mental. The streets of busy towns and the forests of lonely mountains are all, without exception, mere constructs of the imagining faculty. *(V13, 21:2.91)*

> Mentalism teaches a view of physical existence which seems to contradict every experience of daily living. *(unpublished)*

Anthony: Remember, we quoted before that mentalism is almost the direct opposite of the naïve belief that we are born with, that there is a world out there and that I am here—that is real, this is real. He'll point out that when you study mentalism all that is going to be destroyed, it is directly opposite. The whole world is a construct, a mental construct that you think.

S: But it still exists?

Anthony: Sure, if you are thinking about something it is existing. But the point is, if you analyze the mountain or you analyze the box, it is a cluster of sensations, ideas, thoughts, images. No matter what it is. Everything is included. Nothing is left out.

> Now the realist assigns a greater degree of reality to that world than to its observer, because he says it will be there even when the latter has passed away. The idealist, however, assigns all reality to the observer because the world cannot be known apart from the latter. *(V13, 21:4.209)*

Anthony: He is saying that to the materialist, the realist, the world is more real than the observer, because the observer will die and the world will still exist. On the other hand, the idealist or the mentalist would insist that all reality comes from the observer. Take away the observer and there is no world. He's laying this out.

S: Well, there is no world for him. But for others there is a similar world.

Anthony: But if you bring in the others then you have to bring in their mind and their experience of their own mind.

S: But the thing is, I have my experience of my world and you have your experience, but somehow they are similar. So there must be some higher faculty that coordinates that.

Anthony: Yes, later on he will bring in the fact that the World-Idea superimposes itself simultaneously on all minds and that is why we have a similarity of experience. But make no mistake about it: when I have pain you don't experience it—it is mine and I can't give it to you, no matter what I do. You say, "Well, when I die then the world goes on for others." Well, sure, their mind is presenting the world to them, to each and every one. Each and every one has his own mind and that mind is presenting the world to him. The world is being presented to each individual mind. So I would be perfectly justified in saying that the only thing I know is what my mind presents to me. When I look at you, you are, so to speak, a thought in my mind. And likewise, when you look at me I am a thought in your mind. And this doesn't cancel out what we're saying when we say that each person's experience is of his mind. As a matter of fact it reinforces it. The point is, they think that there is going to be a world, but if you took away all minds, would there still be a world? That would be nonsense, because the only way you can speak about a world is if there is a mind that is observing it. If you take away the observer, then what are you talking about? The observer enters into every observation, which means that the observation and the observer are united. You can't have one without the other.

S: Could you say that if all observers die away and there is no one there to observe anything, then the world would not exist manifested, but there would still be a world unmanifested?

Anthony: There would be the World-Idea. The World-Idea won't be destroyed. But what the nature of the World-Idea is—that's a whole different ball game. Nevertheless, if we analyze human existence in its entirety we find that it consists of a world of objects and an observer of these objects.

> Everything that falls within the compass of human experience is known only to the mind and could never be known otherwise. What then are these mental reports? What could they be but ideas? *(unpublished)*

Anthony: Now you see what he is doing. When you say that the image on the retina goes up to the brain and triggers off neuron firings, he is saying, "Aren't these ideas too?" Even when the physiologist says, "Well, I can show you these processes going on," PB is saying, "But aren't these ideas too? Are they something outside the realm of ideas?" So even there he'll trip them up.

A lot of scientists think that they can explain the nature of mind or consciousness by describing the process. But that can't be done because you have to start out with thought to begin with. You have to first observe it. But if you observe it . . . you know, like Bertrand Russell said, when the surgeon thinks that he is looking at the brain of a man on whom he is operating, he is mistaken—all he has is an image in his own mind. Bertrand Russell is a materialist, not a mentalist, but he saw that point. He saw a lot of things. But in the final analysis, when you put his doctrines together, you can see that he believes in the existence of matter. And if you believe in the existence of matter you can't be a mentalist.

S: What does that mean, to believe in matter?

Anthony: You believe that there is something else besides mind. This next quote is difficult, but it's good.

> We may note the fact of being conscious, but we can never ordinarily note the fact that we are conscious of being conscious in the same way that we are conscious of everything else. *(V13, 21:5.144)*

Anthony: He is basically saying that we know that we are conscious, and we don't know that we are conscious of being conscious. That is a kind of unusual experience when you see that you are conscious of consciousness. In other words, the mind perceives itself functioning, that is equivalent to living in an enlightened state.

S: But in the dream state you can be the dream person and observe the dream at the same time. Sometimes you can be in that dual position, not often.

Anthony: You mean when you know that you are dreaming?

S: No, I don't know that I am dreaming. I am dream me and I act in a dream universe, but at the same time I watch the whole situation.

Anthony: If the dream person knows that he is dreaming, he usually wakes up. If he *doesn't* wake up, then he could have the experience of knowing that all he experiences is ideas. In other words, the world in that kind of a situation—the dream world—is very fluid. He sees that there is nothing fixed, that everything is like the metamorphoses of ideas taking place. Let's try again. Let us say I am dreaming and I am looking at a mountain. And to me that is a mountain and I am looking at it. I do not have the experience that the mountain is an idea. But if it were possible for me to wake up while I am dreaming that I am looking at a mountain, to wake up in the dream, then I would have the experience of knowing that I am experiencing an idea. And occasionally that could happen. It is almost like a *satori*. You suddenly experience the unreality of the world. You experience the world as idea, and that could happen even when you are awake. In the ordinary wakefulness you could have the experience that the world is an idea and you know that you are experiencing the world as idea. When you have that, it is a kind of consciousness that you ordinarily don't have. And some people can establish themselves and stay in that condition and know that the world is idea. Schopenhauer had that for a little while.

> The world is never really given to us by experience nor actually known by the mind. What is given is idea, what is known is idea, to be transcended only when profound analysis transforms the Idea into the Reality. *(V13, 21:2.105 and Perspectives, p. 281)*

Anthony: It is what we were talking about before when we gave the example that the sun rises and you know, because of your developed rationality, that the sun doesn't rise. It is the appearance of an arising. Now when you very intensely study something like that, you know as a fact and you experience in your own understanding the sun's rising to be an illusion, an appearance that the senses present you with. That is a fact that is known because of this analysis.

Let me see if I can think of a drastic example. If you are a scientist and you have been a scientist for many many years, you know that this chair is not a solid reality. It is not a thing. You know it to be the form, the flow, the structure of electronic energies. While you are looking at the chair you know it to be a kind of energy, but your eyes go on seeing the chair. So it is only through this very profound analysis that you gradually convert your naïve beliefs into an understanding which takes root and then can't be destroyed. In the same way, when you analyze the nature of your experience very intensely and recognize that it is an idea, and you keep going through this process, there comes a time when you recognize that all your experience is idea. There is no longer any doubt. Just as the scientist knows without doubt, "My eyes see a chair but my mind, my reason, just as clearly has shown me that it is nothing but electronic energies." That is why the development of the rational mind is so important. Without the rational mind a person will always remain at the level of primitive belief. You are born with these beliefs. You have to get rid of them. You are born with the belief that the earth is solid and standing still and the sun rises. And you have to destroy those beliefs. Otherwise you'll go on living like a primitive: "Oh, the sun rises, the world is a center."

S: So that is the only way, to develop the thinking?

Anthony: That is why this is a very unpopular subject.

S: So why is meditation important here?

Anthony: In meditation you will also experience these things. He says somewhere that first he had the mystical experience of mentalism and then he was able to explain it. [Anthony is referring to V13, 21:4.273—ed.] It can be reversed, too. You can study these things for many years and then get the mystical experience of the truth of these doctrines. Usually it happens that way. You have to spend many years in profound study and reflection and then you get the experience of the world as an idea, but only after you have gone through a very lengthy study.

The idea of meditation is to teach your mind to be very calm, very quiet, and go into itself. Also, in meditation your thinking has to get very, very sharp, like a surgeon's knife. You can't make a mistake because if you slip you are going to come up with the wrong notions. So the development of your rational faculty, the ability to concentrate for long periods of time, the ability to keep the mind quiet and still, all these things are necessary to realize and bring about the truth of who you are and what the world is.

S: But don't you develop your thinking through the mystical experience, too?

Anthony: Yes, it works both ways. As a matter of fact, the trouble is that most of the time if people aren't prepared philosophically in their understanding when these experiences come, they won't know what is happening. That's always a big problem. You could get an experience and it could blind you to what is going on. That is why they insist that you practice and that you understand. In other words, theory and practice have to go together.

> Mind and matter are incommensurables. Mind can enter into relations only with something allied to its own subtler nature, not with something wholly dissimilar, as matter is said to be. That which the mind knows must be relevant in relation to the Mind itself. There must be a community of kind between the two, a common identity of substance. The world as known cannot possibly be extra-mental in nature. Hence the characteristics of what the mind knows must be mental—that is, they constitute our ideas. *(V13, 21:2.162)*

Anthony: In other words, the mind can know only mental things. It cannot know something which is not mental. So it can know only thoughts, ideas, feelings—which are all of a similar nature. Now if there were such a thing as they speak about as matter, then the mind couldn't know it. It can't know something outside of its own jurisdiction, outside of itself. Whereas the realist would say that what the mind knows is a material thing, PB is saying, "How could that be? How could you bring together two things that are diametrically opposite to each other?" There is a lot of fun in modern physics with this because they found out that they don't even have matter. They can speak about energies which are tendencies and possibilities which could take a form, but matter—they don't know what that is anymore.

> It is seldom that the meaning of mentalism is immediately grasped; this is why it needs both explaining and approaching from various angles. *(V13, 21:4.49)*

Anthony: Well, that you will find out, I am sure. You see, the difficulty is that all your life you believe in the existence of a world of things, a reality which is non-mental. And when reason confronts you with the fact that you can't know anything except your own ideas, you try to excuse yourself by saying, "Well, regardless, there *is* something out there. It is true that I can know only my ideas, but my ideas are telling me about something out there." And they always try that, you know? In a sense, it is like the people who believed that the world was flat. No matter how much you explained to them, they always said: "Oh, but it comes to an end over there, you'll fall off."

You have to remember that if for many many lives we believed in a real world out there, outside of us, you are not going to be able to abolish a belief which has grown into you. You are not going to be able to abolish it with a stroke of a pen. It is going to take a lot of effort. Because these are beliefs that are ingrained, inborn, innate. I know that many psychologists don't believe in innate ideas, but the fact remains that when you take a child and toss him up in the air he'll startle, he will automatically exhibit an instinctive reaction of fear. And he never had the opportunity to learn that. Then why is he exhibiting fear? Well, it is built into the organism. I say the organism is mind. What's the difference between what the psychologists say and what I say? They say it is an instinct, an unlearned behavior response. They don't want to say it is an innate idea, so it is an unlearned behavior response.

S: Is the idea of "inside and outside" a false idea?

Anthony: Well, this chair is in this room and not outside the room. But I can't say this chair is in the mind because that means that the mind is like a big box and I've got the chair inside.

S: So would you say that "inside and outside" is a false idea?

Anthony: It is not applicable to the mind. It is a relative truth. There is an inside and outside. The universal truth of mentalism does not abolish relative truths. When I say that mind is the ultimate reality I am not at the same time saying that the distance between two objects does not exist. From the point of view of the mind itself, they don't exist. From the point of view of the objects, they do exist.

When we gaze at the world outside and think of that which ultimately gazes—the mind—we assume naturally that the two are distinct in themselves. This is the first untutored reaction. *(unpublished)*

S: What does untutored mean?

Anthony: Uninstructed. It's a reaction without any consideration. This is the way we all are, right? We look at the world, we gaze at the world, and our first reaction is that there are two distinct things here—the world and I who am looking at it. That is our first reaction. Immediate. But he points out that that's a reaction that is untutored. And we all are like that. After a while, culture tells you that if there is no observer, there is no observation. If you reflect very carefully you can see that there can't be one without the other. It isn't that the world is out there and the mind is here, looking at it. It is like two ends of one stick. You can't have one end of the stick. Either the two or none. But when we first have our experiences we are immature and as we look, we say, "Well, that's the world out there and this is me here, the mind here," and we think of them as two distinct things. And it takes a little reflection to see that no, that can't be. It can't be.

S: What is the cause of this?

Anthony: Well, you can look at it something like this. For millions of years, nature has been developing animal bodies. And these animal bodies operate with the instinct that there is a dinner out there, right? Like when a fox sees a chicken running, that is his dinner. So the fox is only interested in having dinner. He is not interested in whether his mind and the world form a unity. He is not interested in that. Now, as we go through many animal bodies and we have this for a background for thousands and thousands of lives, it is built in, it is automatic. It is what they call "the unlearned behavior response." You might call them inherited ideas. They are built into the body, automatically, if I can use that description. Actually they are built into the mind. The mind has learned to look at the world as though it were "out there." And it takes a tremendous amount of culture, reflection, study to start turning all those things upside down. In other words, we are born ignorant. Period. We are all born in bondage. We are not born free. We are born in bondage to our ignorance. But as we mature, as we reflect, then we start changing those things.

S: Is that ignorance what Santayana calls animal faith?

Anthony: Yes.

S: Could you call that matter?

Anthony: No, you can't call it matter.

S: Is it because of our karma, then?

Anthony: Karma would be the way we acted in the past, yes. But if you believe something intensely, over and over and over again, it gets built into you. You automatically react that way, you accept it. That is why it is so important to use your brains, to question things that happen: Is this the way it really is? Do you know what the Jesuits and also the dictatorial governments used to say? "Give me the child for the first five years, and then you can have him." After that the child does what they taught him to do. We are like little automatons, you know. They fix all the screws in the back and wind us up in a certain way. And then we just live out those ideas that they put in our minds.

Here is a question:

> The world *appears* to be outside us. But is it? *(unpublished)*

Anthony: For instance, the white on that wall, is that outside you?

S: I experience it as outside of myself.

Anthony: Yes, but the whiteness out there is an idea in the mind. Right? Whiteness is an idea in the mind. But if whiteness is an idea in the mind, then your mind has to be out there, too. Let's make it worse. You are looking at a cloud a hundred miles away. And it is a nice white fleecy cloud. If you analyze the experience of whiteness, it's an idea in your mind, right? Then that white fleecy cloud is in your mind. Well, where is the limit? There isn't any limit.

S: But I don't know that!

Anthony: No, but you have to constantly analyze and understand, because if an idea can only exist within the mind, then you can't put the world outside and the mind here. It has to be in the mind. So all the ideas that you have—ideas of whiteness, ideas of size, whatever the idea—have to be in the mind. And if the whiteness on the top of the mountain is a thousand miles away and you are looking at it, well, the mind includes you here and the whiteness over there. Because the mind has no size, no dimensions, no shape, no form. It is formless. So the whiteness is in your mind. And so is this body in your mind. And all of that is within the mind. The whiteness can't be out there and you here and a separation between them, because then that whiteness wouldn't be in your mind.

> We have now been able to discover that our ordinary sense of self is a muddled one, confusing thought and thing, mind and body. It may be thought that the statement of mentalism contradicts our natural belief in the solidity of the material world. But as a matter of fact it does not really contradict either of the aforementioned beliefs; it merely corrects them. For it does not deny that the world is external to the body, and it does not deny that all tangible things are solid to the touch. What it does say is that the world is internal to the mind and that its solidity is likewise present in the mind alone. *(V13, 21:2.17)*

Anthony: Generally when you speak about mentalism to people they get the strange idea that you are denying the existence of a certain object, whereas what he is saying is: "No, we are just telling you what that object is. It is a thought. We are not denying its existence, we are explaining it."

> The human mind can enter into relation with—that is, become aware of—that which is of the same nature as itself, that which is correlated to it, that which is also mental. It is impossible for material things to enter directly into the immaterial consciousness of man. *(V13, 21:2.16)*

S: That sounds like he is presupposing that there are material things.

Anthony: No, he's presupposing that the materialists believe that there are material things. See, this is a response to the realists who say that there is consciousness here, or the mind is here, and there's the object out there, and the object comes into the mind, into consciousness. He is simply pointing out that that is impossible.

> Tolstoy, when a mere youth, caught a glimpse of mentalist truth but fell into solipsistic fallacy. He thought he alone existed and that he merely had to withdraw his attention from the world-idea, and then it would completely vanish. Sometimes he even turned round abruptly, hoping to see this vast void! *(V13, 21:4.105)*

> Man feels himself powerless to shake off the sense and conviction of the world's externality and materiality. *(unpublished)*

Anthony: That is how powerful the belief is.

S: What is the difference between externality and materiality?

Anthony: Externality means that the world is out there. Materiality means that it is a thing: it is outside of the mind, and it is a thing. These are the two overriding, compulsive beliefs that are ingrained in our mind.

S: Could you say that space and time are the same as matter?

Anthony: No, I wouldn't say that. They're modes by which the mind operates or functions, but I wouldn't call them matter. They're modes of the mind's functioning.

> In these enchanted moments, all life takes on the shadowlike quality of a dream. *(V14, 22:6.151)*

S: Does this experience of the world as a dream or dreamlike have a sense of more reality—does it feel more real than to experience it as static?

Paul: Wouldn't you say that more of the sense of reality is put on the mental principle and not on the things that appear?

S: Yes, but does it feel *more real, accurate, or that it is more proper?*

Anthony: When you experience the world as a dream you know you are getting closer to its reality. It is not the reality yet, but you know you are getting closer. It is an intuitive understanding that dawns—that the mind projects the world, then experiences the world that it projects. And all that it could project is its own ideas. So you know you are getting closer to the nature of the reality.

S: So then I see the projecting *of the world, and that is what makes me experience it as more accurate. I mean, it's not like a dream which you have at night—because then you don't experience that you are making the dream. But when you experience* this *world as a dream, you also see that you project it. That is what makes the experience more accurate.*

Anthony: Well, it's not a question of accuracy. When you experience the world as a dream, rather than the way you experience it now, there is an intuitive understanding that arises with it at the same time that you are coming closer to the very nature of the mind. You are getting closer to it—you can almost feel it with your fingers, if I could use incorrect language. Because as long as you experience the world as stiff, hard, rigid, you will always think of it as non-mental, as a material thing. But if, while you are looking at that very world, you start experiencing it as a dream, as shadowy, as unreal, then you are getting closer to the mental processes that produce that idea. Go back to the example we used before, when we said that if you wake up in a dream and while you are awake in the dream you experience the dream, you come closer to the fact that you are experiencing ideas. And when you get this feeling that you're experiencing ideas, it is like you are getting closer to the mind-stuff, which is not rigid, not a fixed hard thing.

> Few can understand quickly this deep doctrine of mentalism. It takes time to do so. *(unpublished)*

Anthony: So that should encourage us to be patient, and keep at it.

S: Do you have to create new habits?

Anthony: But of course.

S: It is not something that just happens.

Anthony: No.

S: But when you have created new habits and when you have been studying this for a time, then it will happen?

Anthony: Well, you have to do it for a while. Goethe had a sign next to his bed, and it said: "The battle for freedom is fought every day anew." Most people say, "Well, I'll try once. That is it." No. It's continuous. A lot of people think, "If I read it once I'll understand and change my life." No! Even when you get a mystical experience, two minutes later the ego comes over, takes over and says, "Hey. Forget about that. *This* is the way it is."

S: You say one has to change one's habits. Could you say what kind of habits you are thinking of?

Anthony: The habits of ignorance. In other words, when we think that there is a thing out there, independent of my mind, that is a habit which was ingrained in us for a long, long time. You get up in the morning and you operate on that basis, and you go to sleep at night and all day long you think that way. Those are habits that have to be rooted out. And the way that you root them out is by constantly going over the teachings, understanding them until they are perfectly clear in your mind. So that when the thought tries to express itself as "that is a thing" you say, "No, that is a thought." In other words, you begin to see, in the precision of your language, that your habits are changing. You get more and more accurate in the way you speak—that could be considered as habit. The mental habits are almost impossible to break. They are so deeply rooted. You remember the saying that a man's character is his fate.

This next paragraph requires a little bit of philosophic understanding. I'll read it, just so that you can see for yourself that you have to build up a background, that you have to ponder these things, that you have to get acquainted with what other people have thought.

> I have tried to study the nature of the mind and to understand its office in knowing. And the end of all my studies brought me to the sequel that I was compelled to testify to Hume's strange statements: "Nothing is ever really present with the mind but its perceptions. . . . We never really advance a step beyond ourselves. . . . Philosophy informs us that everything which appears to the mind is nothing but a perception, and is interrupted and dependent on the mind, whereas the vulgar confound perceptions and objects, and attribute a distinct, continued existence to the very things they feel or see. There is no question of importance whose decision is not comprised in the science of mind; and there is none which can be decided with any certainty before we become acquainted with that." *(V13, 21:4.207)*

Anthony: Here is a man who, independently, came to the same conclusion—David Hume. He was forced into it. But you know, it kind of scared him. Still he stuck to the reasons, and he followed them to the end, and he came up with the conclusion that the only thing that accompanies mind is its own perceptions. There isn't anything else. There is mind and what it perceives and nothing else. And he says the vulgar keep on confusing perceptions with the objects. They actually think there is an object and a perception of the object. And he is saying: No, there is only the mind and its perceptions—there isn't anything else. But people insist on saying there is an object there. What they mean is there is a perception there.

David Hume really scared the pants off Immanuel Kant, and got

Kant to work this whole theory out, because Kant was really shocked after he studied Hume and he realized he didn't know anything. He spent a dozen years before he even wrote or did anything, just thinking about this, and he is one of the really great minds of the Western world. So you know, if you don't understand it all at once, don't be surprised.

> This doctrine is the spinal column of the whole body of philosophic teaching. *(V13, 21:4.34)*

Anthony: That is why if you don't understand mentalism you are not going to understand any religion, any philosophic tradition. It is out of the question. I have always tested a man by what he understood of mentalism.

> It is not only a doctrine to be believed but also a truth to be understood. *(unpublished)*

> The existence of the world is not a testimony to the existence of a divine creator, but to the constructive capacity of the mind. *(V13, 21:2.51)*

> The impact of this discovery that the mind is merely dreaming the world around him and that the senses are merely contributing to this dream, may be quite unsettling for a long while afterwards. Our life may be deprived of purpose, our existence of reality, our will of its power, and our desires of their vitality. For those who have been too attached to earthly things, such a mental state may be useful medicine to cure them of their excessive attachments. But man does not live by medicine alone; he needs bread. Therefore, we must put this discovery eventually in its proper place along with all the rest of philosophic truth. If we succeed in doing this we shall recover our balance, we shall live in the world but not be of it, we shall be adequate to our responsibilities but not be enslaved by them, we shall be active but not let activity destroy our inward peace. *(V13, 21:5.43)*

Anthony: Well, we have read enough quotes for you people to start talking now. We are friends here, right? You don't have to feel uneasy.

S: Can you explain further why we experience things as outside us? You say that we have always lived in an animal body and had to chase after food. Is that part of why we experience things as outside us?

Anthony: It became a habit. We think that it's outside.

S: Is it also a habit that we experience space and time?

Anthony: Yes.

S: What is the cause of that habit? Why did we develop it?

Anthony: That is the way—the best way it knows how—that the mind could represent to itself the World-Idea: by putting it into images, one after the other. That doesn't mean that it cannot do it in other ways. There are other kinds of beings that experience the World-Idea differently than the way we do.

But you should be concerned with "how" rather than "why"—because "whys" are forever. The "how" is what you want to know.

S: Do you mean that the mind has always been this way?

Anthony: As far as we are concerned—not that it has always been this way for others. As far as we are concerned, this is the way the mind has understood the World-Idea, by making an image, a picture of it. And then another picture, and then another picture.

S: And is it for the same reason that we experience the world as outside? I mean, it's not just a habit that developed because we have to get food for the body?

Anthony: No, it is more fundamental than that, insofar that picturing the idea is the way the mind makes that idea available to itself. It could do it in other ways, and very often people can experience the world differently than the way we experience it in space and time. Those are habits of the mind, not an absolutely fixed structure in the mind. The mind's natural way of being is really to be itself. But when it is provoked into activity by the World-Idea, the only way it knows how to express that Idea is like we just said: thinking or producing perceptions. There are other ways; you could perceive the World-Idea without making a perception, grasp it directly, without any intermediary. But that's a whole different thing.

S: When you realize mentalism, would that mean that you also stop identifying with the body?

Anthony: Temporarily it happens that you don't identify with the body.

S: But if it's permanent?

Anthony: Well, a sage is not identified with his body.

S: So, you have to be a sage?

Anthony: If you are speaking about a permanent condition where you know that you are the soul or the mind and not the body—permanent. That would be a sage. Whereas for most people who do get a glimpse that they are the soul or the mind, when the glimpse passes then the identification with the body returns. All right, the ego claims it . . . but the identification is considerably weaker now. Much weaker than it used to be before. Before the glimpse, a person has no doubt that he is this body. After the glimpse he knows that at the time he experienced that, he was not the body. So when he resumes the identification, it is like the *intensity* of that identification, the *compulsion* is loosened, is weak. So he doesn't take it as intensely or as seriously as before the glimpse.

S: You said that we shouldn't be so concerned with "why" as with "how." Was that for a particular question? For me it would be natural to be more concerned with "why" rather than "how."

Anthony: Well, questions on why the mind does it this way are really questions that are too advanced right now. They are questions on the nature of the powers of the mind and why it is manifesting the World-Idea the way it is doing it. These are questions that are much more advanced. I want to restrain ourselves to a discussion of the mind, that you are the mind, to get a feeling that you have always been that mind, you have never been anything else, even though you have been misinformed about it—all right?

We all are misinformed, because—did you ever watch little children? They have no sense of "me" when they are babies. It is something that grows up gradually. After two or three, then they begin to say "me" and they recognize that they are a person and all that. But in the beginning they hardly have any sense of that identification. It takes a little time. When that identification gets built in, you can't get rid of it until you actually go through the experience where you disidentify yourself from the body—the actual experience. You know, people have reported the fact that they have been lying in bed in the hospital, and all of a sudden they are looking down at their body in bed. They see their body objectively as "out there." And very often that produces within them the feeling that they are not their body, they are their mind. The body is something given to them, to make use of. Experiences like that very often help a person become more objective.

Now, in all these things you have to remember we are not saying that the body—your body or my body—is not important. It is important. What we are saying is that we are *not* that body, which is a different thing. We have to have a body to have experience of the world. Without a body we cannot experience the world as we see it and understand it. What we are saying is that it is important to understand that you, your "I," is not your body. If someone cuts off a leg—or two legs—you don't feel that the "I" is now less. I am not saying you won't feel pain. I am just saying that your sense of "I" is not based on whether you are eight feet or four feet tall. It is an immaterial presence that you can experience all the time. You know that there is an "I" in you somehow, but to understand it is another story.

S: Is there any connection with Kirlian photography where you can cut off part of a leaf but the aura of the whole leaf will be visible on the picture? Does this have anything to do with what you are talking about?

Anthony: No, because the "I" cannot be seen, with a machine or without a machine. You cannot see the "I." If you look at the aura of a person you can tell that maybe he has certain illnesses or you can tell something about that body's operational mechanism, but you can't indicate through it the mind or the sense of "I" that a person is. The point is that your I-ness, when you get to it, is a truly spiritual, immaterial, placeless, spaceless, nameless being. It is not any kind of thing whatsoever. And they won't be able to bury it when you die. You know, they asked Socrates, when he was being poisoned to death, "Where shall we bury you, Socrates?" And he answered, "If you can catch me, you bury me." You can bury my body, but you can't bury *me*.

S: But what is this aura, then?

Anthony: That has to do with the primal germ, the idea. In other words, the body is based on a certain idea, an archetype of the body.

They call that the aura, the auric egg, and it can be seen under certain conditions. That belongs to the whole animal organism, the way it has been built up. It has to do with the animal organism. It has nothing to do with this principle that we are speaking about, the principle of mind.

S: *Anyway, somehow it is closer to the soul or the idea than the physical body.*

Anthony: No. These are two different notions: on one hand the mind and on the other hand anything that is produced by the mind. The mind always remains in itself—spaceless, formless, intangible, omnipresent—whereas anything that has to do with a body is always related to space, time, causality, and so on. So they are utterly unidentifiables. They are incommensurables, if I could use the term, or there is an absolutely asymmetrical relationship between these two. I generally don't like to talk about this, because people get involved in occultism, they get all these strange ideas. And what we are discussing is, really, in a sense, straight philosophy. We are leaving out any kind of talk of occult phenomena.

You'll see that philosophy goes directly, pointedly, to the issues. Everything else is thrown aside, disregarded. What is the difference if you say "I am clairvoyant and I see things in clairvoyance" or if you are just an ordinary person and you say "I see a tree"? The problem of epistemology remains identical in both cases. If you take it up into the occult realm or bring it down to the sensible world, the problem of epistemology is "How do I know?" So if you want to say that you are clairvoyant, then I'll ask you, "Clairvoyant, how do you know?" It doesn't matter. So you get right to the point. Philosophy pushes aside all those irrelevant details and gets to the issues. And they are really quite fundamental. You remember Plato? He says we are sleepwalkers. We are walking around in our sleep. And if you tell people that they are sleepwalkers they say, "No, I am perfectly awake!"

S: *One thing that I think we all have difficulty with is not so much to understand the mentalist concept intellectually, but to make conscious the part of experience that we view as objective, to see that it is manifested by one's own higher individuality, to see how intimately connected it is with oneself. We think that our experience comes from without, and we don't want to see our subjective contri-*

bution, our own resentments or desires, for example. That is always the block, even if someone understands this.

Anthony: Yes, that is exactly the problem. If a person doesn't understand this, then he blames the world outside for his misfortunes. Nobody will blame himself, ever. But when he realizes that he is producing the world all the time, then even if he has to endure unfortunate situations or circumstances he is not going to blame anybody. He knows that ultimately he produced it and somehow is responsible for what is happening to himself. When this has happened, then if suddenly the world just crushes you—it says, "I am going to teach you," and it crushes your ego—then you can let go of everything. And for a moment the world comes in and informs you of the situation. In those brief moments, a person wakes up. But most of us are not like that. Why? Because we believe that the world is "out there," forcing us to go through certain situations. The world does this, the world does that, all the time we are feeding one lie with another.

S: That is a discipline that one has to undertake in order to get understanding, isn't it?

Anthony: That is exactly the price we pay. If we want more consciousness, we know that a certain amount of suffering is inevitable. Because we have to give up certain ignorances that we accept and live as the gospel truth.

S: But why is what you are talking about so much easier to grasp and understand and accept than the notion that we produce "material things"—a tree, or whatever? What you are talking about now is clear and evident. But that I produce a plant—I drop out there. Why is the one thing completely clear and the other one so terribly difficult to understand?

Anthony: See, what she can't accept is that her thinking has produced the world that she sees, the lamp, the tree, the mountain . . .

S: That is what is hard to understand.

S: There are levels of understanding, I think. Some of these things are easier than others to grasp.

Anthony: Yes, you remember when Galileo saw the moons around Jupiter. He called over the theological students and said, "Now, you look and you can see for yourselves." And they looked through the telescope and saw the moons circling around Jupiter. They said, "I see it, but I don't believe it." Remember? You know, they tortured that man!

When you start attacking beliefs, whether yours or someone else's, you are undertaking a Himalayan task. You just have no idea of how deeply rooted these beliefs are. It is easier for me to take a hammer and knock that wall down than for me to take a hammer and knock that habit out. She can't accept the fact that her mind produces her body and the world she experiences.

S: When you learn to look through the illusion of matter, or try to do so, isn't it an inner work? Don't you have to confront those habits, or work on them within yourself in a much more intimate and real way than just believing it?

Anthony: Yes. You see, you can't go by what I say—my understanding is not yours. It can't be yours.

S: You have to confront the idea of matter within you, in your own body, isn't that true?

Anthony: Well, basically, in your own mind. This is the way the mind has functioned for so long, and to change it is going to require many, many years of active doing. In other words, every time a thought comes out, it has to be corrected; over and over again you keep going over this process. And then, of course, you have to try to get the experience, too—the mystical experience of everything being thought. Once you get the mystical experience that everything is thought, then it is easier to accept the fact that your mind produced the world-experience. But if you don't have the experience that the world is a thought, then it is going to be very hard for you to believe that your mind produced the world, the World-Idea! You first have to get the understanding that the appearance is thought, you've got to get that first. Then and only then can you say, "Well, of course, if it's only thought, then my mind did it! What other mind could do it?" So, that means that you have to go through this constant analysis of your experience, tear it down to its rudiments and see that it is only, so to speak, ideas. And you have to keep doing that. And then on top of that, you have to be able to try, in some kind of meditational experience, to actually *feel* it.

S: So what you say is that one has to go through this over and over again, your experience with the complete work.

Anthony: Yes, this is what they call the Work. The Great Work. The world is such stuff as our dreams are made of.

S: So every time you have experience of a door, or a bird . . .

Anthony: Every time you have experience, you look into it and analyze what your experience consists of. If you wanted, I could prescribe for you a kind of reading where these ideas are constantly analyzed. So you could read Berkeley, you could read Hume, you could read Kant, Schopenhauer, Fichte, right? Gradually, little by little, you hammer away at it, until you change these beliefs.

S: And would you say that a person could reach the same results through a recognition, come to the same truth about life through another "door" than the intellectual?

Anthony: Yes. You can go through what they call the devotional path. Saint Teresa of Avila was one who had experienced the truth of these things. As a matter of fact, she even told one of her students: "Don't believe in your ecstasies, in your raptures. There is a truth that is greater than all of that." She was an exceptional woman.

S: Could you reach enlightenment without understanding it?

Anthony: No. What do you think enlightenment is—for fools?

S: What difference does it make in practical life if you have this understanding of mentalism? Would you still think it would be easy to imagine that everything is mental if I punched you in the nose?

Anthony: When Johnson heard about Berkeley's ideas on mentalism, he kicked a stone and said: "See, I refuted Berkeley." What does that prove? If you punched me in the nose, then I would have to go through the same process to understand what happened. Well, a certain velocity of your arm hits this bone, and I feel pain. But in order for me to feel pain, let us see, the nerve had to go all the way up to the brain and . . . now wait a minute, how come I experience this pain? So it isn't a question that if I punch you in the nose I refute mentalism.

S: I understand that, but would there be a difference between an ordinary person and a sage in the way they experience pain?

Anthony: I was looking at PB. He cut his finger and I was looking at him. I was very ignorant and I figured: "Well, he is a superior being, a sage." I said, "Does it hurt?" He looked at me and said, "Of course it hurts!" That is how stupid I was! Because if it is only an idea, then it doesn't exist, right? He says, "No, wrong! It does exist!"

We are explaining *things*. We are not explaining them away.

S: But isn't there a difference if you are identified with the pain?

Anthony: I'll tell you a story about a lama who was captured by the Chinese. He was put through tremendous torture, and for some reason or other the soul took him out. It raised his consciousness. And he said he had the experience as though someone else were suffering the pain. But the pain was still there.

S: But it was easier . . .

Anthony: It was easier, yes. And sometimes that happens in the case of certain saintly people. When they are being tortured, the higher self comes in and takes their consciousness out of the body so that the pain is lessened considerably. Those things can happen. But the fact remains that it is your body and that your soul is working through that body and will experience the states of that body. We have a very intimate connection with our body, and until our time is over with that body we will experience the states that the body has to go through. This body is part of the world, part of the whole circuit, and the changes that are going on in the cosmos change the body. There is always a reaction, and in order to experience the World-Idea the soul must identify with that body. Do you think Nature went through all this trouble of developing this wonderful brain so that you could say, "No, nothing doing"? That's how the soul finally becomes aware of itself, through the experiences it gets through body after body. It grows that way.

Paul: A sage could be aware of the world, or he could step out of the world.

S: He can choose?

Anthony: Yes, but usually the sage accepts his karma. The pain is lessened, not taken away completely. In the example I used of the lama, he said the pain was there. It seemed as though it were happening to someone else. But it was there.

S: Was it a special case with this particular lama, or could it happen to anyone at that level of development?

Anthony: It probably could happen to anyone else at that level. A higher state of consciousness could happen to a person. It is as if the soul becomes much more prevalent, or let me put it this way. Sometimes a person is about to die and something comes into him which gives him the strength to accept it. And you see a peace and a calmness in his bearing which wasn't there before. You know something has happened to the person. He doesn't have to be a sage. Very often he is not. I have read of many cases of people dying. They were in severe pain and a presence came to them and they felt relieved. The pain was there, but not as intensely experienced. There was a loosening of identification with the body.

The Buddhists say everything is illusion. But they don't say that about pain. They say suffering is real. They don't try to minimize it, it is real. As a matter of fact, that is one of their cardinal doctrines. Life is suffering. And the sooner you find that out, the better. But most of us won't find that out. We get little disappointments and we keep trying for more.

S: What is the reason for pain?

Anthony: Well, that's a subject all by itself—the spiritual value of pain and suffering. But first of all, pain is real. It's a part of the World-Idea and even the sage has to know pain. Even the Buddha died in pain—after eating some food that was poisoned or bad. But you have to remember, a sage's experience of pain isn't like yours. When we have pain, we feel that the self is completely negated. If I get into pain, for example, I feel like God abandoned me, left me to my own devices. I know nothing but a denial of my self. A sage doesn't experience the denial of the self, but he will experience the pain.

There are some schools of thought, like the positive thinking schools, who say that pain or evil doesn't exist. Those people are crazy. After all, that's one of the ways in which the ego gets instructed. You will notice that when a person is in pain he becomes humble. Ordinarily he is not humble. Get a little pain and you'll learn humility fast. But let the pain go away, and the arrogance comes back.

So, very often we are put through pain to learn certain lessons. I can't say what they are in general, because every case is individual. But it always has a spiritual function.

S: When we say we are not our body, wouldn't it be more correct to say that we are not only our body?

Anthony: Yes. We are our body, but we are much more than the body. Anyone who denies the body is a fool. I mean, how do you go about in the world? Many of the people who write on spiritual subjects simply don't know what they are talking about.

S: Before you said mind has these habits of thinking. Do you use "mind" in two different ways? PB uses mind with capital M and little m. Can you say Mind has habits? Or do you mean the personal mind?

Anthony: Let me put it to you this way. If you say you know something—you know that two plus two is four, for example—who is this knower? Little mind? Big mind? Middle-size mind?

S: But isn't the personal mind somehow a part of a bigger mind—the World-Mind? And Mind itself, in the biggest way that you can use it, cannot have habits, can it?

Anthony: You mean the World-Mind? No, it has no habits. Or do you mean your higher mind? The highest in you? The Overself? No, it has no habits.

S: But you said before that mind has habits. So you used the word "mind" in another sense.

Anthony: Yes. There is a part of the mind which is always interested in getting embodied, in having a body. And it is *that* part of the mind that has certain habits, which it picks up in every incarnation as it goes along. That is usually referred to as the lower mind, or we can call it the lower soul, or that part of the mind which has a desire to have earthly life. That is the part of the mind which is always involved with bodies. That is the part of the mind that has to learn how to get out of bodies, to learn what it has to learn and then release itself from the compulsion to have bodies. But it is basically still your mind.

S: It is very important to know that there are different parts of the mind.

Anthony: Not different. It is not really different minds. It is one mind. But it has various powers. It has the power to reason, it has the power of memory, it has the power to perceive—so one and the same mind has all these powers. Now, some of the powers are more interested in experiencing a sensible world. Other powers of the mind are more interested in abstract reasoning. But in general we apply the generic term "mind" to all of that. So it is your mind in the sense that it is one mind, one mind with many powers.

S: *Can you say that the person's psychology and character is somehow part of mind, or an aspect of mind?*

Anthony: Well, when the faculties of the mind—memory, perception, reasoning, and so on—have to operate through a body, then you have a psychology. But prior to their operation in a body you don't have any psychology. Look, doesn't it appear strange that the mind—the whole mind—could be present when I get a pain in my toe and when I get a pain in my ear? The whole mind is present there and present here. Isn't that baffling? If you think of the head of a pin, you use your whole mind, and if you think of the continent of Australia, you use your whole mind. You don't use a little piece of the mind to think of a little pinhead, and a bigger piece of the mind to think of Australia. It is a very mysterious entity, this mind.

S: *You use your whole mind just to . . .*

Anthony: . . . to imagine the little head of a pin, yes. And you use your whole mind if you imagine the whole continent of Australia.

S: *That's very strange.*

Anthony: The mind is a strange thing. Our ignorance about it is unbelievable. Have you heard of some of these mathematicians that are born prodigies? They can multiply seven-digit numbers by seven-digit numbers in their heads and give you the answer before you are finished working it out on paper.

S: *You said that when the mind operates through the body, it becomes your psychology. Could you be on two levels somehow? Can you be your psychology and at the same time be witnessing it? That seems like your mind can split in two: mind taking one form, the psychology, and mind taking at the same time another form, witnessing the psychology.*

Anthony: What form is it taking? In other words, when you experience yourself as the Witness-I, your psychology, your personality, becomes very objective to you. You see why the ego is doing certain things. And at the same time, you are the ego doing those things. Does that mean that you have two minds?

S: No.

Anthony: That is what I mean when I say that the mind could be totally present when I have a pain in my toe and when I have a pain in my ear. It is both places. Totally here and totally there. That's enough to baffle you.

S: So mind is present everywhere.

Anthony: No, everywhere is present to mind. Right? Mind isn't present everywhere. Because what you're doing that way is putting mind in space, whereas what I'm saying is that mind is present anywhere and everywhere. Or let's put it this way: wherever you want to go, the soul is already there, mind is already there. It isn't that it has to seek you out. Can I repeat what I said? It's not that the mind is everywhere. Because then that would be like saying: mind is in space, and any place you go, mind will be there. But what we have to say is that mind is not in space, it is not *where*, it is not in some place. But mind is present to every place. If there is a place, mind is present. Mind is not in space and you cannot look for it in something. Space is within mind.

S: Space is a thought in the mind.

Anthony: Space is a thought within the mind, yes. Space *is* thought. If you had no thought, there would be no experience of space.

S: If it is a thought, that explains that it is in the mind.

Anthony: So we do live in a mystery all the time, don't we?

S: Are thoughts always pictures, not words?

S: Everything is thoughts—words, sounds, not only pictures. When you hear things, that is also a thought. Sounds, smells, everything.

S: Or you can say ideas. Some ideas you call pictures, some ideas you call something else.

S: Are thought and idea the same thing?

Anthony: Very often the word "image" is used in that way. You could have an image of something formless. "Image" is used in a very extensive and broad way today.

S: Do you use thought in one way and idea in another, or do you mean exactly the same thing by them?

S: They would be synonyms to me. Ideas in our mind or percepts in our mind would mean the same thing.

Anthony: When I use a term like "percept," that includes an abstract thought or image or picture, even a feeling. "Percept" is very comprehensive and includes any kind of presentation to consciousness.

S: We are trying now to educate our thinking, and that obviously can be done in different ways. We meditate, we discuss philosophic questions—these two things are tied together, they complement each other to produce a better understanding. But how can we learn to create more constructive habits? We need practical ideas on how to do this. Reading these things, constantly trying to get it little by little, is this the only way?

Anthony: In the beginning that is the main way. Because you have to be informed that you are misinformed. You have to start there. I don't know if you ever read Plato's *Alcibiades*? It is about a man who wanted to be emperor because he thought he was the greatest. And Socrates talks to him and tries to find out why he thinks he is so great. By the time Socrates finishes with him, he demonstrates that he is no better and no worse than any other Joe Blow. But the whole discussion finally ends up in the fact that Socrates points out . . . here is a man who is ignorant, well, that is pretty bad, but what makes it really bad is that he doesn't know that he is ignorant. There is ignorance and then there is ignorance of ignorance. And the second kind is deadly. Because if you don't know that you are ignorant, you can never do anything about your ignorance. But once you become aware that you are ignorant, then you can start working on it. It is really quite a beautiful dialogue of Plato. You should read it together in class. It is not very long. It is very, very beautiful and to the point. This is the fundamental problem, that we are ignorant that we are ignorant.

S: Is it really hard to find intelligent questions?

Anthony: But of course. As soon as a person asks me an intelligent question, I don't even bother because he's on his way. If you can ask an intelligent question, that shows that you already understand. To formulate a question precisely is already quite a feat of knowledge.

THREE
Focusing the Mind

Anthony: Last night we discussed mentalism and tonight we will let your brains rest and we will discuss meditation. In these notes PB covers an enormous amount of ground and those of you who want to take up meditation may find enough hints here as to what to do, how to go about it. These are aphoristic statements, not a long logical sequential treatment of the subject. Sometimes they run a couple of sentences. But basically they are very pithy, they are making a certain point. And as we read them we could discuss them. So we will start out with the simplest ones I could find.

> Meditation without purification may be dangerous. *(unpublished)*

S: What kind of meaning would he put into purification?

Anthony: It covers the gamut. Purification is something that you gradually keep adding to. You don't try all at once to do everything. But you try to live a more ethical life, you try to take care of your body. You attempt to leave out any unethical actions. If there is hatred in a person's heart, for example, he really can't meditate. If there is preoccupation with some greed or lust, all these things must gradually be weeded out. So it is in the grand sense that purification must be taken. And we can only do it a little at a time. As long as a person is constantly striving to improve his ethics, his character, his morality, then it is all right. But people who sit to meditate with their heart full of envy or hatred are asking for trouble, because it boomerangs, comes right back. Do you remember we pointed out that meditation is very creative? The kind of thoughts you think in those periods when your mind is concentrated inevitably have to get manifested. So meditation without purification may be dangerous.

All aspirants should be warned that self-development in meditation without some co-equal effort and development in morality, intellectuality, and practicality may easily lead to a state of unbalance which would unfit them for the ordinary obligations and duties of life. *(V4, 4:1.458)*

Since meditation forms an essential part of the Quest's practices, a part of the day must be given up to it. It need not be a large part; it can be quite a small part. The attitude with which we approach it should not be one of irksome necessity but of loving eagerness. We may have to try different periods of the day so as to find the one that will best suit us and our circumstances. This, however, is only for beginners and intermediates, for one day we shall find that any time is good enough for meditation time just as every day is Sunday to the true Christian. *(V4, 4:2.35)*

The press of house duties can be repulsed for a few minutes to make place for this valuable and important exercise. ***(unpublished)***

Anthony: In other words, you could wash the dishes later.

Once you have caught this inner note in your experience of your own self-existence, try to adhere firmly to the listening attitude which catches it. *(V15, 23:6.228)*

S: Could you say something about that?

Anthony: In meditation, when the mind is very quiet and the thoughts have subsided somewhat, there is a feeling attitude that a person operates with. It is as if you are fishing around and you pick up the scent of your own being. It is the kind of attitude like, for instance, if you are listening to a piece of music and you are following the thread theme or the motif every time it comes; because you are listening, and you are in a state of expectation, you'll pick it up as soon as it comes. Now, in meditation, very often when you are listening inwardly you can pick up what you might call the life-current in you. And it is a kind of certification of your own being. It is a feeling that you are authentic. I don't know how else to put it. Do you have any notion of what I mean when I say that you have a feeling that you are authentic, that you are for real?

It is a very delicate subject, this listening attitude that you acquire when you meditate. You have an attitude where you are very attentive. You know there is something there but you just cannot quite get to it. Nonetheless without that attitude of listening and paying attention you would miss the whole point. Again, imagine you are listening to a great piece of music. You know that at a certain place there are a few very important measures that are very melodious and very inspiring, but you are not listening and they go by. And you are not there. But if you were in the attitude of listening and expectation and you were watching for it, the moment it arises you would immediately pick it up and you would feel it. In a similar way, when this current comes through you or passes through you, you pick it up and you hold on to it and it takes you deeper and deeper into yourself. And they call that the life-current. Some people refer to it as the I-current. But you have to look for it. We'll circle around and try to get a picture as we go along.

> The more inert the ego can be during this exercise, and the more passively it rests before the Overself, the fuller will be the latter's entry. Obviously this condition cannot be achieved during the first stage, that of conscious effort and struggle with distractions. *(V15, 23:7.253)*

> He must lock himself in a room for a few minutes every day with the fierce determination to tame his mind which jumps about like a monkey. He must choose a topic and then keep his thoughts rigidly fixed on it. He should concentrate all his attention on it and try first to provoke and then to develop a sequential logical line of thought about it. He must wear down its resistance by unremitting daily practice of this kind. *(Perspectives, p. 44)*

S: *Does that mean that you choose a subject and keep concentrating on it? I didn't get the point that you could also develop a thought as long as you keep it on the topic. Is that what he meant?*

Anthony: Yes. In the beginning the procedure generally is that you take a certain topic. Maybe I can give an example. Let's say that there is a paragraph in an inspired book that you particularly like and feel drawn to. You memorize the passage so that you don't have to refer to it. Then you sit down and meditate on the passage. Let us say you repeat the whole passage, and then you take one sentence at a time, or better still, one phrase or unit meaning at a time. You concentrate very intensely on it and make sure that you understand, or you try to extract the meaning from it. And you do that, meaning by meaning, until you finish the whole paragraph. Then you go back and do this a couple of times so that the essence, the quintessence, of the meaning of that paragraph is drawn out for you. And you elaborate on this meaning. You expand it, you amplify it. You draw out all these relationships from the center, so that by the time you are finished with the subject you feel as though you thoroughly explored every facet of it. Right? And you got absorbed into it. That would be the first phase of meditation.

Then the next phase would be where you restrict your attention to one facet and you don't move from there. You take one facet and keep repeating it in your mind and there comes a point when you feel as though you are just gazing at it. You are not thinking any more—the discursive mind has come to a halt. But the idea is right there in front of you all the time. Now you are no longer discursively ruminating and spreading out, magnifying, amplifying, but you are on one passage, you are on one particular idea, and you are not moving away from it any more. You stay there. That would be the second stage of meditation.

And there is the third stage where the intensity of your gazing upon that facet, the very intensity, elicits an absolute self-absorption. The mind doesn't move. You are now in a state of contemplation, completely self-absorbed.

He'll go through some of these. But most of us have to start at the level of discursive exercise. Not to plunge into, try to do advanced exercises until we are ready.

> We habitually think at random. We begin our musings with one subject and usually end with an entirely different one. We even forget the very theme which started the movement of our mind. Such an undisciplined mind is an average one. If we were to watch ourselves for five minutes, we would be surprised to discover how many times thought had involuntarily jumped from one topic to another. *(V4, 4:3.25)*

Anthony: I think we are all familiar with that. Our mind is like a grasshopper. We don't even know which way it is going to jump.

> When it is said that the object of concentration practice should be a single one, this does not mean a single thought. That is reserved either for advanced stages or for spiritual declarations. It means a single topic. This will involve a whole train of ideas. But

they ought to be logically connected, ought to grow out of each other, as it were. *(V4, 4:3.79)*

Anthony: All right? That was the first part of what we were speaking about in the previous quotation, where you start meditation at a discursive level, and you take a paragraph and you memorize it and you repeat it in your mind. You try to understand every shade of meaning, every nuance, any possible association. You draw everything out. That is discursive meditation. Now, most people don't consider that meditation. I think they are mistaken. I think it is meditation. If you can keep your mind unswervingly to one topic and not deviate, you are getting concentrated.

Meditation can be learned by the orthodox as well as the unorthodox, by the atheist as well as the theist, by the rationalist as well as the mystic. *(V4, 4:1.51)*

Anthony: It doesn't matter what you believe, or don't believe.

These concentrations begin to become effective when they succeed in breaking up the hold of his habitual activities and immediate environment, when they free his attention from what would ordinarily be his present state. *(V4, 4:3.81)*

Anthony: You know how often you put on a piece of music because you just want a moment of inspiration to get out of your humdrum environment and your meaningless existence? So many of us will put on a piece of music or read a piece of poetry just to have even a few moments of inspiration for the day. With meditation that can be done very systematically.

Some of these notes are very advanced. I'll read this one anyway.

The "great void" mentioned in my book is not synonymous with death. Death conveys the idea of the loss of consciousness. There is no loss of consciousness in this state, but the consciousness is transformed indescribably. The state is so blissful, moreover, that there is no worrying about the loss of the ego. However, it is a temporary state because so long as we are living in the flesh we are unable to sustain it and are drawn back by the forces of nature—first to the ego and then to the body. But anyone who has been through that experience even once cannot possibly regard the ego and the body ever again in the same way, because their limitations are clearly felt.

In any case, one need not worry about the absolute condition but rather should await its arrival—then judge whether it is worthwhile or not. *(V15, 23:8.72)*

Anthony: Like I said, this is advanced, so we won't worry too much about it. Here's an easier one.

Meditation is a very delicate technique and incorrectly done may do some harm as well as good. Moreover there are times when it is even necessary to abandon it, in order to strengthen weaker parts of the personality which might otherwise affect the meditator adversely as he becomes more sensitive through the practice. *(V4, 4:1.459)*

S: What kind of things would have to be strengthened?

Anthony: There are times, there are certain periods when, for instance, a person may be ill, and it might be wise not to meditate because that might exaggerate the state of mind. It is a delicate thing, because sometimes when a person is going through a crisis it might be wise to meditate. The situation has to be judged individually. In some instances it is wise to go on meditating because a crisis is developing, let us say in your outside world, in your business relations or marriage or whatever. It really depends on the individual to try to get the clue or the intuition from within whether he should sit or not. And very often, by sitting, a person will gain the necessary calmness, the repose, to help him. But also very often, because of his condition, it is unwise to sit. Not only because he cannot concentrate, but also because the state of mind gets exaggerated in the meditation process and what you could handle before now you have difficulty handling. I can't give a straightforward answer on this one.

One of the causes of the failure to get any results from meditation is that the meditator has not practised long enough. In fact, the wastage of much time in unprofitable, distracted, rambling thinking seems to be the general experience. Yet this is the prelude to the actual work of meditation in itself. It is a necessary excavation before the building can be erected. The fact is unpleasant but must be accepted. If this experience of the first period is frustrating and disappointing, the experience of the second period is happy and rewarding. He should really count the first period as a preparation, and not as a defeat. If the preliminary period is so irksome that it seems like an artificial activity, and the subsequent period of meditation itself is so pleasant and effortless that it seems like a perfectly natural one, the moral is: more perseverance and more patience. *(V4, 4:3.2)*

Anthony: Most people have the experience for the first few years when they meditate of the difficulty of practicing concentration, of trying to keep the mind still, or, let's say, concentrating their mind on one thought. You know, you sit down and you have your mind on the subject, and you start trying to get concentrated, and a thought will come in. You push it aside. Another thought comes in. You push it aside. You move, you start thinking about the subject, another thought comes in—you push that aside. Anger comes up, you push that aside, and it goes on and on and on. And it can go on for years. Of course, you can shorten it by the determination, the ferocious determination: "I am going to stop this." You can shorten the length of time, but basically we all have to go through this period where the mind is continuously revolting against any attempt to discipline, to think and concentrate on one point. Try to remember that. The mind will not willingly surrender its own sovereignty. It is not going to preside over its own liquidation with joy. Don't have any illusions about the way the mind can trick and deceive us.

He should fully understand and accept the importance of being punctual in keeping his unwritten appointment when the meditation hour comes around. If he is careful to honour his word in social or professional engagements, he ought to be at least not less careful in honouring it in spiritual engagements. Only when he comes reverently to regard the Overself as being the unseen and silent other party with whom he is to sit, only when he comes to regard failure to be present at the prearranged time as a serious matter is the practice of these exercises likely to bear any of the fruits of success. It is a curious experience, and one which happens too often to be meaningless, that some obstacle or other will arise to block the discharge of this sacred engagement, or some attractive alternative will present itself to tempt him from it. The ego will resent his disturbance of its wonted habits and resist this endeavour to penetrate its foundations. He must resist this resistance. He must accept no excuse from himself. The decision to sit down for meditation at a stated time is one from which he is not to withdraw weakly, no matter what pressure falls upon him from outside or arises from inside. It may require all his firmness to get away from other people to find the needed solitude or to stop whatever he is doing to fulfil this promise to himself, but in the end it will be worthwhile. *(V4, 4:2.370 and Perspectives, p. 39)*

If the reverie attains the depth of seeing and feeling hardly anything outside him, being only faintly aware of things before him or around him, that is quite enough for philosophical purposes. A full trance is neither necessary nor desirable. *(V4, 4:3.100)*

S: What is meant by a full trance?

Anthony: You become unconscious of the world completely. You break off completely from it. It has some disadvantages for us, a full trance. We live in contemporary society. When you are in full trance and somebody comes banging at your door, you'll be shocked off to oblivion. The phone will ring, I can assure you. Better still, somebody's baseball will come through the window. There is a little danger in full trance, because of the shock condition that you are subject to. Nonetheless, if you can get to a state where you are in a reverie, the world is far away—it is there, but very far away, very dim, and you hardly give it any attention anymore—that is good enough, because that will get you into the mental world.

The only way to learn what meditation means is to practise and keep on practising. This involves daily withdrawal from the round of routine and activity, of about three-quarters of an hour if possible, and the practice of some exercise regularly. The form which such an exercise should take depends partly upon your own preference. It may be any of the set formal exercises in books published, or it may be a subject taken from a sentence in some inspired writing whose truth has struck the mind forcibly; it may be a quality of character whose need in us has made itself felt urgently, or it may be a purely devotional aspiration to commune with the higher self. Whatever it is, the personal appeal should be sufficient to arouse interest and hold attention. This being the case, we may keep on turning over the theme continually in our thoughts. When this has been adequately done, the first stage (concentration proper) is completed. Unfortunately most of this period is usually spent in getting rid of extraneous ideas and distracting memories, so that little time is left for getting down to the actual concentration itself! The cure is repeated practice. In the next stage, there is a willed effort to shut out the world of the five senses, its impressions and images, whilst still retaining the line of meditative thinking. Here we seek to deepen, maintain, and prolong the concentrative attitude, and to forget the outside environment at the same time. The multiplicity of sensations—seeing, hearing, etc.—usually keeps us from attending to the inner self, and in this stage you have to train yourself to correct this by deliberately abstracting attention from the senses. We will feel in the early part of this stage as though we were beating against an invisible door, on the other side of which there is the mysterious goal of your aspiration. *(V4, 4:1.231 and Perspectives, p. 38)*

The first quarter-hour is often so fatiguing to beginners that they look for, and easily find, an excuse to bring the practice to an abrupt end, thus failing in it. They may frankly accept the fatigue itself as sufficient reason for their desertion. Or they may make the excuse of attending to some other task waiting to be done. But the fact is that almost as soon as they start, they do not want to go on. They sit down to meditate and then they find they do not want to meditate! Why? The answer lies in the intellect's intractable restlessness, its inherent repugnance to being governed or being still. *(V4, 4:3.9)*

The first thing which he has to do is to re-educate attention. It has to be turned into a new direction, directed towards a new object. It has to be brought inside himself, and brought with deep feeling and much love to the quest of the Soul that hides there. *(V4, 4:3.83)*

Anthony: Well, you see you are getting involved in something very difficult. So if you have no illusions about how difficult it is, you won't get disappointed too quickly.

The mind can be weaponed into a sharp sword which pierces through the illusion that surrounds us into the Reality behind. If then the sword falls from our grasp, what matter? It has served its useful purpose. *(V4, 4:3.84)*

Whoever wishes to pluck the fruits of meditation in the shortest time must practise with both perseverance and regularity. This advice sounds platitudinous, but it happens to be true within the experience of most students. Such is the law of subconscious mental unfoldment and it is by understanding and applying it that success can be attained. *(V4, 4:2.365)*

Anthony: As far back as you could study in history, men have been interested in reaching and finding God, whether you say it is within themselves or whatever. And no one is going to stop that, because it is inherent in man to do so. Now, for most men that isn't true; but there are always a few, somewhere, for whom that is all they want. And they will do anything to get there. And PB, of course, was one such person in my opinion. So once you decide, once a person from within wants to find God, it doesn't matter what his personality says, what his ego says, what friends say, what father and mother say, what the government says, it doesn't matter any more. He will find a way to find that.

How long should the period of meditation be? The demands for a concentrated attention upon his mind and for a still posture upon his body exhaust him after a certain time. The attention flags and the posture becomes a strain, the interest tires and the innate restlessness of the human psyche makes it unprofitable and unreasonable to continue his practice when this time has elapsed. He cannot stand this further strain. *(unpublished)*

It is an obstacle to success in meditation if he times himself by a watch or a clock. This will create a subconscious pressure diverting his attention intermittently towards the outer world, towards his affairs and schedules in that world, towards the passage of time—all things he had better forget if he wants to remember the Overself and reach its consciousness. *(V4, 4:2.293)*

S: What about using an alarm clock?

Anthony: Yes, you could. You mean the kind that rings? That is better than watching a regular clock. Some of us have to use a clock. Any time I meditate with a group I use a clock. Or I use a timer. I set it for forty minutes or fifty minutes and then it goes off. But it is true that if you go by the clock, you will feel a certain amount of pressure, and every now and then, you'll see that you stop meditating to look at the time. So you are better off without those things.

Do not carry your own troubles or your temptations or other people's troubles and situations straight into your own meditation. There is a proper time and place for their consideration under a mystical light or for their presentation to a mystical power. But that time and place is not at the *beginning* of the meditation period. It is rather towards the end. All meditations conducted on the philosophic ideal should end with the thoughts of others, with remembrance of their spiritual need, and with a sending out of the light and grace received to bless individuals who need such help. At the beginning your aim should be to forget your lower self, to rise above it. Only after you have felt the divine visitation, only towards the end of your practice period should your aim be to bring the higher self to the help of the lower one, or your help and blessing to other embodied selves. If, however, you attempt this prematurely, if you are not willing to relinquish the personal life even for a few minutes, then you will get nothing but your own thought back for your pains. *(part of V15, 23:6.58 and Perspectives, p. 322)*

Anthony: This is an exercise, obviously, for an advanced practitioner who has made it a point to help people. And it is a fact that doesn't have to be advertised. He does not have to say anything. And you will find, in many of these quotes, how you can help others.

S: What happens if you attempt it too early?

Anthony: You won't make it if you do it prematurely, because you first have to have the light in you. After that you could bring your request to that light to help someone, but to prematurely request help for someone when the light is not yet within you would be just a waste of time.

He has to stand aside from himself and observe the chief events of his life with philosophic detachment. Some of them may fill him with emotions of regret or shame, others with pride and satisfaction, but all should be considered with the least possible egoism and the greatest possible impartiality. In this way experience is converted into wisdom and faults are extracted from character. *(V4, 4:4.189)*

Anthony: This is one we could all do, which is really quite famous. It was used, for instance, by Pythagoras, Plato, almost all the Western sages.

He should from time to time pass in analytic review the important events, the experiences, and the attitudes of his past. It is not the good but the evil emotions and deeds, their origins and consequences, that he should particularly attend to, mentally picture, and examine from the perspective of his higher self. But unless this is done with perfect honesty in an impersonal unconcerned detached and self-critical spirit, unless it is approached with a self-imposed austerity of emotion, it will not yield the desired results. It is not enough to mourn over his errors. He should carefully learn whatever lessons they teach. *(V4, 4:4.109)*

S: *He mentions a similar one at the end of* The Wisdom of the Overself, *where you look back, starting from the evening, going through the whole day, trying to find the highlight of what happened this day, and analyzing it in this way.*

Anthony: He has that exercise in *The Wisdom*. He has many different versions of it. All of us unconsciously do it when we are caught in a situation and try to understand what happened. We reflect and think over it. But this is a technique that has been used by almost any school of philosophy, where you go over in your mind the preceding events of the day. You try to understand what they mean to you, and then make the necessary corrections or adjustments that you think your personality needs. But even if a person doesn't go that far, and every night, before he goes to sleep, just reviews in his mind, "What have I done wrong, what have I done right, what did it mean for such and such a thing to happen?"—if he does this every night, after a while he begins to see himself in a very detached way, he begins to look at himself very objectively. And it has been used as far back . . . even Pythagoras used to give this to his students, and that is going back quite a few thousand years.

This is the basis for the way I understand astrology. For every individual insofar as he is an individual, insofar as he is part of the World-Idea, there is a meaning in his life, a pattern of events, situations, circumstances. There is a growth of understanding that's taking place because of the interaction of this person with the world. When you understand astrology you can see how the meanings, the pattern of events, are peculiar to this individual and no one else. If he really penetrates into the meaning of the events and circumstances that are going on in *his* life, he is getting at the quintessence of the meaning of his life to him. I think that this is really the fundamental purpose of astrology, this is what astrology should help a person to understand. Never mind if he is going to meet his beloved, or if he is going to make money on the stock market. That's all a waste of time. But in this way astrology can be a really spiritually potent tool, so that the person could try to be aware of what significances are blossoming as his life. He's living these ideas, he *is* these ideas—why not try to consciously understand what is going on? But most of us, of course, are living in the world like sleepwalkers.

S: PB also has another exercise in The Wisdom *where before you go to sleep you figure out the way events will happen the coming day and in a similar way try to analyze and take the position of an observer. Would you comment on that please?*

Anthony: Meditation on the future—when you go to sleep at night you think of the kind of person you'd like to be? Oh, yes. That exercise is unbelievable for its power. Most people unconsciously practice it at some time or another, although they don't know it. Maybe I could put it this way. When we are very young and romantically inclined, a person will think of the one he loves. When he goes to sleep, he will have all kinds of fantasies about that person, and to that extent, he will be predetermining his future. He will bring it to pass, if he does that intensely enough. So many people use the exercise and don't know it.

S: He will bring that to happen?

Anthony: Sure, if you can intensely imagine something about yourself. For instance, you say, "I am going to get rid of my anger. I am not going to get angry ever again." So at night when you go to sleep, you imagine yourself in the most perilous situation, where you are arguing with somebody, but you remain calm, dignified and noble. You see yourself in your mind's eye and you say, "That is the way I am going to be." And then tomorrow you are arguing again and all of a sudden you are about to explode, and you catch yourself—the image comes up in your mind and you say, "No, I am not going to blow up." You try it, you see if it doesn't work.

It is a remarkable exercise because what it does is to use the creative power that is in the imagination to formulate your character. And, little by little, you can bring your character into accordance with the ideals that you have in mind. Now, I don't say you can completely succeed, but . . .

S: But don't you have your karma?

Anthony: Don't worry about that. I know what you are going to say. Your karma is to go on being angry. Try it! You don't know what your karma is until you try it. It may be your karma to get rid of your anger that way.

S: *In this exercise on the future, don't you have to beware of involving others in your imaginations? I mean, you can do it with your own character, but as soon as you involve others it touches on magic, doesn't it?*

Anthony: Yes. As soon as you bring other people in and you want them to subserve your purposes, you are dealing in black magic. So there is always a call for ethical understanding. And that goes even for purposes that you consider worthy and good. When you consider purposes as worthy and good, be twice as careful.

S: *But you said before that at the end of your meditation you could think well of others.*

Anthony: I would say that any person who meditates realizes after a while that at the end of his meditation he should face the four directions, one at a time, and send out his compassion and love. One direction at a time, you wish all living beings well and wish them happiness. Face the east and say that. Face the north and say that. Face the south and say that. Face the west and say that. And then your meditation is over.

S: *So what you should be careful about is not to have any specific thoughts about persons, but just to try to send out love.*

Anthony: You mean in reference to her question?

S: *Yes.*

Anthony: Well, you see, she might be doing something like this. She might say, "Well, I imagine myself as a noble, calm person who is not subject to anger, who will not demean myself in that way." She cannot at the same time say, "But he has to learn to get down when I say something!" You see, you can't bring that in. That would be unethical. In other words, if she thinks in her mind that he should pay attention to her, then she is trying to manipulate him. That is black magic. Some people can practice it and succeed. I have met people who could hypnotize you to do anything they want and you don't know it.

S: *But even if you think that something is good for another person and wish that to happen . . . is that wrong?*

Anthony: She may think it is good for him, but what she thinks is good he may not think is good. So, she has to stick to her own development and not worry about someone else's.

S: You could try to send out love, but not be specific about it, not think that this person should do anything or should change in any way, but in a neutral way just try to feel love.

Anthony: But that wouldn't be called for. The exercise calls for you to imagine the qualities that *you* want, regardless of how the other person acts. You are not interested here in the other person. You think to yourself, well I must learn to be the kind of person who could put his anger aside, walk away from it, not accept it. And you have to then imagine, make a picture in your mind, hold it steady for as long as you can, and fall asleep with it. When you wake up the next day, you will have forgotten it, of course, and you go about your business. But then the situation arises when you meet this person and you are having a discussion with him. You are about to get angry and that image will come up to your mind and reformulate the way you are going to act. It will help, actually help. Most of us haven't realized the tremendous power of the imagination to be creative, to create for us the world we live in.

S: Once I asked PB if I could in any way help a person who has died recently. He answered that it is possible, by thinking of the most intense glowing white light, and then thinking of the person being in that light. Is that possible also with living persons?

Anthony: Yes. A person may come to you with a problem and you can't help him, you don't know of any way to help him. But you take it into your meditation, and when you reach a certain point of intense concentration you hold the image of the person in that white light, and that light will help. It isn't you or I personally who helps, but the higher power that helps. If it is meant to be, it will be that way. But the trick there, of course, is to be able to conceive or imagine the white light and hold it. That is what is difficult.

S: If you intend to help a dead person, that person must exist in some way. What does PB think about life after death? How does the person exist?

Anthony: You mean what kind of existence do we have when the body is taken away? The same kind that you have now: as the knower, as the real person, the real being, the true being that you are. That can't die.

S: *But if the body limits you so much, why do you live this life in a body?*

Anthony: Well, for one thing, experiences in the body are so intense, in comparison to experiences outside the body, that you learn much faster what in the spiritual worlds may take you many, many years to learn. And I am speaking about hundreds and hundreds of years. Experiences in the body are so intense that sometimes one experience is all you need to learn. The body provides the means whereby our experiences are intensified to the *nth* degree. You can experience pain here that you can't experience elsewhere, you can experience joys here that you can't experience elsewhere, because of the very intensity of the mechanism by which the soul is operating in the world. On the question as to the mode of existence when you have no body, I would have to say that the mental being that you are cannot be harmed in any way. You cannot cut it with a sword, you can't burn it in a fire, because the nature of the soul is of an immaterial principle. We spoke last night about the fact that as the knower you are not anything physical. When you refer to yourself as the knower, or the Witness-I, or the spectator, you can't physically locate yourself. Can you follow that? If in essence you are consciousness, then nothing can destroy, obliterate, burn, cut up that consciousness that you are. Because it is not a thing; it is an immaterial, spiritual principle. How could you get to it, how could you kill it, how could you hang it? You can only do that with physical things, not with a spiritual principle. So if you think of yourself as pure consciousness, pure awareness, then what can you do with it?

S: *So it is always developing, the I, the soul, even if it is not in the body?*

Anthony: Even after life, in death, a certain amount of learning goes on. And usually, for many years, you are preoccupied with assimilating the experiences that you had here.

S: *You don't get the wisdom when you die?*

Anthony: No, we remain just as foolish when we are dead as when we were alive. People that are dead aren't smarter than they were when they were alive. If you communicate with them, if you get in touch with them, you'll see that they are still as stupid there as they are here. Wisdom is going to be bought at the price of experience, understanding, reflection. It is not going to come, you know, gratis. You are going to work for every ounce of it.

S: *If you see your life as an opportunity to work on it, do you have a chance to get further in a much more rapid way?*

Anthony: That is what these studies are about—a chance to proceed much more quickly. In other words, to bring consciousness to bear on your own evolution means that you want to develop much more quickly. You have to apply, in a conscious way, your understanding. You have to go into meditation and things like that. But the ordinary person who is not concerned about these things, he lives the ordinary life; and then when he reincarnates and comes back, he repeats the same things over and over again. That is the long hard way. This way is a little shorter, because you want to get to the goal much more quickly. And that means that you have to step in and control, bring in conscious control over, your own growth.

S: *But it is also easier for a man like PB who when he was born was already . . .*

Anthony: Well, that is because he did a lot of it before. And before that. And before that. In other words, we ourselves must bring our will to bear on our own conscious evolution. Otherwise it doesn't happen. A lot of people think that we are going to evolve, that we are going to get smarter as time goes on, automatically. I can assure you, it will never happen that way. It will never automatically happen. Assuming that you say, "Alright, I believe in reincarnation, that I will keep coming back"—assuming that you accept that—well, it doesn't mean that just because you keep coming back you are going to get smarter. You can also get more stupid; you can go backward or forward, it depends on you. So what we are saying is that once a person recognizes this, then he takes a hand in his own evolution. He starts applying these things and tries to grow in the direction of the goal that he has set up for himself. And the other point that we were making is that evolution will not happen naturally. You have to get involved, because there is no guarantee, by anyone, or by any circumstances or conditions, that things are going to get better. They are not. They usually get worse.

S: *Do you think PB will come back again and learn yet more?*

Anthony: Well, somewhere in one of his notes [V8, 12:5.342—ed.] he says something like: "I have to laugh about this. Soon I will reincarnate." Now how much time I can't say, and it varies with different people. He says, "And it is going to be humorous, because I will be reading my books and be enjoying this man's writings because I like this kind of stuff. I'll go right to it." In other words, these are traits that you take along with you. If you are preoccupied with a certain line of development, then when you die, it is not broken off. When you come back it continues.

Think of a man like Mozart. At three years of age he was playing his piano. At six or seven years he was writing sonatas. At fourteen years, from memory—after one hearing—he wrote down the whole of Allegri's *Miserere* that he had heard in Rome. I mean, this kind of genius you can see as the development of a particular faculty in a person. It is there. It didn't happen by accident. It didn't happen by heredity.

S: Do you think men like Buddha and Christ are men that have come a long way in this development?

Anthony: Oh, yes. That is what it means to be a Buddha—you have brought yourself to the acme of human evolution through your own efforts. I mean, you can't go to public school and have someone there guarantee that you are going to get it. It won't work that way. You have to do it. You have to decide, "I am going to be honest. Period. That's all."

S: Is it similar with Christ?

Anthony: Well, Christ was different. He was a being sent from a higher plane of existence. The Buddha was a man who through his own efforts succeeded in attaining the evolutionary goal that man is striving for. Christ represented a spiritual principle sent down from a higher plane of existence to help mankind. Among the early Christians, it was known that the descent of Christ was experienced as a huge light coming into the earth long before Jesus appeared. So they're different. There are different possibilities of spiritual evolution and we had better not get into discussing that now. It's too complex. Let's read some more of these notes.

> Meditation must begin with lulling the physical senses into quiescence. We cannot begin to put the mind at ease unless we have earlier put the body at ease; and we cannot make the intellect

inactive unless we have earlier made the senses inactive. The first reward and sign of success, marking the close of the first stage, is a feeling of lightness in the body, of numbness in the legs and hands, of having no weight and being as light as air. This shows a successful detachment from the thought of the body. After this, the second stage opens, wherein a deep intense half-trancelike absorption in the mind itself is to be achieved, and wherein the body is utterly forgotten. *(V4, 4:1.232)*

Command your thoughts during this first period of meditation; direct them by the energized will towards a definite and specific subject. Do not let them drift vaguely. Assert your mastery by a positive effort. *(V4, 4:3.10)*

He is not asked to devote more than a short part of the day to these exercises. If he advances to a stage where it may be necessary to desert active life for a time, the Higher Self will bid him to do so by inward prompting and will arrange his circumstances in a way which will make this possible for him. But until it happens it would be a mistake on his part to anticipate it by premature action or impulsive emotionalism. *(V4, 4:2.366)*

All possess the power of reflection but few use it. When this power is turned outwardly, we look upon the physical body, its organs and senses, as our self and so plunge into the bustling activity of this world without hesitation. But if this same power of reflection be turned inwardly, we begin to forget our activities and to lose knowledge of the physical body and its environment. For we become so deeply indrawn into the world of thought that for the time being this inner world becomes for us the real world. Thus we are led gradually by repeating this practice to identify ourselves with the mind alone, to look upon ourselves as thought-beings. *(V4, 4:4.11)*

His attention should, in theory, be wholly concentrated on this single line of thought. But in practice it will be so only at broken intervals. *(V4, 4:3.165)*

Anthony: Well, any comments, no, yes, on meditation?

S: When people hear that you are to have no thoughts, that state is often confused with the state of ordinary plain unconsciousness when you sit and are not aware of all the millions of thoughts that are in your mind. They think that their mind is void, but it is not, it is just unconscious. They just don't know of the thoughts that they have, and how that differs from the thought-free state.

Anthony: I think what you are saying is that very often you come across people who are so unreflective that they are unaware that thoughts are going through their mind all the time. You think that it will take only a little reflection on their part—if they sit down and look at their mind—to recognize after a short while that they have thoughts, plenty of them, one going after the other so fast they are toppling over each other. But for a person who is very unreflective, I don't think you really can do anything; it has to come eventually of its own accord. His own growth will force him to recognize that thoughts are constantly going on. If a person is constantly extroverted, he certainly won't be aware of the thoughts that are going on inwardly all the time. But that is not unusual, considering the contemporary society where extroversion is almost like a disease. I mean, a person actually is preoccupied with his relations with the outer world to such an extent that there is a complete unawareness of his inner life which is going on. Yes, it's quite common. I wouldn't engage those people in a conversation about the fact that they are not in a void state. I wouldn't get involved in that.

S: Maybe you could just describe the void state a little, so that one would know what is not that. What kind of heights and intense attention can a person reach in an introverted state?

Anthony: PB does have some very nice quotations here on the void: that the mind is stretched out to infinity and that there isn't a ripple, or the slightest murmur, or the slightest motion, that the person is almost like in a breathless state. But those are very advanced states. There is an exaltation of mind which is indescribable. I mean, there's no sense trying to speak about it. There are things that we have to wait for.

So why don't I leave it to you people to discuss some of these ideas. Let me see where you're at in your understanding of these things.

S: If you concentrate on your mantra or whatever you are concentrating on, should you be conscious about the thoughts coming in?

Anthony: If you're concentrated, they can't come in.

S: When I try to concentrate, sometimes I am concentrated on one thing, but feel some thinking going on at some other level.

Anthony: It doesn't have to be at some other level. It is at that very level. In other words, your concentration is imperfect. It's like this murmuring going on as you're trying to get concentrated. But that simply means that your concentration is imperfect. When the concentration is perfect you won't hear any murmuring. You won't hear any other activity. There won't be any other activity except that you'll notice that you're surrounded by a silence. That's when you get concentrated. So for a while, of course, you will experience this imperfect concentration as though there were other activity going on simultaneously. What you have to do is to intensify your concentration. It will get so intense you'll reach a point where you won't hear anything else. You'll be paying attention only to that object which you're concentrating on.

S: Couldn't you be aware that you are projecting the world, but that the stuff of the world is the same as the I—I mean that the world is consciousness too? That I am spreading my feeling of "I" also to that microphone or to that wall?

Anthony: It's very rare for a person to be aware that he's projecting.

S: It's a sort of unity, but you're still sitting in this body and seeing all this stuff. You are not the microphone but still you are in some way feeling some affinity with it.

Anthony: You could try this. The first instant when you wake up in the morning, in the very first image that comes, your ego and the world-picture both have the same status. An instant later, you recognize your ego as distinct from the total image. Do you know what I mean? The first moment you wake up, the very first image that comes into your mind, in that image there is no distinction between I and the world. The next instant that distinction comes into operation: all of a sudden one distinguishes that his ego and the world are two separate things. But that's the next instant. You can make an exercise of trying to see that in the morning, when your first image is presented. Then you can see that you are projecting the world in that instant and you're not making a distinction between the I and the not-I in that projected image.

S: But couldn't you be aware of that, too, by concentrating on a certain object?

Anthony: Yes, you can reverse the procedure. You can take, for instance, a vase. You put a vase out there and you concentrate very intensely on it and you can momentarily succeed in subtracting your ego from that image. In a state where a person is very relaxed, calm, and attentive to, let's say a vase—he's concentrating on a vase—there will come a moment when he won't be experiencing the distinction between I and the world out there. It's a unified world-image, it's a unified picture of the world with your ego as part of it. That can happen, sure.

S: So you can reach a witness state through the object, without letting go of the object or without turning inward?

Anthony: Because what you basically do when you're concentrating, let's say on the vase, is that you're eliminating all thought. And if you succeed even temporarily in eliminating all thoughts, the moment that there's no thought the I and the not-I are seen as basically part of the same image.

S: Isn't inward and outward only an idea in your mind? If so, can you concentrate on anything to reach a state without thoughts?

Anthony: The difference is this: in the exercises where you turn inward and you learn concentration, this is a long drawn-out discipline that you're practicing so that you can evolve, develop your concentration. The exercise that I'm speaking about now won't evolve, won't foster your abstract concentration. Ultimately you have to be able to keep your mind on an idea. So in the beginning it's very often wise to close your eyes and concentrate inwardly on an idea, because that's the ability you want to develop. But that doesn't mean it can't happen the other way. You could sit outside and watch the sunset and identify with it so extremely that for an instant you lose the sense of being distinct from the world. But that's fitful, that's a glimpse, whereas what we're talking about in meditation is the ability to be able to concentrate on a point and stay with it as long as you want every time you sit down. That's what you're evolving towards, so it's a little different.

Many people get momentary glimpses. They're sitting outside, there's a beautiful scene, and for a moment they forget everything and they're very peaceful and quiet; then the next moment thoughts come in and it's all over again. After a while you'll see that that is the very nature of thought. I mean, you begin to recognize that thought seems to have one function and that's to keep you in a state of agitation. It actually keeps agitating you. Every thought you get is like a little devil coming in with a pitchfork. Now I'm not saying that thought in itself is wrong; you know, a thinker, an artist has to concentrate, has to think and use his mind. But most of us when we're living the ordinary life are not thinking, we're just letting thoughts come in one after the other. Any thought that wants can come in. It doesn't even knock and say, "Let me in." It just comes in, runs through your apartment, rips down the curtains, kicks the sofa aside, runs out, another one comes in, does the same thing. And people sit there stupidly: "Gee, why should I think of that? It's upsetting." You don't have to think of it. STOP IT!

You might find it very delightful if you could be without any thoughts for a minute. Just try it. It's delightful. Someone took me to a restaurant and asked me how I liked it. Up to that moment I hadn't been thinking about it at all. Once she asked me that, then I was disturbed, I didn't like it. My usual state is that I'm aware of facts but have no thoughts about them, a peaceful state. But as soon as she asked me how I liked it and I had to bring in a thought, and another thought came in—there I was, agitated and disturbed.

It's very hard to believe, and yet, a moment's experience will guarantee you that if you have no thoughts for a moment or two you would be naturally very happy. People actually inflict punishment on themselves. They have to always keep thinking about something. You've had experiences where thoughts just come up randomly. Well, you know why? Because the ego doesn't want you to have that moment of peace. The ego has one job, and that is to make sure that you don't get any light. That's its function, to block the light. You get up in the morning, the first moment you're awake you have no thought, you're still enjoying the happiness. The next moment, as soon as a thought comes in, you watch and you see the day started.

S: Doesn't the ego want to refine itself?

Anthony: Well, the ego is a mixture, you know. It has good tendencies and bad tendencies. One morning you get up with a good tendency and another morning you get up with a bad tendency.

This is a quick way to refine the ego: don't think. Most people don't know or don't accept the fact that if they had no thoughts they would be happy. That they don't know is a disadvantage. But they should know, because when you're sleeping you're happy, you have no thoughts. If you have one thought you get disturbed, you have a dream or a nightmare. But before thoughts arise you're very happy. Now the trick is to be awake while you're sleeping, in other words, while you have no thoughts. If you could be awake while there are no thoughts, you would experience the same happiness as when you're sleeping. That's a preliminary stage of meditation. When you get to a certain level your mind gets less and less noisy, has fewer and fewer thoughts. You're quiet, you can enjoy a little peace. Then there's a deeper stage where you have no thoughts at all, and the serenity gets very intense and you feel quite happy.

S: Can I achieve that goal you were talking about before without meditating, but through intense praying?

Anthony: Yes, prayer could do it, sure. You mean the goal where you keep all thoughts away? Yes, you can practice it during the day. You know, every time a thought comes up you say, "NO!" Cut it right off. That's a very famous exercise in most of the Eastern traditions, where they tell you: every time a thought comes up, cut off its head. Don't let it come in. Cut it off, cut it off, keep cutting it off. It's very strenuous, but after a few months you begin to get a little success here and there and you begin to feel the quietness around you. In Zen monasteries that's one of the favorite practices. It's called the *Hua T'ou* exercise, and it's really very simple and very direct.

Imagine this: after a rain, you're outside looking at the earth and, all of a sudden, a worm pops up. You've probably seen that. In a similar way, you keep looking at your mind. Now it's quicker if you do this during meditation because that gets you started on the right track. But once you've learned the trick, then you could do it while you're washing clothes or dishes or sweeping or anything of that nature. And the trick is something like this. In the same way as when we spoke of looking at the earth after a rain, you're looking into your mind. You're looking very intensely into that darkness. You're looking and you're looking, just in case a thought comes up. If a thought comes up, you're going to cut it right down. You are not going to let it come up. Just like when that little worm pops up, you're going to cut off its head, you're not going to let it come out. So in the same way, you keep looking into your mind. A thought comes up and you stop it. And you keep doing that for a while. Now that practice is very good because within six weeks, if you do it intensely, you become aware when a thought is quietly sneaking up behind you. And after a while you can almost feel—it's like you develop a sixth sense—you can feel the thought is trying to come in.

I don't know if you're familiar with some of the Zen tradition. There was a movie I saw, *The Seven Samurai*. Do you remember when the Zen warrior walks in through a door and automatically blocks the man hiding inside from hitting him? As he was walking in, he already knew psychically that this man was behind the door, and he blocked the man's blow. Now in the swordsmanship that they used to teach young samurai, one of the things the students had to learn was that when they were engaged in swordplay they had to keep their mind absolutely blank, and their mind would tell them what the next move should be; but if they had one thought they were defeated immediately.

Here is a story, for instance. There was a very famous swordsman, a samurai warrior who was known to be a very powerful man, victorious in many battles. And it happened that he was free from duty for a while and was staying in his residence. A young man who served him at home had an envy towards him and hoped to one day become a great swordsman and challenge him and defeat him. The young servant always had this thought in his mind and the master swordsman used to walk around and turn around quickly, sharply. He was doing this for a couple of days and then the young man asked him, "Is there something bothering you? Can I help you?" He said, "I had the feeling of the presence of an enemy." Because his mind was still, he was picking up what this young man, his valet, was thinking. So when the mind gets very still you can feel and you are aware of the presence of what is around you.

At any rate, let's get back to the point we were making about prayer. Brother Lawrence used to practice the Presence of God, which meant that he always had to keep all thoughts away and keep his mind recalling and remembering that at one time he had the experience of the Presence. And he tried to repeat that all the time in his mind. With that exercise, he was keeping away all other thoughts and eventually his mind became very, very calm, without any thoughts. Such men emanate a great peace. You can feel it when you're near them. If you're sensitive you can pick it up. You don't know what it is, but you know that there's a certain amount of peace there.

These are very well known and famous exercises. And the nice thing about the Zen school is, they meant business. When you went into a monastery, you were given a discipline. Within a few months, if you couldn't make it you were thrown out. They're very intense.

S: *What about various spiritual feelings, should you cut them off also? Should you cut off everything?*

Anthony: If you're going to do the exercise you have to cut off everything. Everything.

S: *Don't you develop aggressive tendencies, if you picture yourself cutting off every thought?*

Anthony: Well, I hope you don't think that you're going to succeed by picturing yourself doing it. You have to *do* it. But for heaven's sake, why all this discussion? When an exercise is given to you, you do it. When I gave her an exercise to do she asked me, "But why shouldn't I think about it?" You can, but then you're not doing the exercise.

S: *I immediately get a picture of myself cutting worms popping up.*

Anthony: Then you go on to greater feats, cutting off the heads of snakes and then the head of the dragon! You see, that's the trouble with theoretical speculation when what's required is that you do something and what you're being asked to do is to eliminate all thought, stop it before it arises. That means that you have to exert the will. That means that you always are attentive inwardly to what your mind is thinking. That means that one of your eyes is turned the other way, looking in all the time. One eye outside and one eye looking inside. These are things that you could talk about and after a certain point it becomes ludicrous. You either do it or you don't.

S: *When I am using the method of TM—Transcendental Meditation—I let the thoughts and pictures come and go.*

Anthony: If I follow what you are saying, you're simply quietly and passively observing the images arise and disappear, whether they are thoughts, pictures, even visions. They come, they arise and they go. But you're passive, you're quiet, you're just looking. And then an occasion may arise where all of a sudden there isn't anything there—

no images, no pictures, no thoughts—and you experience momentarily a kind of peace, of stillness. Sure, that could happen. And I think you will notice that the moment that you experience, or preceding the moment that you have the experience of stillness, you're very, very relaxed. If you could completely relax—if anyone here could completely relax—you would immediately get very still, absolutely still.

There is no disagreement here. The variety of techniques that have been employed by the hundreds of different schools and sects are not in disagreement with one another. They're different approaches. And basically I think if you follow any of them persistently, if you follow through, you're bound to get some results. One of the famous uses of the mantra is in the Hesychast school where they use the Lord Jesus prayer. They just recite the mantra over and over and over again. And after a while the mantra and your breath come and go together. Then after a while you don't say it any more physically, it goes on mentally by itself and it goes on all day long. You're at the level where you reach one-pointed concentration. Your mind is on only one thought. And then all of a sudden it will stop, the mantra will stop, and you'll feel very, very elated. You're in an exalted state of peace and quiet.

These are all techniques. All these techniques come to one thing: trick the mind somehow to stop thinking. They all come down to that. The highest state among the Hindus, for instance, is *nirvikalpa samadhi*, which means no thought, period. None. And of course you can go into a deep trance with that. Einstein is a good example. He had worked for many, many years on his general theory of relativity, and when he got up one morning, his mind was an absolute blank. Very peaceful, very quiet. The next moment he came out and formulated the theory of relativity. He had experienced *nirvikalpa*. In that moment he understood the theory in depth, but there was no verbal formulation, there was no thought, nothing. When he came out of it, then he started formulating it. I have seen over and over again, in many great men who were subjected to tremendous inspiration, that when inspiration came it was basically this silence, absolute silence. And then after the silence, they knew. They found out what they wanted to and they went to work to bring it out. So the silence, the stillness, is the source of this tremendous inspiration that we can have if we only take the trouble to keep at it, to keep going at it.

The student should not feel bound to follow rigidly a devotional-meditational program laid down, as it needs must be, on general lines to suit a variety of people. He should feel free to express his individuality by improvising additions or alterations in it should a strong prompting to do so come to him. *(V4, 4:3.217)*

Each exercise in meditation must start with a focal point if it is to be effective. It must work upon a particular idea or theme, even though it need not end with it. *(V4, 4:3.77)*

If any light flash or form is seen, he should instantly concentrate his whole mind upon it and sustain this concentration as long as he is able to. The active thoughts can be brought to their end by this means. *(V4, 4:3.98)*

He should not be satisfied with a mere glimpse of the pacified mind. He should hold on to it long enough to make the meditation period a glorious success. *(V15, 23:7.299)*

Anthony: Very often when a person has some kind of success in these matters he doesn't know enough to persist, to push it for everything it's worth, to go deeper and not to stop where he is caught in the attitude of repose and calmness and stillness. Most of us make the mistake when we get there of saying, "Ah, I will take a rest here," and so we stay there. And the next time of course it becomes more difficult.

Most of the preliminary techniques are to get you to the pacified mind and then, when you get to the pacified mind, to vigorously employ the pacified mind to introvert into itself. But there won't be any strain when you do that. It isn't that you have to grip your mind and say, "You stay here." It won't be that hard any more; it will be very easy going. A pacified mind, a mind that is quiet, can introvert on itself very intensely without any effort, without the person feeling any strain. It is a very relaxed kind of meditation. It is what we call the second stage. Then there's a third stage, the contemplation exercise where you go much further.

It's enough in the beginning to get a person interested and started at trying to get it for himself. If he gets a genuine glimpse once, he's hooked. He'll know then that there's something in him that's worth seeking and he'll come asking, "What can I do?"

But there are two parts to the problem. The first is to get a person interested in the quest, and the second is to keep him on it. The first part is easy, easier than the second: keeping him on it. My experience has been—and I think this is an experience many have had—you can get ten people interested and they'll listen to you for a while. But only one or two are going to stick it out. It has always been like that. You can get them going, get them started. But to keep them going, that's the hard part.

When I went to California many years ago I met a man who was getting on in years. He began to feel that he had to do something, because all his studying and his meditation had gotten him nowhere, and he didn't get a glimpse. So he decided that he was going to go to bed early, get up early in the morning, and meditate every morning from about four o'clock to six, because then he had to go to work. And he was going to do that until he got some glimpse. This to me is unusual because usually it sounds like too much ego. So he worked on it very hard, for about a year and a half. He would get up at four o'clock in the morning and start meditating and meditate right through to six. And then one day it happened. All the strain was over, everything broke down. He was able to concentrate with a minimum of effort. Within five minutes after he sat down, he told me, he got very concentrated, pulled in, and then all of a sudden the glimpse broke and it lasted for about four months. He knew, he identified with, the soul. He experienced himself as soul. He experienced himself as a witness consciousness. Everything was within him, everything. He extended to the outermost reaches of the universe and then as it started leaving him, started contracting, little by little it contracted until finally he was himself again. And he was close to seventy when he decided, "I am going to have it or else I am not going to die."

> Let it be granted that the practice of concentration is hard to perform and irksome to continue for weeks and months without great result. Nevertheless, it is not too hard. Anyone who really makes up his mind to master it, can do so. *(V4, 4:3.89)*

> The inward stillness which is attained during meditation affects the character in this way: it shows the man a joy and beauty beyond those which animal appetite can show him. It gives him a satisfaction beyond that which animal passion can give him. This he discovers and feels during meditation periods; but its after-effects also begin to linger more and more during the long intervals between such periods and to permeate them. *(V4, 4:1.295)*

Anthony: In these writings on the meditation category, PB gives a description of practically every technique that I've ever come across. When you get finished with this category, you will be acquainted with all the basic techniques that have ever been devised on how to approach this. And some of them, although they sound simple, have a profundity which is like an abyss. Here's a simple one.

> If the turning wheel of thoughts can be brought to a perfect standstill without paying the penalty of sleep, the result will be that the Thinker will come to know *himself* instead of his thoughts. *(V4, 4:3.3)*

> It is not merely an intellectual exercise. All the piety and reverence and worship gained from religion are needed here too. We must pray constantly to the Soul to reveal itself. *(V4, 4:4.5)*

> The method of this exercise is to maintain uninterruptedly and unbrokenly the remembrance of the soul's nearness, the soul's reality, the soul's transcendence. The goal of this exercise is to become wholly possessed by the soul itself. *(V15, 23:6.213 and Perspectives, p. 318)*

Anthony: That's the difference between a man who knows and those who theorize. Well, are you all inspired to go home and start meditating?

S: Is it best in the morning?

Anthony: It's always an individual affair, always. I have found that at times certain times of the day were better for me and then years later other times of the day were better. There's no fixed way. There was a time when I used to meditate only at four o'clock in the morning. I used to work at night and there was a time when I could meditate. It was the best time. If I tried now I'd probably fail miserably. But when you decide what time is best, then try to stick to it until it's a habit. A lot of people who are used to meditating at a certain time of day tell me that even when they don't sit down then, they can almost feel their mind starting to slow down, get quiet automatically. So the habit becomes so strong that when you're not doing it the mind just gets quiet anyway and slows down almost as if to say, "Why don't we stop?" You can actually have that experience.

FOUR
The Mental Nature of Experience

It is not possible to explain intellectually how sensations of the physical world are converted into ideas, how the leap-over from nervous vibrations into consciousness occurs, and how a neurosis becomes a psychosis. No one has ever explained this, nor will any scientist ever succeed in doing so. Truth alone can dispose of this poser by pointing out that sensations never really occur, but that the Self merely projects ideas of them; just as a man sees a mirage and mistakes it for real water merely by his mental projection, so people regard the world as real when they are merely transferring their own mental ideas to the world. *(V13, 21:2.78 and Perspectives, p. 286)*

S: How could two totally different substances, mental and material, have any real relationship? How could you know anything about matter if it is not mental?

Anthony: So he's saying that the physiological analysis of sensation—where the scientist says that the retinal image travels through the optic nerve, goes to the occipital lobe and then gets converted into an idea, into consciousness—will never, under any conditions, ever ever ever succeed in explaining that. Do most of you here have an understanding of that gap? You know, if you have a chain, a very big strong chain made out of iron, and there's one link in it made out of cotton, you know the chain is going to break where it's cotton, right? And what he's saying is that here's a line of reasoning which is fine up to this point where they speak about the molecular activity in the brain getting converted to consciousness. He's pointing out that this is the weak link in all their reasoning which shows that it will not hold.

A good part of *The Hidden Teaching Beyond Yoga* is concerned with making that very, very clear. In the theoretical exposition of the physiology of perception, PB goes through the reasoning process step by step. He tries to show how the modern scientist is going to explain perception and he repeats their arguments, describes their experiments. When he gets to the part where they say it reaches the brain and then becomes consciousness, he says this is where the problem is. Because they are going to have to explain to us how a sensation which is supposedly a physiological happening gets converted into a process of knowing. That's an important point because unless you see what the argument is about, unless you see the problem, you don't even know that there is a problem.

We're born into a situation where our ignorance is so pervasive and so dominant that we can't fight our way through a paper bag. Any time that a person has a sensation of something, he automatically assumes that there's a material object out there—isn't that so? If you have a sensation of anything, no matter what the thing is, you automatically assume there's an object of which you are having a sensation. And obviously, if this is so strongly built into the very processes of our thinking, our mental functioning, then we're never going to find out what the truth is. We assume that we already know it. So the question that we're discussing is, how do we know something? And when we try to analyze the steps involved in the process of knowledge—PB takes you through that in *The Hidden Teaching*—you find out that you can't explain knowledge through that process.

So I have to find out how familiar you are, not with the answer, but with the problem. I don't care about the answer. Unless you see the problem, there's no sense worrying about the answer.

S: Consciousness as I know it, being conscious, is nothing that you can touch.

Anthony: Good, good, it's not a material thing. When you say that you know something you're not speaking of a piece of iron, a stick, or a rock.

S: But the explanations physiologists give are altogether material. They study processes that they can look at and manipulate. One thing they don't consider is that they have to be conscious in order to do these things. Consciousness is presupposed.

Anthony: That's very good so far. You see if you dwell on that problem and you think about it very seriously you might get pretty scared. Because one of the things that you become aware of is that knowledge is a mystery. You don't know what's going on. But nobody walks around thinking that knowledge is a mystery—what's the matter, you don't see the chairs? What are you, blind, you can't see the chairs?

S: But of course you take for granted some things in your ordinary life.

Anthony: But then if you take that for granted, it's like you feel comfortable that you're living with your ignorance. You feel very comfortable. You say, "It's all right, I could live with it. It doesn't bother me."

S: No, I don't think it is so comfortable.

Anthony: No, it isn't. It isn't. You see, we regard this ignorance as one of the fundamental problems of mankind that brings about more evil and misery than anything else—because if you have a mistaken idea about that, then everything else is going to be mistaken. You know, you're building all your knowledge on a theory made of quicksand. It reminds me of a mystic of Islam, Al Ghazzali. He went into a cave and he studied. He spent ten, eleven years in the cave. It must have been very uncomfortable. He came out pulling his hair, screaming, "Knowledge is a mystery!" And he was one of the really wisest men. He's still considered one of the official doctors of the Islamic tradition.

> Truth alone can dispose of this poser by pointing out that sensations never really occur, but that the Self merely projects ideas of them; just as a man sees a mirage and mistakes it for real water merely by his mental projection . . . *(part of V13, 21:2.78)*

Anthony: What does he mean here when he says that the Self merely projects ideas of the sensations?

S: I think he reverses the process. Previously he talked about the sensations starting "out there" and going inwards. Now it goes in the other direction: the ideas are projected, which means outwards.

Anthony: All right, the point you're making here is that the sensation is something projected by the Self. But you have to notice that what you said in that statement is quite comprehensive. You are projecting the ideas of sensation. You are projecting the ideas. There is no such thing as sensation, but ideas of sensation. If we take the dream example, there in the dream you are looking at a pink elephant and the pink is a sensation. Are you projecting a sensation or an idea?

S: It's the same thing.

Anthony: Yes, but there is a little distinction that I am trying to bring out. Isn't it true that the color is the idea that is being projected? It is a projection of an idea. It's not a sensation. There is no such thing. Those are just technical abstractions which after a while started becoming real to these people. But the fact of the matter is that you project the ideas or your mental functioning and when you see the colored elephant in front of you, what you projected was an idea. In *The Hidden Teaching*, PB shows that the way to solve the problem is by making the idea first, and everything else will follow. If you make the idea first in the chain of reasoning, the thought comes first and then this thought becomes concretized as a perception. If you start out with the thought, you end up in a sequence of reasoning which is correct.

> Such is the make-up of our habitual outlook that we take it unquestioningly and immediately for granted that the presence of a sensation in our field of awareness indicates the presence of an external *material* thing. *(V13, 21:2.14)*

Anthony: Now, isn't he saying here that we are so constituted and dominated by our ignorance that we automatically assume that if we have the sensation of whiteness, then there has to be something there which is white?

He's more or less asking you to refer to the kind of presuppositions you work with. And he's saying that if you have a sensation, regardless of what, you automatically and naturally are absolutely convinced that there is an external independent object there besides the thought or the sensation of the object that you have. Is this basically what is being said in this quote?

Let's take the dream example. In the dream you see a green table. You automatically, unconsciously, swiftly, immediately assume that there is some thing there that is independent of the thought of the thing that's there. Do we operate like that? Now, still staying with the analogy, when you look at the dream from the point of view of wakeful consciousness, you would say that the man dreaming was very stupid to believe that there was something in the dream besides his thought. There was only his thought there. There wasn't anything else there. But all of us assume automatically, swiftly, quickly, immediately, with absolute certainty, "I have a sensation, there's something out there, something which is independent of my thought of it." We have to wake up to the ignorance that we're always living in. So when I perceive an object or when I have the sensation of an object, I shouldn't automatically assume that there's something there which is independent and external to my thought of the thing.

S: We must change our habits then.

Anthony: Yes. You have to first try to understand that the thinking that we are constantly carrying on is faulty, to use a British understatement.

S: So we are all here in this room, we are thinking each other into existence.

Anthony: No, I don't want you to go that far yet.

S: It helps to think of when you are hypnotized, because you can see that in that state you take things to be real when they are not.

Anthony: Yes. All that the hypnotist did was to impress a thought on your mind and you concretized it and believed that there was something else besides that.

S: How do you wake up?

Anthony: Nobody wakes up. For heaven's sake, do you want the picture to be over? To wake up is a long arduous process of reflective concentrated thought. It won't happen in a flash of lightning. Every now and then you get glimpses of the fact that you are living in a world that in your thinking you have brought into being. But they are rare glimpses and they have to become more and more frequent.

S: Intellectual understanding of it is a kind of waking up, too, isn't it?

Anthony: Yes, intellectual understanding, reflective consciousness, employed constantly to analyze your experience, helps you wake up.

> The fact is we have never seen more than our idea of the external world, never known its physical nature, the latter being our own imagination or mental projection. *(V13, 21:2.23)*

Anthony: You see it is the assumption that we all make when we look out there at that rock—two tons, big rock—we assume that there's something more there than our thought. Everyone assumes this. No one is assuming, "Well, that's only my thought." Everyone assumes, "Well, I see that rock, there's something out there more than my thought, other than my thought." So, it's like an ingrained animal instinct, this belief that there's something other than my thought.

S: If you wake up does the world continue to exist then? Or do you live in a totally empty world? If sensation is only imagination, then the world is not real, is it?

Anthony: It's not real, I agree, but what's wrong in saying that it's your imagination if it is so?

S: If you wake up, the stone isn't there any more?

Anthony: You mean if I were a sage, a man who was aware of pure consciousness all the time, I wouldn't see the stone anymore? You see, that's a common answer that people have—that if I wake up the world is going to disappear. That's a misunderstanding. Why is it a misunderstanding?

The idea doesn't go away. The idea, the thought of a stone that weighs two tons doesn't go away because you wake up to the fact that it's a thought. That's why Einstein criticized Jeans, who was a mentalist. He said to Jeans, "Why bother studying what doesn't exist?" Jeans was an astronomer; he'd be looking at the stars and Einstein would say, "Why bother studying them? They don't exist according to your theory of mentalism." That shows how much Einstein understood about mentalism. The thought remains. Later on we'll go into why it must remain. But right now what we're preoccupied with is pointing out that to recognize the nature of the world does not dissolve it. Like for instance, I'm having a dream and in the dream I'm looking at this rock that's two tons. I'm looking at it and I realize that it's only a thought. As long as I am having the dream, that rock will go on being there and I will be looking at it and it will still be there. So if the dream character in the dream recognizes that the rock is of the nature of an idea, that doesn't make the rock disappear.

Do you follow that? If you follow that you got a big point. Just look at the situation that would happen in the case of a man, a sage, who realizes that everything is mind. According to your theory, there would be no sense in his sitting down to eat anything because when he recognizes that everything is mind, everything will disappear. But that doesn't happen. What happens is that you understand the mental nature of everything that you see. You see that it's made of mind, that like the dream, it's not a material external thing outside of mind.

S: Are we also made out of mind?

Anthony: Yes. As you go along, as you study this doctrine, you will see that it will answer every question—but you can't try to get them all at once. You have to go one at a time. Whereas if you study many other teachings, you'll see that many things are impossible for them to explain. For instance, materialism says that everything comes out of matter. You would have a problem explaining how feelings, emotions, intellectuality, sensitivity, artistic creativity, all these things come out of atoms—which by the way don't even independently exist. Physicists ultimately found that atoms are mysterious tendencies or probability distributions. Prior to their manifestation as wave or particle we don't know what they are. So even scientists have come to the realization that there isn't any such thing as independently existent matter. They can't figure it out either, and they've been battling for fifty years.

Well, I'll read this one here. It's a very difficult one. If you can get even a little bit of it you are getting a great deal.

> Hume rightly pointed out that the mind is a mere series of sensations but he wrongly concluded that the series is destitute of any connecting thread. He saw nothing in the world but momentary perceptions, and in perceptions he saw nothing at all. They arose and faded into a void. Thus it might be said of the Scottish thinker that his doctrine was a Nihilistic Idealism and his universe a meaningless one. "Everyone keeps a distance," he complained. "I have exposed myself to the enmity of all metaphysicians and even theologians; and can I wonder at the insults I must suffer?" *(V13, 21:4.206)*

Anthony: David Hume has very often been compared to certain Buddhist schools of thought which claim that the World Image arises and fades, another instant another World Image arises and fades, and there's this constant flux of one picture after another with no meaning in the whole thing. Now if an image arises or a perception arises and then another and then another, and you are included in that perception and there's no meaningfulness in the images, then he also has destroyed any belief in the identity of the soul or the continuity of the soul or both. So many people look upon him as a real atheist, a thorough-going nihilist. He just abolished everything. He is a very, very perceptive thinker, I mean, I'm not trying to put him down. I spent a lot of time with him. He's an extraordinary genius. But if you look at his view of things, then you could see why they would refer to him as a nihilist. Because how could you believe in anything? An image arises, fades away, another one arises, fades away. They come from nowhere, they go nowhere. And in between there is nothing. It could be pretty devastating.

S: But when you say perceptions, then you are presupposing someone having those perceptions.

Anthony: That too is included in the perception, according to Hume. He would say something like this: You are artificially connecting the contents of this perception with the contents of the next perception and then the next one. You are joining together what is not joined together. In other words, the continuity of your "I" depends on memory. But he shows that memory is nothing but a series of stills, that you remember these pictures. Therefore, he says, you are superimposing on this series of images a meaning that they don't have. You are constructing a fiction. So for him there is no self.

S: But this is partly true, isn't it? You build up some kind of personality, but for your inner self this may be a very fictitious entity. But he didn't believe in any self at all?

Anthony: No, for him there is no such thing as a self.

S: There must be something watching this?

Anthony: That, too, is part of the perception for him. When you say there's someone watching this, he would say that's part of the perception. There is no "someone."

S: But there must be a thought.

Anthony: Yes, but it wouldn't matter to him whether you called it thought or whether you called it perception. He's partly right. But in other ways he's wrong. We will try to answer this question later on. Right now all I'm interested in is showing how this man saw perception and why he is often referred to as the Buddhist of the West, because there was a school of Buddhism which referred to themselves as the nihilists. They didn't believe in the existence of anything except these momentary flashes of images, one following upon another, and they said that there was no meaning to any of them either singly or put together. You can see a certain amount of logic in that. But you must understand what he means by perception; you cannot exclude anything. When you say, "But isn't someone watching it?" he answers, "No, that someone is included in the perception. Who is it? It's the one that you're making up." In other words, the thoughts that you have are also included in the perception. So you can't go outside the picture and say there's someone looking at the picture. No, no, no. He says there isn't any thing out there. What else do you know besides the image that you perceive? He's not naïve.

S: Knowledge could be matter at a different level.

Anthony: He would ask you, "What matter are you talking about outside of and independent of the perception?"

S: It could be in the perception.

Anthony: But what is this matter that you're referring to? Isn't that an inference? In other words, Hume would say: Here is an object. When I analyze this object, all I get in my analysis are certain sensations: color, taste, touch, shape, all of these sensations, all together. When I analyze the cup completely, and in my analysis reduce the cup to all the constituents that make this cup into my perception of it—if I take away these constituent characteristics of the cup, what will I have left? You say, matter. He'll say, what matter are you talking about? Is the matter the whiteness, is the matter the shape, is the matter the taste of the cup, is the matter the feeling of the cup? He'll ask you point blank what do you mean, matter? The same way I would ask you. If you told me that there is a matter here that exists independently of the qualities or characteristics that I perceive in it, I would ask you to show me what you're talking about. Because if you analyze an object—a chair, a table, a brick—and you analyze it in depth, you'll come up like the modern scientists and say there's no substantial thing there, there's only whirling protonic and electronic energies, there's nothing there, no *thing* is there.

The Buddhists will do the same. They'll analyze it and show you that there's nothing there. The perception of an object is purely a mental affair. In the nineteenth century, Western scientists believed that everything was ultimately made out of atoms. In the twentieth century, they broke down the atoms into neutrons, protons, quarks, hundreds of different kinds of particles. Finally, do you know what they came up with in quantum mechanics? They find that all you have is a package of tendencies which is not an independent thing of any kind. Ultimately it's neither a wave nor a particle. This is what twentieth-century analysis has come up with. So whether you speak about a Buddhist or whether you speak about a man like Hume, he would ask you how, if you analyze this stuff, are you going to come up with a "matter"? That's a concept, that's a fiction. Twentieth-century scientists have come to the same position.

S: What are these tendencies in the scientists' explanation?

Anthony: They can't say. The tendencies have no kind of objective existence.

S: Aren't they talking about some kind of energy?

Anthony: They'll tell you point blank: "We can't tell you what it is. If we tell you what it is, then we are talking about some thing, an atom. We can talk about an atom, but when you break down the atom to the particles that constitute it, when you get to the ultimate particles and break them down, then you don't have particles any more." What do you have? And all they can tell you is, "We have certain tendencies, a matrix of possibilities, which can get converted into either a particle or a wave; but until that happens, we don't know what those things are, what that is." They will not speak about it as an objective thing. That's what twentieth-century quantum mechanics has come to.

In a sense what will be required on our part is to get acquainted little by little with some of the work that has been done in the twentieth century, too. You have to remember we are not Neanderthal men or women, we are in the twentieth century. The bomb has exploded. They have found out that matter and energy are convertible terms. And that means that there is no such thing as a thing. One of the reasons why I recommend the reading of twentieth-century scientists is because it's amazing to see that they came to the same conclusions—a few of them, not all of them, because many of them are still holding out; they just can't go this far, they can't believe their own eyes. But twentieth-century physics has come to this conclusion which is pretty frightening, that there is no matter.

S: But there still is a thing outside.

Anthony: No, there is no thing outside. I just tried to point out that when you break it down, when the particles are broken down, there isn't any substantial or independent thing there anymore.

S: Well, quantum mechanics would still say that this matter . . . electronic stuff . . . is outside of your thought.

Anthony: As a matter of fact, some of the modern physicists are saying there's *nothing* outside your thought. Men like von Neumann have refused to accept anything outside of thought.

> We must firmly grasp this principle, that the only objects we know, the only world of our experience, have no existence apart from the mind. They do not and cannot subsist externally by themselves. That which projects them into space is mind, and as space itself is within the mind, their independent existence is sheer illusion, or *Maya* as Indians call it. We must look behind their illusory independence into the mind from which they spring. *(V13, 21:2.81)*

Anthony: You see, I am sitting on the floor just like you. I am only a student. These things I could read a hundred times and I still have to go back and make sure. See if you can just pull out the essence of the idea. That's all. And that means that you have to zero your mind in like a magnifying glass, focus it on just one point. And at the same time you'll be learning meditation.

Paul: One of the key points there is that spatiality in the perceptions is something supplied directly by the mind. In *The Hidden Teaching*, PB has a whole section on illusions. You draw two lines. If you look at it one way it looks like a vase, and if you look at it another way it looks like two faces. And the spatialness to those two lines is provided by the idea in your mind when you are interpreting that experience. Now which way is the true way? He has a whole series of examples that illustrate how the spatiality comes from your own mind in the perception. It is not an attribute at all of the phenomena being investigated.

S: Would you say the same about time?

Paul: I think even more so. Time is the form of all thought. But I think in this case he is speaking about space in specific. Spatiality is the relationship that gets established among the sense qualities in a percept. You're dealing with a totally mental object: the form of the sense impressions, spatiality, and then the sense qualities which are, again, an interpretation of the functioning of the mind. According to the scientists' explanation, the qualities in an object come from your own physical organism—the pressure on your fingers, or the vibration of light in your eye. The sense functions are always a modification of your own body. They have nothing to do with the object. The quality of whiteness is an interpretation of your physical organism. So is the spatiality. That's just normal everyday science, that somehow the sense qualities are an interpretation by the organism.

Anthony: You could see that very clearly in the dream, right? In the dream you create a huge city, walls around the city, buildings. And then you're in the dream, and you're looking at the wall, you're counting the bricks, feeling them, seeing the color. And you say, "That brick is good, that's a big 8 × 4 brick." All the time you're talking about what? An idea. There isn't anything there but the idea. Now when you wake up you say, ah, that was just a dream. Now I see the real world. But in both cases you have just an idea. With the dream you can't avoid coming to the conclusion that all you experienced was the idea. With the dream you can see that you create the space. Inside the space that you created you put a city and then you populated the city. You have all kinds of sensible qualities—tastes, smells, odors. You're walking through the ghetto part of the city. All of it is made by your mind. You can see that when you wake up and analyze the dream. Now, if you analyze the experience of your wakeful consciousness in the same way, you will see the same thing.

S: But there is some difference between dreams and the waking state.

Anthony: Yes, there are a few differences. This dream takes a little longer than that one.

S: But there must be other differences.

Anthony: When you're speaking about the basic substance of the object, there aren't.

S: But isn't it important that I experience this world as more real than the dream world?

Anthony: But when you're in the dream, that dream world is real for you.

S: Yes. But in the dream world I don't reflect on this world and think that this world is less real than the dream world.

Anthony: Why should you insist that the standard of reality in the dream world should be this world? You don't insist that the standard of reality for this world should be the dream world.

S: No, but I still experience that this world is more real than the dream world.

Anthony: But you experience in the dream world that the dream world is real.

S: When I am in the dream state I can't compare the dream with waking experience in the same way that I can compare them when I'm awake. That's why I know that this world is more real than the dream world.

Anthony: When you are awake, you're not dreaming. So how could you compare them? But let's go back to the essence of what we're discussing. We're not discussing that this world of wakeful consciousness has continuity, that there seems to be a thread of meaning running through it. What we are discussing is more like this: that the substance of the dream world is your mind, that the substance of the wakeful world is also your mind. That's what we're really discussing. If you analyze the dream world you could very clearly see that it's nothing but your own mind functioning. If you analyze this wakeful world, you will see the same thing: it's nothing but your own mind functioning. This is the gist, the essence, the kernel of what we're talking about.

S: Yes, but . . .

Anthony: No buts! The whole point here is to stick to the point. We'll get to why the dream world in comparison to the wakeful world is less real. Let's not worry about that now.

S: We once discussed the notion that if physical objects are thoughts then it follows that the mind is where they are. You can't separate thoughts from the mind. Everybody agreed until someone said that where the furthermost star is, there your mind is. Then a very heated discussion ensued, because that was too hard to understand.

Anthony: Too hard to understand? Or to *believe*? But a long time ago they used to believe that the world was flat. A long time ago they used to believe that there were unicorns. They used to believe all kinds of things with such a tenacity that they would burn you at the stake if you disagreed with them. Belief is not enough; reason has to come in and support it. So, when you're looking at a white cloud way up in the sky, is the whiteness an idea? Yes. Is it an idea in your mind? Yes. Then your mind is beyond that cloud and includes that cloud no matter how far away that cloud is! But that means that my mind has no size, no shape, no form. Yes! Of course! That's the whole point!

S: But what's the difference between the mind and the self?

Anthony: It depends on how you use it, but generally when capitalized they're the same.

Can we get back to this point then? Insofar that I see a star, then my mind is beyond the star. There is no size to my mind. It isn't two inches, four inches. It's not in my head. Now this is scary. You remember the biography of C.G. Jung. After his heart attack he had a vision and he experienced himself looking at the world from 4000 miles away. Now where was his mind? His body was in bed. He was in an unconscious state. He couldn't move. But he had this vision and he saw the world moving in its orbit just like an astronaut looking out of a space ship would be looking at the world. Now, if you asked Jung, "Tell me sir, how big is the Self?" he would want to say, "You cluck, you're infinite." But he wouldn't tell you that because he doesn't want to disturb you. He doesn't want to unsettle you, so he says: "Well, you're a tiny little man walking around on the street." And this is what people will go on believing. So if you believe that, then how could you believe that the white cloud is in your mind, that the whiteness is an idea in your mind? How could you believe that? You can't. If you say that your mind is in here and the whiteness is out there, then you're never going to bring them together.

S: Was Jung's experience a Witness-I experience?

Anthony: Yes, I'd call it that.

S: But why didn't he experience that he was united with the world then?

Anthony: Just because a man has a mystical experience, that doesn't make him a sage. What was the point in bringing out this example of

Jung? The point would be something like this: evidently the mind of Jung is not to be confined to his head because his body was lying in bed in an unconscious condition, under very careful supervision by the doctor. Yet this experience shows very clearly that the mind of Jung was still functioning. It was not restricted to the body, it wasn't tied to the body, but that mind was capable of functioning nonetheless. And not only was it capable of functioning, but—being dissociated from the body—it was able to take the position of what we call a Witness-I. And it went as far as its limit.

S: If you have that experience in a room, would you call that also an experience of the Witness-I?

Anthony: Yes, that would be a Witness position. Very often sick people or dying people get this: they see their body lying in bed. That's the Witness position. You're not identified with the body. You're free from the body. You're looking at it as another idea, an idea like all the other ideas.

S: So, it doesn't matter if you are 8000 miles away or just two meters up in the air.

Anthony: There are many different grades of manifestation of the Witness-I. You could experience yourself as the Witness-I in a bedroom when you're sick and you look at the body. You could experience the Witness-I as including the whole universe. You could experience the Witness-I as including just the world you're living on. There are various manifestations of that. But if we get into that, we're going to lose sight of the point we were driving home, that the mind is not the head. You can't put your mind in the head.

S: But isn't it also true that you can't put your consciousness or your mind in your body?

Anthony: Yes, that's true. And yet your body is not excluded from your consciousness. Your consciousness is immediately present to any and every part of the body. Like, for instance, mind is present to both feet, yet that doesn't mean that the mind is in the feet!

Paul: Any level of object—whether in the dream, whether in Jung's experience, whether in this present state of consciousness—all are subject to the same analysis. Every one of those states is a content to consciousness. And that's the whole purpose of the philosophic enquiry, to get at the truth. The truth is not going to deviate, it's not going to change. Any mystical state, any dream state, any wakeful state is a content and an object of consciousness. Different ones are going to demonstrate different characteristics, and there's going to be an indefinite array of possibilities, but the point to be grasped is that every one of them is an idea to consciousness and that the mind puts forth its own ideas and then experiences them.

Anthony: If you go to a higher level than this one, it will still be a content of consciousness; and if you go up to an even higher level, or even to the level of being itself, there will always be a content of consciousness. Unfortunately this is an idea which neither Ouspensky nor Gurdjieff could grasp. Although Ouspensky speaks about the fourth state of consciousness, he fails to understand that it could be analyzed just as at the empirical level or any level. When I analyze my experience, whether the experience be that of a dream world or of a wakeful world, any experience insofar that it is the object of consciousness is subject to the same analysis. And when someone talks about clairvoyance I will point out that the object of clairvoyance is an object of consciousness and is subject to the same analysis as well. That's why it is so important to grasp this principle firmly. Hold on to it, because with it you will be able to analyze all experience and tear apart any misconceptions you have.

So PB says we must grasp this principle. The only objects we know, the only world of our experience, can have no existence apart from the mind. They do not and cannot subsist externally by themselves. That which projects them into space is mind and as space itself is within the mind, their independent existence is sheer illusion. We must look behind their illusory independence into the mind from which they spring.

This is true of all the seven levels of existence, even if you live in the angelic world. So if someone came from another level of existence and said, "Yes, but your analysis doesn't hold for my plane of existence" I would say, "Is it a content? Is it an experience for you? Is it a world that you are perceiving? Is there a perception taking place? You know it? Yes? Then it's subject to the same analysis." That's how it cuts through everything and that's why this teaching is direct and the most comprehensive one you will find. This teaching has been around for thousands of years and it won't disappear. We'll disappear before these teachings do. Now you ask yourself, each one of you ask yourself, "What is my world?" And you will see that the world that you know, the only world that you could know, is the world that you perceive. There is no other world. You say, "Well wait a minute, wait a minute. I'm looking straight ahead and I can see a whole different world which is different from the physical one." Fine, good, you're wonderful! Now is that an object of your consciousness? Yes. Subject to the same analysis. That's how comprehensive the teaching is. It goes right to the core. Now, this next quote will hurt you even more:

> My fellow creatures are themselves but ideas, no less than the inanimate objects against whose background I see them. For they too are known to me only as reports of my mind. Nay, more, the very fleshy frames whereby they take individual shape before my eyes, and in which they are embodied, are but sense-images whose habitat is entirely subjective. *(V13, 21:3.18)*

Anthony: You are an idea to me. Remember in *Alice in Wonderland* where little Alice is crying and says, "But I'm real," and Mr. Rabbit or Tweedledum says, "No, you're not, you are not real." She says, "But you see, I am crying." And he asks, "But what makes you think that your tears are real?"

You see, everyone lives in his own world and doesn't know it. He thinks he's sharing the world with others. This is something that we don't like to accept. It is very, very painful. It's full—if I could use the existentialist term—of dread, anguish, loneliness. I don't want that. But you think about it for a minute. If what we say is true, if all that you could experience is what your mind reports to you, then you live in your world and that's it. That doesn't mean I can't get in touch with you, but that's another question.

S: We have a mind in common also.

Anthony: We have a mind in *common*? God *forbid* . . . [group laughter] What are you trying to do, give me nightmares?

S: We think that we live more separately than we do. Isn't it an illusion that we are totally separated?

Anthony: No, the illusion is that we think that we can get in touch with each other. Like when a man embraces a woman. "She's mine." Oh no she's not! You're only embracing your own idea.

S: The further we get into our souls the closer we get to each other. Couldn't you say that?

Anthony: No, what you are trying to get to is that when you recognize, when you come into contact with your soul—really get into contact with it—then you know other souls are like yours. Insofar that your soul has real being, true being, and you understand that, you experience that, you realize that, then you know that all other souls also have true being. And there you have, so to speak, the recognition that the divinity exists in every soul. But that is something else.

> We all firmly believe in the existence of this material world and we all appeal to common sense and common experience in support of our belief. Idealism retorts: That a world of which we are conscious exists is undeniable; but that this world is material in nature is disputable. *(V13, 21:2.10)*

Anthony: Disputable—in other words we'll all agree that we are conscious of a world. But when someone says we are conscious of matter, I am going to argue with that. If all I know are my ideas and you say no, my ideas are about things that exist in themselves, then I'm going to argue that point, because you will never be able to prove it to me.

Many people refuse to face squarely the conflict between reason and habitual belief. The British philosopher Bertrand Russell is one good example. He admits in his book *The Problems of Philosophy* that when the position I'm expressing here is properly understood, it cannot be logically refuted. But he wasn't able to *believe* it. He is basically a materialist, and he just couldn't believe what his own reasoning was telling him. So instead of staying right there and working out all the implications, he more or less says, "But since we know that can't be true, let's forget it and go on." That a man of Russell's caliber could do this shows that when reason comes into conflict with our most cherished beliefs, we will throw reason out the window and keep our beliefs. It was inevitable that Russell was going to deceive himself and come up with a notion that real philosophy must be concerned with materialism of some kind. And I would say that the philosophy that he developed is the result of a refusal on his part to be intellectually honest.

> When we say the world is not real, we mean that it lacks *intrinsic* reality for it is only an idea in a mind, an *appearance* to something else. *(V13, 21:1.44)*

Anthony: That's pretty straightforward, isn't it? One of you asked, "Suppose you have no senses?" You can rest assured you won't see the world the way it is now. Or let's do the reverse. Suppose that instead of five senses we have seven or eight senses. What kind of world are we going to see? It certainly won't be the one you see now; it will be completely altered.

Given that the soul or consciousness must operate through five senses, then it will see a certain kind of world. If it operates through ten senses, then it must see a different kind of world. No senses, what do you see? You might see the world as it really is. Well, you would have to see it with the mind.

S: But the senses are also an idea in your consciousness. The senses are an idea in the mind. If someone is blind, that must be an idea in the mind, too.

Anthony: Yes. But that's very hard to understand. If we go to the dream analogy, you appear in your dream. You see the dream Maria. And Maria in the dream is looking at a tree and says, "I see the tree." Is that true or false?

S: It is false. Because it is not Maria in the dream who sees the tree.

Anthony: Do you think you see with your eyes, or smell with your nose? You do these things with your mind. That is complicated, but let me build up a little more and then you will begin to understand that you do not see; it is not you, the person, who sees. It is the Witness-I that sees all the time.

S: Isn't it wrong to say that you smell with your mind? Shouldn't you say that you project an idea of smelling with the mind?

Anthony: You project the idea of smelling with the mind. Yes.

> When this truth of mentalism strikes our mind with vivid lightning-flash, we have gone a long way on the quest. *(V13, 21:5.106)*

> "I was often unable," Wordsworth says, in the preface to his great "Ode," "to think of external things as having external existence, and I communed with all that I saw as something not apart from, but inherent in, my own immaterial nature. Many times while going to school have I grasped at a wall or tree to recall myself from this abyss of idealism to the reality." *(V13, 21:4.223)*

Anthony: You've heard of William Wordsworth, the English poet? He has written some very beautiful mystical poetry. The one that PB is referring to here is the "Ode on Intimations of Immortality." If you can, get it in English and read it. You will enjoy it tremendously. He is a very mystically oriented poet, like Shelley, A.E., and a few others. But in this quotation you get a feeling for William Wordsworth, the kind of inner being, the kind of personality he had, how evolved he was. You see, a lot of people think that a mystic is just a mystic, but you find them everywhere. You find them in painting, in poetry, in science, everywhere. It's a stage of evolution that a man or a woman reaches. It's not something that is artificial. It's a natural growth.

Do you remember the story of when Ramakrishna touched Vivekananda on the head and Vivekananda started going into a trance and said, "Stop, stop! What are you doing to me? I'm disappearing!" Vivekananda was a very advanced soul and soon after he came into contact with Ramakrishna, Ramakrishna just touched him and he started going into a trance. In other words, he began to experience himself as an immaterial being and saw everything is within.

It's like when you wake up from a dream and you say, "Everything was inside me. While I was dreaming I thought it was out there, but no, it is all within me." Well, in this wakeful state also you could experience everything as though it's within you, not out there. It is not something out there; it's all within you. But we are so fragmented. "I am here; the world is out there, and you've got to stay out there. Don't try to come here." We are quite alienated, in our times, from ourselves.

> If the mind did not have its primacy in us, did not exist prior to our experience of the world outside us, we could not know that world and could not even know that we existed at all. By its power all is made possible. Yet foolish men, forgetful of the fact that the eyes never see themselves, deny the reality of mind and imagine it to be an effect of a material action. *(unpublished)*

Anthony: What is the most immediate experience you have? Your Self. All the time. The only thing is, you say "He said *me*." No, I said your Self! This is the immediate experience you always have. Another way of putting it would be like this: you are immediately experiencing your mind without any interruption ever.

> Does the world turn to a mere shadow when its mentalistic nature is revealed? Are we less fascinated then by its beauties, less repelled by its horrors? Is every man—and not only every inhabitant of an insane asylum—a victim of these successive hallucinations destined to lose his firm hold on life when the truth frees him from them? *(unpublished)*

Anthony: What is he saying here? When I recognize that a rock is an idea, it doesn't become a ghost. I could still go on enjoying it. When I explain something, I don't explain it away. That's what he is saying. When I understand the nature of my experience, it doesn't disappear. I understand the nature of a flower. I understand that it is a thought in my mind and that this thought has different kinds of structures or modes of being. It doesn't make the flower disappear and I don't enjoy it less.

S: But couldn't the flower sometimes change very quickly, depending on your sensations?

Anthony: No, the flower goes on remaining a flower, a rock remains a rock.

S: You could also have the experience that the world is very friendly.

Anthony: Yes, when you understand that the world is your idea the world becomes a friendlier place. What do you think—it's your world.

S: But I just wonder—could you have the experience that the world is changing, like a cubist painting? The world would have a very dreamlike quality.

Anthony: That's only when you realize it. When you realize that the world is an idea, then it has a dreamlike quality. That is true; that is a stage in the mystic's development.

S: This realization that the world is an idea, that goes beyond all this . . .

Anthony: Intellectual analysis, yes. But you have to go through the intellectual analysis. That is, most of us have to go through it. I don't know if you have heard of the sage Ramana Maharshi. He lived perpetually in that state, where the world was of a dreamlike quality. He only experienced the world the way you and I do now at the end of his life, when he got cancer and the pain became so intense that it brought him down to this level. PB told me he didn't experience the world the way we do. The world was always dreamlike. It had none of that fixity, that rigidity that we have. It's as if you wake up in a dream but you go on dreaming, and you see that it has a different texture than when you're awake.

But that's a stage of realization of these teachings. You see, the nice thing about these teachings is that a person who is willing to pay the price can experience the truth of them. These doctrines can be proved. You can experience that the world is an idea, if you are willing to subject yourself to the discipline needed. I don't have to go on believing them—I can find out if they are true or not. But some people go on reading about them for twenty-five years and never want to go through the problem of realizing them in experience. When they get to a certain level where they are sick of reading, then they say, "I want the real stuff." You know, like at a restaurant, if you keep reading the menu, reading it, and reading it, you are going to stay hungry. You have to eat some of what the menu is talking about, so you've got to do what the doctrine is telling you! Jesus meant the same thing when he said that those who do the doctrine know it.

S: It would be nice if we could talk about these disciplines sometime.

Anthony: Sure, you read about them in *The Hidden Teaching*. PB's works have a tremendous amount on that. He has six categories in his notebooks devoted to various kinds of disciplines: the purification of the emotions, the disciplining of the ego, the refinement of the personality, the cultivation of the higher feelings. All these are disciplines to help you get there. It is the greatest contribution I know of. But it won't be for our times; it will be for maybe 200 years from now. People are not ready for this stuff. They are too interested in flying spaceships, punching out computers. They live in a toy world. But there is a growing interest. I can assure you that when I was your age I couldn't find these books. I used to pay all kinds of money for various books on mystical philosophy and today you can go out and buy them in paperback—the good and the bad and the indifferent. So there has been a growth, an expansion, as if this knowledge is being thrown at us. But that is also because we live in such evil times. Read another one or two.

> If mentalism turns our universe upside down for us, further comprehension of it brings the universe back again into position, but transformed, divinized, and divinely supported. *(V13, 21:5.101)*

Anthony: A Zen monk said, "When I first studied Zen, rocks were rocks, trees were trees, rivers were rivers. Then I studied for a while, and rocks were no more rocks, trees were no more trees, rivers weren't rivers. But I kept studying, kept studying. Then rocks became rocks again, trees became trees again, rivers became rivers again." So in the beginning it is confusing.

S: But there is a difference between the first experience of the river and the last.

Anthony: Very much. That is what he means when he says now the world is divinized for you. You recognize that the world is a receptacle for the work of the gods. But you'll have to go through that phase where for a while you feel completely confused, lost, and you're wondering if you understand, if you're crazy, if they're crazy. And during that time, it can help if you're with a group or if there is a student around who's a little older than you, who can keep pointing out, "You've got to take the next step and then the next step . . ."

S: But this intermediary stage when the rivers aren't rivers and the trees aren't trees, wouldn't you be sort of lost in the world?

Anthony: Yes, that may happen.

S: So then you are a little frightened about coming to that stage.

Anthony: Yes, but that's why it is worthwhile to know someone a little older than you, to have a friend or a guide or a teacher. It doesn't necessarily have to be a master. It could be someone who is just a little older than you, who already has travelled part of that path and knows, "Don't go that way; go this way." Yes, sometimes it's so scary that you don't want to come out anymore.

It's very important that you always maintain your reasoning, you always employ your reasoning. Never give up your reasoning until you get to the void. As long as you are in this world, and you're struggling and you're trying to learn and understand, never give up your reasoning. It will keep you going in a straight direction.

> The necessary action of human reason when at its best and sharpest, and when directed inwards upon itself, leads it to this irresistible conclusion—that the whole experience of this world is but the end-product of a process of the human mind. *(V13, 21:2.54)*
>
> It is true that the world is an individual creation, but it is not the whole truth. *(unpublished)*

Anthony: Do you know what he means by that last statement? You see, right now we're talking about the fact that you experience your world and I experience my world and yet there's something common to both worlds. He would say that's because the World-Mind is simultaneously present in all minds and its idea of the world, its World-Idea, is what you must experience. Right now what I'm emphasizing, for good pedagogical reasons, is first to understand that all you can experience is your mind. Then we will worry about why our minds seem to share a world in common. But you must remember that this comes first, that your experience is of your mind. When you hear a sound and I hear the same sound, the sensation that you have and the sensation that I have are two different sensations. They are similar, but they are not identical. Yours is yours and mine is mine. So that's the first thing.

S: So you are an idea in my mind?

Anthony: And you're an idea in my mind.

S: But how can I know that you exist?

Anthony: Well, how could you know that anything exists? There are certain means of knowledge that are employed, and there are ways of checking out your knowledge. If the knowledge is valid you can check it out. If it's not valid, you can check that out too. In other words, knowledge has certain rules by which it goes that make it work. So if you want to find out if a piece of knowledge is correct, there are certain rules that you can employ. You have different kinds of logic: symbolic logic, formal logic, transcendental logic. And you employ different kinds of logic and reasoning to see if what you thought is so. A scientist does the same thing. He gets a certain theory; it's an idea, and then he has to prove it. If he can't prove it, he won't buy.

Now, for instance, I make a statement something like this: "The presence of consciousness cannot be denied." And I tell you that's true. You try to disprove it. It's what you would call a self-evident principle. You can't prove it and you can't disprove it. If you say, "Well, I'll show you that consciousness doesn't exist," you've just proved it. So there are ways of certifying the validity or nonvalidity of your understanding.

S: You can start from a wrong proposition.

Anthony: Yes, but you first have to start from a proposition. I apply reason always to the premises before I start thinking anything out. If the premises don't hold, I don't bother to reason further.

Let's take an example in logic, since you want to get into this. "Man is mortal. Socrates is a man. Therefore Socrates is mortal." Is that an example of syllogistic logic? Yes. Why don't I accept it? Because of the premise "Man is mortal." Now I'm not saying that this is so or not, I'm just trying to give you an example. I cannot assert that every man is mortal and start out with that and then draw consequences. In reasoning, when you want to follow a chain of logical thought, one thought following upon another and then another and another, you always have to examine the very first thought you start out with. Because that's where your mistake is going to be. The premise is where your mistake is going to be, and only reason—not logic—will point out if the premises are correct or not. Logic can't do that. Reason is like the general intelligence that a person has. Logic is a particular application within reason.

S: Isn't reason a belief?

Anthony: Reason is not a belief. Do you think there will come a time when two plus two does not equal four?

S: No. I don't think so.

Anthony: You had better not, because if you doubt that you're going to doubt your sanity.

S: But couldn't it be that it's only a belief I cling to because I have to feel secure?

Anthony: For heaven's sake, aren't there laws that govern the universe that are independent of how you feel or how you think?

S: How can I know that?

Anthony: That's what you have to find out. Are there such things as reason principles that never change? You'll find out that there are, and they don't care how you feel. You can't decide that because today you don't feel so good, then two plus two will be three instead of four.

S: Could you see reason as a habit?

Anthony: Reason is not a habit. It never was a habit and it still is not a habit. For you $1+1=2$ is a belief. For me, I have to understand the reason principles. I have to understand the nature of the integer 1 to be able to prove to you that $1+1$ is 2.

Let me give you an idea of what reason is. In the divided line that Plato works with, at the very lowest level he puts the perception of shadows. At the next level he puts belief, opinion. At the next level he puts reason, understanding. And at the highest level he puts insight. Now, don't think you know what reason is. It's something you are going to have to investigate.

S: I thought you said that he put reason on the last level.

Anthony: No, on the last level he puts intuition, intelligible intuition. It's the perception of reality by reality. In other words, you perceive the ideas directly as they are. Plato refers to that as intelligible intuition or insight into reality. Below that he puts reason. Then he puts belief and opinion. And then at the very bottom he puts conjecture, assimilation of perceptual shadows. Now, what's the difference between reason and belief? Well, you see something out there and say, "Oh, wait a minute, it's got two arms, two legs, a head—that's a man." Now reason would have to tell you why it is a man and can't be anything else. Reason is firm, it doesn't move. Platonists refer to reason principles that govern the universe and don't alternate. The principles that are being discovered in science, in mathematics, and in the various branches of knowledge—this knowledge is a discovery of reason principles. Once you get to them, you are getting to sure knowledge.

S: So reason principles couldn't be relative in any way?

Anthony: I didn't say that. Relativity is another reason principle. In order for relativity to be true, it has to be a reason principle and not something else, right? Therefore it cannot itself be relative. Do you follow? If relative knowledge were completely relative, you would have no knowledge. There wouldn't be anything to talk about.

My point while I'm here is to inject a little mentalism into you. I have to leave aside everything else I would like to teach. I would like to teach you a lot of other things because I know how necessary they are. When I studied all these different systems like Theosophy, the Gurdjieff school, Christian Science, if I didn't have my reason I would have sunk all the way to the bottom. I would have drowned. The only thing I had to hold on to was reason. When a man makes a statement that I can show is unreasonable or that he is not using reason, I move on. It's the only safeguard we have.

S: But you don't equate that with logic?

Anthony: No, reason is greater than logic. Reason includes the application of intelligence at all levels. Logic is restricted to the coherence and the syntactical structure of your grammar.

S: We can't think of a Swedish word equivalent to the way you are using this word "reason."

Anthony: It would be good if we knew ancient Greek or Sanskrit, because they have a word for every metaphysical idea, a word that you cannot mistake. Now if we all knew Sanskrit or we all knew Greek, then we'd be well off, because then I could say anything I wanted and you would know precisely what I was talking about. I often use words that have different connotations for you, and you have to try to make sense out of what I'm saying. These ideas are difficult, they are not simple.

S: Could you say that reason is when you experience the subject-object relationship of your knowing as lessened, when you feel that you are closer to the object of which you are thinking?

Anthony: No. The use of reason doesn't imply the diminishing of the intensity of the subject-object relationship. Some people of the greatest intelligence, who have tremendous capacity to reason, have no experience that the world or the ideas are getting closer together or that the subject and the object are getting closer together.

S: Would you say it is reasoning if you have a witnessing faculty that is testing what you experience according to a standard that never changes? A higher witnessing faculty?

Anthony: There is some truth in what you're saying. When you investigate and get into the nature of reason, you are getting into the nature of the way the mind functions. And the way the mind functions is what is reason, because it doesn't alter. So it's really a faculty of the soul. The soul has all the reason principles or the ideas with which it can manifest itself. And those are firm, they're abiding.

Why don't we continue with mentalism?

> Those who can lay proper hold of its knowledge will find that it carries power instead of depriving them of it as the superficial critics believe. *(V13, 21:5.34)*

Anthony: Once you understand mentalism and start applying it you will find out that it is powerful medicine. You can apply it, even though you haven't been able to reason it out. You have faith. You know that it's there but you haven't worked it all out. But in applying it, you will see that it works—that as you change your inner nature, your inner life, your outer world changes too.

> The mind exists and develops on its own latent resources and needs nothing from outside. There is nothing outside. Nevertheless, its imaginative and creative power calls into play an environment which seems to be outside and which elicits those resources. *(V13, 21:2.69)*

S: Elicits?

Anthony: Draws forth. In other words, if I put you into difficult circumstances, the situation draws forth from you the potential strength you have to fight back. This is a very interesting quote. If you examine what he's saying, you will see he's saying something like this: There's only mind. Now, how does mind draw forth from within itself its own powers? It creates.

Imagine an animal that lives in a cave and can't see and knows it has to be able to see and then, after some number of generations, develops eyes. The point is this, each animal also lives only in its own mind. The mind, so to speak, uses this body of the animal to manifest its own powers. How? Well, the animal thinks, "I've got to see, I can't see anything. I have no eyes." And it keeps on working until it develops the organs it needs by which it could see. The potential is from within the mind.

If we think of the mind as a function, then this function could create the organ through which it could operate. The mind creates an eye through which it can operate. It develops its own function through a body. Then it develops, let's say, talons. What it's bringing forth, it's bringing from within itself.

Now, it's the same way with an individual man. His mind wants to draw forth from itself its own potential, so it puts him in a situation where it is forced to use whatever potential it has to make better what it is. So, unless a man is brought into confrontation with circumstances, he will not develop the potential that is in him.

S: Doesn't it also limit itself?

Anthony: Yes, it limits itself, surely. The mind has to limit itself. It says, "Now, I am this body. Now, through this body I've got to operate, and through this limited body I've got to acquire knowledge of what I projected out." So it is forced to develop. All development is imposed on us. It's an ongoing process, it goes on and on and on. You develop more and more faculties. If, for instance, you want to see more intensely and the eyes aren't enough, it will force you to develop clairvoyance.

S: You could develop inwards, or you could develop your physical organs more and more.

Anthony: Sure. Creatures that are much more developed, let's say entities that live in different realms, like the stars in the inerratic sphere, could have highly developed bodies—extremely sensitive bodies. These bodies are organs for their own development; whereas in comparison our bodies are gross, like mud.

S: What is the reason for the mind to develop itself?

Anthony: It wants to know more about itself. Don't you like to know more about yourself?

S: Mind wants to know about itself? But mind already knows all about itself.

Anthony: Yes, but that kind of knowing is like unknowing. It's like a state of total universal consciousness. It doesn't know any particular thing and it wants to know itself in a particular way.

S: The mind is . . .

Anthony: . . . is in the process of knowing itself, realizing itself. Each one of our individual minds. Just like the World-Mind knowing itself as millions and billions of minds. But ultimately when you want to ask why is there manifestation at all, the question is not admissible. Nobody knows why.

Unreflective minds are amazed, then scornful, when they first hear someone deny the existence of matter. Reflective minds are equally amazed but less scornful. If they take the trouble to investigate the assertion, they may be left with an uncomfortable suspicion that there might be something in it, even though they feel it too deep or too difficult for a final judgement. *(V13, 21:4.88)*

Anthony: There's an old saying, "When you talk about mind to an ordinary man, he will get scared."

> What is the use of maintaining that the universe has an existence of its own, entirely separate and apart from that which our minds give it, when we have never been able to know it and obviously can never know it except through our minds? Any such statement is a mere assumption for which we have no grounds at all. *(V13, 21:2.24)*

Anthony: All he's simply saying there is very direct. Why bother to believe in something existing outside of your mind when all that you know is what your mind tells you? What possible advantage would it be to say to yourself that there is a universe outside of your mind? What use could that possibly be? All you could know is the ideas in your mind, so why not remain content with that and work with that?

> The simple notion that the world is just a machine, that God is the mechanic who puts its parts together and that matter is the stuff he began with and used to make these parts, belongs to the primitive levels of scientific thinking. It is for those who are just beginning to form the conception of an orderly universe in their enthusiasm for the early discoveries of science. *(V13, 21:4.179)*

Anthony: In other words, if you believe that, you're still at a primitive level of intelligence—at the level where science used to think that the world was a big machine and God put it together.

S: If you are content that you can't know anything outside of your thinking, of your experience of your thinking of the world, why should you worry about explaining it? Why should there be science then?

Anthony: Why shouldn't there? As a matter of fact, you may come across a real science then. You may get knowledge that will boggle your mind once you understand the laws of the mind. Don't ever think that the people who understand mentalism don't know what science is. They have a greater conception of what science is than scientists do.

Why do you reason that only if I believe that there's a universe outside of my mind will I investigate it? Why *shouldn't* I investigate it if I know that its phenomena are only ideas in my mind? Why shouldn't I investigate and find out the way these ideas operate, the way they work? Why shouldn't I understand the World-Idea which is in my mind?

S: If you are one with the world, why should you worry about trying to explain it?

Anthony: But for heaven's sake, why *shouldn't* I? Why can't a sage be a scientist too? He wants to realize his own mind and he wants to understand how it works. Why do you have these objections? I am a scientist, I am also a mystic. I want to realize myself, I also want to understand the World-Idea. Why do you find that contradictory? You see all these objections to mentalism are really nonsense.

Why shouldn't a sage be interested in helping others? In other words, do you think that if Edison had been a sage he wouldn't have been interested in making the electric light, the incandescent light?

S: Why not?

Anthony: That's what I am saying. The sage would say: sure, make the electric light. Only an idiot would say don't do it. You have some strange ideas of what it means to be self-realized! You think you sit in a corner like a little plant and germinate? [laughter] A sage knows that the essence of everything is mind and to that extent he knows that we are all of that essence. But he also knows the forms that he sees. He knows both. Try to remember that. It isn't that he just knows that everything is mind. He knows that, but he also knows the forms of the mind.

> Plato, on Mentalism: "What a superior being would have as subjective thought, the inferior perceives as objective things." *(V13, 21:4.212)*

Anthony: What a god thinks, we would have to perceive.

S: But if you say that we are all participants in the World-Mind's thought of the world, then why don't we experience the same world?

Paul: I think it would be more correct to say that all our thinking has a common source, but each one of us experiences a creation from our own soul's envisioning of that Idea.

Anthony: The *what* is provided by the World-Mind and the *who* provides the *how*. In other words, the World-Idea is provided by the World-Mind, but each individual mind determines how it is going to experience that World-Idea. The individual has to put that World-Idea in its own time and space.

> A curious example, but one helpful to the inquirer, exists in the case of bodily pain. It is utterly impossible for us to imagine pain in the abstract—existing without any mind to be conscious of it. The word becomes quite meaningless if we try to separate it from someone or something to perceive or feel it. Its very existence depends entirely on being thought of, on being related to a conscious percipient. The sensation of being felt, this alone gives reality to pain. This fact refers equally to past or present pain. It should be easy to apply this analogy to the case of mere ideas, for the latter, like pain, can never come into existence without something, some mind, to think of them. Consciousness, on the part of someone or something, alone can make them real and factual. *(V13, 21:1.32 and Perspectives, p. 287)*

Anthony: It's impossible to think of pain existing in the abstract. If pain exists, some mind is there—otherwise it's a sheer abstraction. Just try to think of pain existing without some mind experiencing it and you see you would be talking nonsense. Pain cannot exist in the abstract. It can only exist in the mind. And that's what I meant when I said before that everybody is a mentalist when it comes to pain.

S: I don't get that.

Anthony: Well, lean back and think it over. Can you imagine pain independent of any mind?

S: I can't imagine anything without someone experiencing it.

Anthony: Well, there are people who say that there are things in the world that exist independently of the mind. And he's pointing out that in the case of pain, here is one case where you can't say that. Absolutely negated.

S: I get it, but it's the same with happiness or any other human feeling.

Anthony: Yes, sure. There you see how obvious it is that happiness or any kind of feeling is a feeling to a mind. It doesn't exist in a vacuum.

There's no such thing as happiness in itself, pleasure in itself. It's pleasure or pain for some mind.

S: So it is the same with the whole psychology?

Anthony: Yes. PB would point out, go further, why stop there? Can there be anything known without a knower? Can there?

S: No.

Anthony: Then how could there be a world without the knower? There can't be. Therefore what is real is the knower. And who is the knower? I am. Then I am more real than the world.

S: Do you think it is a good attitude to take—that I am more real than the world?

Anthony: Yes, *if* you know what "I" I am referring to. The "I" I'm talking about is not part of the world in that sense. That means that the ego-and-its-world is an object to a superior consciousness.

> At the centre of each man, each animal, each plant, each cell, and each atom, there is a complete stillness. A seemingly empty stillness, yet it holds the divine energies and the divine Idea for that thing. *(V16, 26:1.213 and Perspectives, p. 361)*

> *Yoga Vasistha*: "There is a mind behind every particle of dust." *(V13, 21:4.271)*

Anthony: The One incarnates in an atom, in a human being, in a solar system and repeats everything that has gone before. Every individual mind will go through this. It's guaranteed. Each and every individual mind will evolve from the stage of an atom and go on indefinitely. There is no beginning. There is no end. Mind is a self-perpetuating intelligence that is always actualizing whatever potential it contains.

S: So it doesn't end with liberation? It just goes on and on?

Anthony: Yes, you go on. But as far as we're concerned that is pretty far. When you reach that level, then you can worry about what goes on after that. But as far as humans are concerned that's it. So most people believe that and you leave them alone at that. The Buddha wouldn't speak about what was beyond. He says first get here, then we'll worry about other things.

But in that one sentence is the most mind-boggling conception ever put down in the history of mankind: that the Universal Mind incarnates in every atom in every particular entity, and that it will go on through this endless process of evolution.

S: When I see a tree, my mind projects the tree. When I turn around so I'm not seeing the tree, and no one is seeing the tree, can the tree manifest itself? Isn't it a part of nature which is also evolving?

Anthony: The only nature that you know is the one that your mind manifests to you. Your mind is constantly manifesting thought after thought. And there is continuous change going on. What do you think of that? That there is a mind behind every entity, whether it is an amoeba, a crawling reptile, a snake, a bird, a fish . . .

S: A pencil?

Anthony: We are speaking about entities. A pencil is not a real entity. I would say, for instance, that a mineral or a rock is an entity. I wouldn't call what we put together an entity.

S: When you have a feeling of "I," isn't that an entity? But a rock doesn't have that feeling of "I."

Anthony: Look at the word in the quote: "particle." So you can go all the way down to an atom.

S: There is an individual mind behind every entity?

S: But didn't you say universal mind?

Anthony: It is universal, the mind is always universal. But if you speak about your mind, not my mind, it is an individual absolute for you. My mind is an individual absolute for me.

S: But an atom has an individual mind?

Anthony: Yes, otherwise all atoms would be the same and there would be one mind for all atoms. And then you couldn't speak about the mind incarnating in every entity.

S: But an entity, doesn't that mean that there is an "I" thought?

Anthony: No, it's not a thought. It's mind. Behind every entity there's a mind. The feeling of "I" doesn't arise until you become self-conscious.

S: By entity do you mean it creates its own world?

Anthony: By entity I mean an organized system of relationships. An atom is an organized system of relationships within itself. And you don't confuse it with another atom, which is another organized system of relationships.

S: Could I rephrase my question? My mind has to project itself in order to know itself and it does that in space and time. But nature doesn't seem to have to manifest or project itself. The tree doesn't have the ability to manifest itself. Its existence in the manifested world is dependent upon my seeing it.

S: Is it right to say that the tree's existence for you is dependent on you, but the tree's existence for itself is dependent on itself? Is there such a thing as the tree's existing for itself?

Anthony: In itself, yes.

S: So the tree is existing for itself when you turn around?

Anthony: On one hand you are speaking about the being of the tree. Does the tree have true being? Yes. What about the tree you are looking at? No, that doesn't have true being. You are manifesting the being of that tree in your perception. Therefore, what is an appearance for you in your mind—this tree that is manifest in your mind—depends on you. But the true being of the tree does not depend on you.

S: But you say that every entity has an individual mind. Isn't the individual mind of the tree capable of manifesting itself to itself?

Anthony: It does. The tree has its own world in which it lives. The tree has a perception of its own environment which is not the way we would perceive our environment, nor our time and space. The Maxwell Equations of electrodynamics show very clearly that every wave only knows its own immediate environment—no other. I know the world that is manifested in my consciousness. I see a tree. It is manifested by my consciousness, but that doesn't mean that I know the true being of the tree.

S: But a tree or a flower or a small animal cannot project a world, can they?

Anthony: They do. Every entity creates its own environment. The mind behind every entity creates the environment in which that entity is living. I create my world. That world is a manifestation within my consciousness. You do likewise. So does a tree.

Look—anything in the world that you perceive is an entity in its own right. But you don't see it in its own right. You only see it as your consciousness is manifesting it to you. Don't get into the question now as to what the ultimate reality of each and every object in your consciousness is. The reason principle that makes a thing to be a rat, a goat, a sheep—that's a whole different ball game. The point to understand here is that all these things are represented in your consciousness. And the amazing thing is that anything that *is* has its own principle, its own mind, and that each and every one experiences the world in its own way. Now what will happen is that you'll balk at the immensity of the conception. You'll get scared. You'll say—how could there be so many?

S: But isn't it right to say that there is an object outside of my individual mind which I am not aware of?

Anthony: Outside of your individual mind? Then how are you going to be aware of it?

Paul: You see, the very calling it outside is stating it incorrectly from the higher point of view. The intellectual world is not in space and time. So, that greater consciousness is not in space and time. The true being of any other being is not outside. It will never be found outside.

Anthony: What you're going to find out is that the whole intellectual world exists within you. But right now I don't want to get into that.

S: What did you mean when you said that a tree is not in the same kind of space and time as we know?

Anthony: Look at this. You have a hundred thoughts a minute, a turtle has one thought a day. You live in two different worlds. He lives in his world of thought, one thought a day. That's all.

You see, the thing that you are not going to believe, but I'll tell you because you insist, is that each person is in a sense a World-Mind. Each soul contains the whole of the intellectual cosmos within itself. You participate in it. But it would be better, in some instances, to put it this way—as Plotinus says in *The Enneads*—that the whole of the Intellectual Principle is within you, within your mind and functioning through your mind. And then at a lower level your individual mind translates, transcribes what's in the Intellectual Principle and manifests it. And then your mind experiences what it manifests. But we are not ready for that, because that's something that you can't accept. You can hear the words but the implications are so vast that it takes an enormous background to realize them. When you say "God is within you," that's what you are saying. It's not going to be a piece of God. God is within you. When you say that, then the full implication is that the whole Intellectual Principle is operating through you, through your mind. It's what organizes and structuralizes the functioning of your mind. But those are questions that come not in mentalism but in ontology—the study of the World-Mind or of the World-Idea.

The important thing right now is mentalism. Make believe I have an iron wedge and a hammer and I'm making a hole in the top of your skull and the only thing I'm going to put in there is mentalism! First I'll do that, okay? And then I'll patch that up and later on make another hole and put in the World-Idea. I only work with one idea at a time. You're not ready to handle a lot of subjects all at once. It's confusing even for people who have worked with it for years. As soon as you get a feeling for mentalism—and after a few days you feel like a blotter, you are saturated—then I'll give you more. You have to be so saturated with it that you could start answering all your own questions. Until you reach that position you are not sufficiently saturated.

FIVE
Life Itself Is the Quest

Anthony: When most of us sit down to meditate, you close your eyes and you look and there is blackness in front of you. Nothing. Right? And after a little while you get bored. You say, "There is nothing here. What am I doing?" And then after a little while you get sleepy and you go to sleep. Some of us, when we sit down and we're looking at that blackness in front of us, that nothingness, ask, "What am I looking for?"

You have to ask yourself, "Who is looking?" Whether there are pictures in front of you, or whether there's just blackness in front of you, or whether there are a lot of thoughts, the question that should come up is, "Who is looking?" You are always looking *at* something, but the *one who is looking*, you always forget. You're always preoccupied with what goes on, so to speak, on the cinemagraph. And you never look at the guy who is looking. It's like when you go to the movies, you forget about yourself and you're just looking at the picture. Well, that's what we're doing all the time. We're always looking at pictures. We have looked at pictures so much that we have forgotten that we *are*. And that's the problem.

So the first thing we have to do is to try to understand, theoretically, something about mentalism. And that's difficult. Then the next thing is, after you have some understanding of mentalism, then you want to be able to realize a little bit of it. If you can do these two things, then everything else will be taken care of.

When a person tries to understand mentalism, he has to think very deeply and profoundly over and over again. Then he tries to realize it in meditation and he gets a glimpse—now he's on his way. There's only one other thing he has to find out. He has to find out about his ego. The only time you become a real quester is when, number one, you get a glimpse, and number two, you find out who your enemy is. Then you are on the quest.

So why not concentrate on something that will put you right on the quest and make you start moving? Because once you get a glimpse, then you know there is no way out. You've got to go to the end. You won't turn back. Before that happens—and most people don't know this—you could think you're on the quest; but until you get an actual glimpse, until you actually feel and know your soul intimately, whether for a minute or for an hour or for a month, it's all theory. So those are the two important things that I feel that we should get very acquainted with. One: understand mentalism. Two: understand something about meditation, so that you can realize what mentalism is all about in yourself. Because no matter how many times you read the menu in a restaurant, your hunger will always persist unless you eat something. You can read the menu a hundred times, but it's not going to fill you up. So you need to understand mentalism more and more, but until you get an actual experience of it, you're not going to be happy.

It's the most obvious thing in the world that most of us, when we close our eyes and sit down to meditate, are faced with a blankness like there's nothing there. We have to confront that, and we have to evolve a method and then stick to that method. If you wanted to learn piano, you would either have to follow a certain method on your own or go to a teacher every week who will instruct you. Then after a few years you could play. In a similar way, if you want to learn to meditate, you have to do it conscientiously every day and you have to know what you are doing. It's not going to happen by chance because it is a difficult art. But assuming that a person understands something about mentalism, he may then get an insight in meditation into the mentalistic nature of everything. And then I'm finished, my work is done. He could go on studying more with me, or he could go away, or he could go to Timbuctoo, or he could become a salesman. And I like to get rid of you people as fast as I can.

S: *How can we tell if what we think is compassion is really compassion?*

Anthony: At a certain level of understanding, compassion is automatically released. When now and then you get a good feeling about a person and you think that is compassion, just wait a while—wait until he does the first annoying thing and see if you still feel the same way. If you don't, you can rest assured that it wasn't compassion to begin with. Compassion isn't going to go away just because the person is annoying. Compassion will always be there. Even if the teacher has to criticize a student he is not doing it to humiliate him. He's criticizing constructively, he's trying to point out something. But a real teacher doesn't feel that one person is better than another, because to him they are all the same. He knows and lives the truth of mentalism, so the consequence is that he can't really have favorites in that sense.

S: *It would be helpful if sometime you could talk a little about the practical trials and problems that we have to work with in trying to assimilate or understand, get an insight into mentalism. The kind of problems that meet us in life and that life is trying to instruct us with—how are we to tackle those, what attitude is helpful? It is always easier if one knows that something is a part of the quest or a trial of the quest.*

Anthony: Yes, but isn't life itself the quest?

S: *Yes, of course. But isn't there a special attitude, or special disciplines, you need to develop in order to meet things and make the best of them philosophically?*

Anthony: I'll give it some thought, but it still is my very honest opinion that you have to learn the philosophic principles and then apply them. No one else could do that for you. For example, very often a person comes over to me and says, "I have been meditating for two years, and I still fall asleep." And the only thing I could tell him is, "I can't give you the will to meditate. I can only explain to you the principles of meditation. I can explain to you step by step what goes, but when all is said and done you have to do it."

When you first get on the quest—when you first hear about these things—you get very enthused, you get carried away and it is like you have extra energy. You can actually get up and do the things that you think you have to do. But after some time, and it varies with individuals, that enthusiasm is not available any more and then you are again faced with what you were, without the enthusiasm to push you through. If enthusiasm were always available—you know, like when you go to the sink, you turn the faucet on, the water comes out—so you could turn the faucet on and get enthused and do everything, well, it wouldn't be much of a quest, would it? It would be a snap.

The fact remains that each and every one of us has to struggle through every one of our problems. And no problem ever gets solved. You just live through it. You endure it and you live through it and you learn from it; but as far as solving them, I've never seen any of them solved. It is a psychological fact that after a certain time the enthusiasm, the energy that you had in the beginning settles down and you are confronted with doing these things with your own strength. No one else is going to give you the strength to do it. So that's a very fundamental problem. But the best way around it that I know of is to learn to meditate. Try to make sure that you do it. After a while, it doesn't take very long, you do get moments of extraordinary peace and tranquility. And when you come out, that will give you the strength and the endurance to see through the next day and the next day. You're going to go up and down. You're going to have good days and bad days. And you're just going to have to learn to push through them regardless of how they are. And then you develop a nice disposition. But it's every day, day in, day out, day in, day out. If you look at the transits in your astrological chart, for example, and say, "I've got bad transits today," you go to work anyway. Tomorrow you've got good transits, you go to work anyway.

So even nature is trying to teach us to persist, to keep going. Then a particular problem comes up. Like a woman comes over to me and says, "I just got my divorce." Then she says, "You know, I just met a man I like." I say, "Wonderful, go ahead, start all over again." We make our own trouble, we have to get out of it. Sometimes everything is cleared for us to go ahead and do the things we always wanted to do. Then in comes a problem. Maybe we should mention that there do arise over and over again what you might call tests. These things do happen. And I think most of us know when that's happening, we can smell it.

S: Could you talk about those kind of things a little so that we would be better equipped to handle them?

Anthony: But that's like trying to anticipate what your problems are going to be.

S: I don't mean in particular, just in general.

Anthony: In general? I never came across general problems. They were always specific.

S: What do you mean by tests?

Anthony: Take an example. You're sitting and meditating and you are succeeding. You're getting on with meditation. You're beginning to get introverted, self-absorbed, and you know that this is beginning to happen. You can see that you are withdrawing from the world, or that the world is not so important to you any more. You are more interested in what's going on inside. Then a man comes along and offers you a fabulous job, but you have to get completely extroverted. Or a beautiful girl comes along and makes goo-goo eyes. Then out you are. You are out there all over again. And you could think about it. You could say, "Wait a minute, why is this happening to me?" And maybe it would be the right thing to do, maybe not. I don't know. Because there is no way of telling ahead of time whether this is what you should be doing or something you should be avoiding. But if a person is meditating, getting introverted, more and more introverted, and then like I said, a girl comes along and makes goo-goo eyes, he knows what's happening. This has happened at this time, now, because of his introversion that's starting to take place. Because the world always wants to keep you for itself. It has a nice glamour. Do you know what I mean by glamour? It has a nice sheen, a nice glamour. And it's always drawing you. It says, "Come here, come here! I've got just what you want!" It doesn't want you to get introverted. It doesn't want you to seek your soul.

S: But it sounds like you are talking about the world as if it has the same role as the ego has, as if it is doing the same thing.

Anthony: Who do you think is doing it?

S: Am I really projecting out, or is it some kind of synchronicity?

Anthony: Never mind about synchronicity. The point is that right then and there your ego is showing its colors. Now, who is the boss, your ego that wants to go out and see that girl with the goo-goo eyes? Or are you going to say, "No! We're going to sit and meditate. Today and tomorrow and the next day. Forget about it. You're not going to go see goo-goo eyes!"

S: Can't you do both? Can't you enjoy the girl with the goo-goo eyes and meditate?

Anthony: Try it, you try it. One thing I think you will notice is that if the tendency towards extroversion becomes powerful and you start relating to the external world again you are going to be outside, out there in the world. You're not going to be able to take that energy and introvert it and bring it down into yourself. Have you ever watched a cork or a rubber ball on the water? You try to push it down and it always comes up. You know, you take a big rubber ball or a cork and you try to push it down in the water. It keeps coming up. Well, if the world, if the glamour of the world is so strong that it keeps drawing you, then it's like you're trying to push the ball down and it won't go down, it will come up. You can't really split the energy in two directions. You can't have a river going in two different ways at the same time. So there has to be a withdrawal of energy from the world. To some extent it has to be. That doesn't mean that you shouldn't do the work in the world that you're supposed to do. You can go about doing the work in the world that you're supposed to do. But you have to remember that the world—we call it the dragon—the dragon always has nice little stories to tell you. "Why don't you come, live in the world, enjoy the world? Drink and be merry, don't worry about tomorrow." And there is something inside of you that says, "Wait a minute. I've got work to do. I've got other things to do." So my own experience has been that I can't do it. A sage can do it, because to him inside and outside are one thing. But when we're talking about our evolution, our development step by step, I find it very hard.

S: *How would you explain that the world is always trying to get your attention? Is it because the world is projected from the ego?*

Anthony: Basically, of course, it is the desire nature which is rooted in the ego which always wants, so to speak, to have the world and the so-called objects. It has a lust for objects in the world. That is its very nature. And part of what we have to understand in this study is that this lust for objects has to be brought under control. There's no limit to it. We are always looking. What's out there? Is there something there for me? You walk down the street, downtown. There is nothing there. What are you looking for? We are like that. You know in English we have a saying, "Everything that glitters isn't gold." It could be tinsel.

The funny thing is that the adverse forces in nature will attack at a crucial time, at a time when it's possible that you may be able to make a little advance forward. And they could attack you with a goo-goo-eyed girl or handsome man, or they could attack you with, "Here is a wonderful job." Any possible way.

S: Now you are saying forces of nature?

Anthony: They are natural things. It isn't that they are devised. For instance, in us as individual beings there is the tendency that anything that happened to us will condition us. If as a child you went through certain kinds of experiences that left a deep impression on your mind, they conditioned your mind in a way that stays with you all the time unless you deliberately go about to undo it. This tendency for the past to remain with us, this inertia of what we've experienced in the past, is part of our very nature. The past conditioning that you've gone through is present here and now.

You follow that, don't you? Past conditioning is always operative. Well, when you are trying to understand something new, that makes it difficult for you to understand something that your past conditioning doesn't at all understand or grasp. So we could think of that as an adverse force in us which always wants to hold us, bind us to the past. I would call that an adverse force.

S: But I thought when you said "adverse forces of nature" you were speaking about forces outside of the ego.

Anthony: You're getting away from the point now. What you're trying to do is to get into an epistemological discussion that there is nothing outside of us, and all that.

I am speaking about the fact that I meet someone out there who makes goo-goo eyes at me and I say that these are adverse forces of nature which are going to try to stop my progress. I am talking—the expression is, I'm talking turkey. This happens; this really happens. There have been quite a few people who have studied for a few years and then something has come up in their lives and they made a complete turn-about and they are out. They are no longer interested in these things. What happened was that they actually got attacked by adverse forces in order to see, "Do you really want this?" And the person finds out, "No, I really don't want this. I want these other things." He has to go after them. So I am not now talking epistemology, I am not talking ontology. You wanted me to talk about practical things and these are very practical things.

You know, a monk lives in a monastery and thinks he is very honest. But if this monk has to live in the world and he has a family to take care of and he rings up the register, he may find out he's not so honest.

S: That is very important. I think that you shouldn't just avoid things. You should train yourself to see things and live with them but, inside yourself, try to be detached. It couldn't be wrong all the time to go after that girl or that job, but it might be a matter of how you do it, if you could still remain detached.

Anthony: Yes, but you see what it comes down to. If you want to find your soul, if you want to get a glimpse of your soul, you have to become very concentrated about it. You can't be dissipating.

I had a friend once—this is many years ago—he said, "Let's take the summer off and finish the quest, so that we can do what we want."

S: Couldn't you use these tests deliberately in your spiritual training?

Anthony: They happen deliberately. They're not accidents. You're going to be presented with these things as soon as you go out into the world and start trying to apply what you know.

S: If you are aware of that, it shouldn't cause you to leave your studies or your quest.

Anthony: Ah, but I don't think you know human nature.

S: The best thing is to have an aim first and then try to follow that.

Anthony: Yes, that's what we're saying. But the point is what do you do when the actual time comes and something is presented to you. If someone comes over, for example, and says, "Here is a box of gold; I want you to do this," what do you do?

S: If I have forgotten my aim I will take the box.

Anthony: Even if you didn't forget your aim, the test is going to be for real. It is not going to be imaginary. It's going to be very real. And it's going to hurt. It's going to hurt.

S: Do these tests get worse and worse?

Anthony: Well, they tend to get more subtle. In the beginning it may be a more material thing, but later on it gets to be a more subtle thing. And more subtle. And your mind has to get more subtle, too, so that it could encounter that adversity and deal with it.

Anyone who has been on the quest for a number of years will sooner or later find the world that he lives in, the world that he knows, blowing up in his face. Everyone who has been on the quest a few years has that experience automatically. It's very rare that things go along smoothly for too long a time. For almost every quester, that's to be understood, in the sense that it can't be helped. It's in our very nature, because of the way we are and the way our whole past history is. Our whole history is of such a nature that when we want to get to the highest part of our being, when we want to touch the soul within us, certain changes have to be made. The way we are is not good enough, some changes have to be made. And usually things happen so that these changes are brought about in the person.

It may be, for example, that you never had the desire to drink, or you forgot about it or gave it up. But then you meet a sage, and all of a sudden you want to start drinking. I mean, it actually happens that way. Now what happened? In the presence of the sage, a past habit which is still alive in you is brought up to the surface and now you have to overcome it once and for all. Get rid of it. It could be any number of things that we all have in our past, that we have to deal with if we want to get to the truth. All these things within you that are blocking you from getting to the truth get activated when you get into the presence of a sage. It's not that he comes personally there and shovels around; it just happens naturally, like a catalytic reaction.

These parts of ourselves that can't serve the higher purpose have to be taken up, brought up into the daylight, into your consciousness. They have to be understood for what they are and then they must be disowned, discarded, or completely dissolved. So very often when a person is neurotic, if he starts meditating, things are going to get worse, not better. Because these problems start coming out into the open. Those of us who have been at it a few years begin to recognize that. You know, "Why is everything going wrong? What's going on?" But that's exactly what to expect and it's good, because if these things are not brought out they will always stay in what the psychologists call the unconscious, the subconscious. And when the right opportunity comes, they'll spring out and you'll find out, "I am not at all the way I thought I was. I'm really a grub, something horrible." But all the time we thought we were 99% gold. So these things happen, very naturally. It's to be expected.

S: Isn't the important thing not what you do, but how you do it and that you are aware of your attitude to it?

Anthony: Yes. The important thing is to recognize the nature of the temptation. Why are you tempted to begin with? If this girl makes goo-goo eyes at me, why am I tempted? There has to be something in me that responds to that. That's what I have to find out. What is it in me that responds to that?

What is there in me that responds to this man offering me a million dollars, so that I want it? That is what I have to go after. Now it's like a tree. It has a lot of branches. You chop off one branch and you say, "Well, I got rid of that." But then you find that there are other branches growing and you begin to realize, "Wait a minute, this can go on forever, where is all this coming from?" Then you have to go to the roots of the tree.

S: But if you are offered a million dollars, you can't say in general it is wrong to say yes. It might be better to say yes and take on the responsibility of what to do with it.

Anthony: You remember the story about the egg? When you boil it for too long it blows up. I'm only giving an analogy. That's why I don't like to talk about ethics.

S: For each one it is different. Each of us is attached to different things. And you have to know yourself and be honest with yourself to find out which they are for you.

Anthony: You see, she is going to say that maybe you need the million dollars and you'll build an institution for the care of the blind, and do good with it. So I can't give you any analogy. Because then this girl with the goo-goo eyes, maybe she'd make a good wife. Get married?

S: Maybe she would.

Anthony: I know. So any analogy I give is not going to work. But the fact remains that here's an example where this man is happily married, everything is going nicely. He has a job, makes a good living, supports his family, and every night he practices meditation. All right? His wife leaves him alone. She says, well, he has this peculiar habit, but it is better than going to the bar. So every night he meditates and he is starting to get very deeply drawn in. And sometimes he can sit for hours, absolutely quiet, peaceful, so peaceful that he doesn't know that there are two things there, him and the world. They're both gone—his ego and the world. Now he knows he is getting close to the secret and that if he could persevere, he could experience the nature of the mind, the void mind. So tomorrow morning, he goes to work, he has a new secretary, a beautiful woman, blond, long hair, six feet tall. Get married, you say. Right? It would be obvious.

S: *But isn't it the attitude that's important? You cannot avoid looking at the secretary, but you should try to see your feelings and that would help you to see how your ego is operating.*

Anthony: Yes, that is the point. But, usually, you will find out in a very murderous way how your ego is operating. It'll take you about two minutes to see.

What you say is true. He can't quit his job. She can't get fired. He has to get through the test. So he's going to go through a furnace.

S: *I think it is very important that you test yourself all the time.*

Anthony: No, I don't want to! If I can get away, I'll get away. I won't do it. It has to corner me. It has to say, "Now you can't get out." Don't go looking for them.

Paul: You usually lose.

Anthony: You bet your life you lose. You don't know how strong your ego is until you encounter it. Then you find out, it's eighteen feet tall. I can see you're naïve.

S: *You want to test the value of what you have obtained.*

Anthony: I don't want to test anything. I want to mind my business. I want to avoid it. Who do you think I am? Saint George? I don't want to fight the dragon. That's all right for Saint George. He fights the dragon, he kills the dragon. But every time I fought the dragon he killed me. I appreciate what you say. I understand what you say. And it's a very heroic attitude. But I'm a coward.

S: *I always have a feeling that you should try it a bit. You go out and say, "Hello dragon, here I am." And then you lose. And then you try a little bit again.*

Anthony: But after you do that a few times and your head is bleeding and you're bleeding from all over your body you say, no more.

S: *Don't call him, he'll call you.*

S: Would you say that if I want to learn how to deal with it, I have to get to know my lower nature and its ways?

Anthony: No, I don't buy that. I don't have to get to know my lower nature. I *know* my lower nature. I have no illusions as to what my lower nature is. It's a creeping reptile, a snake, a rat. You want me to get to know it? That's like the psychologists who tell you to start practicing the primal scream and be aggressive. No, I don't need it. I know what my lower nature is. And you have to be really naïve not to know what your lower nature is, you've got to be a babe in the woods. I know that I'm vile, I know that I'm a liar, I know that my ego would do anything to have its way, to fulfill its desires—I don't want to go on. I know it. I'm too old, too old.

S: There is an expression, "Everything you give your energy to, grows."

Anthony: Yes, that is why I give my energy to other things and try not to give it to the ego. If anyone thinks that he could live out the shadow, that's like adding fuel, you know, gasoline, to the fire and hoping that it will go out.

S: Jung writes that it contains a lot of energy.

Anthony: He speaks about the shadow as this inferior aspect of our personality which didn't develop sufficiently and has a lot of negative qualities, is still rooted in the unconscious, is not differentiated from the unconscious. Yes, he says that the inferior function has its roots in the unconscious and that if you follow it through you will tap these primal sources of energy. That is what he said. I don't need that energy. I don't want it.

S: But if you talk about it as a creature, if it's like a wild animal which you can tame to drag your wagon or to ride on?

Anthony: The only time you are going to tame the ego is when you go through the mystical death. Until then it will always try to overcome you.

S: So you mean you can't develop your will?

Anthony: Yes, of course you have to develop the will to put it in its place. But what I was specifically talking about is that the approach of identifying with and living out the shadow, so that you could exhaust its potential and reach the source of its energy, I consider very dangerous.

S: Did you say it was dangerous to try to exhaust the shadow?

Anthony: Yes, exhaust or live it out.

Paul: If you try to follow through with an ideal, you are going to meet your shadow immediately. You try to set up a schedule—say, you are going to study every night. You don't have to go seeking it. It is going to show up at your doorstep every day. I think that is the point. As soon as you start developing a little consciousness, you are going to see it. It will be at your doorstep as soon as you get up in the morning.

S: I've been going into my shadow. I went into primal scream therapy. Many people told me it was wrong, but I found it was positive.

Anthony: I don't know enough about your personal problems, and I don't want to go into that. But it's very possible that what happened could be interpreted differently than the way it was interpreted to you. You have to remember that in psychiatry, psychotherapy, and psychoanalysis there are half a dozen different and contradictory hypotheses explaining one and the same illness. So I have reason to suspect that they may not know what they're talking about. They do seem to succeed sometimes in helping a person, but when they tell me the explanation of what helped I have reservations that their explanations make any sense. So I still feel that for a normal person to go out looking for his shadow is asking for trouble.

The example Paul gave just now is very true. As soon as you set up an ideal for the life that you want to live, the way you think you should live—you want to embody nobler ethics, finer ideals—then immediately the shadow will be there attacking you. Because there are parts of our being that will not accept the ideal. And those are the very parts that have to be transformed.

I'll give you a personal example. I took a job working nights, twelve to eight, so I could study all night. Every night I went there with my books. All I had to do was be there—I didn't have to do anything and I could study all night. At 12:05 I was fast asleep. Every night this would happen. I tried to read, study, but in ten minutes, twenty minutes, I would be fast asleep. This went on for six months. I stopped the job. I said nope, I can't handle it, evidently I don't have the strength. And I waited two years and then went back and tried again. It was a real struggle. But the only way I could get any studying done was to get a job where I could be left alone. I had four boys at home then—who is going to study with four or five boys at home? I raised six sons, so I would never try to study at home. I go down into a cave, into the cellar, into a toll booth, into a car—go anywhere but home to study. So I used to get jobs where I could do that. And it was really a struggle. The resistance would come up and it would be so strong that I would just fall asleep. I would try to meditate, and I'd fall asleep; try to fast, I would be twice as hungry. Every time I attempted to do something, the opposite would happen. And I began to realize the power and the strength of the adversity in me. You know the adverse forces are very strong.

You get another example of that adversity if you try to see a person the way he is, without any prejudgments. And you will see your mind rushing in and superimposing on that person all kinds of nonsense. So you say, look, why can't I see things the way they are? Well, that's the way the mind has been conditioned, that's the way it is going to work. And if you want it to work differently, you are going to have to struggle with it and reform it to do what you want it to do.

So I became convinced in my experience and by the experience of others that as soon as you set up your ideals and try to live them the shadow is right there, fighting you tooth and nail. He is not going to let you do it, and you are going to have to come up with a tremendous will to overcome that. You're going to have to do it. Nobody else can do it. You're going to have to do what *you* think is the right thing. First of all, you have to think it out, try to be sure that it is the right thing. If I think it out for you and say that is the right thing, that is wrong for you. What good is it if I do it? Because then the benefit is mine, not yours. Everyone has to think his way through and apply what he believes to the problem, and he has to persist and endure to see it through. There is no other way. Otherwise none of us would be here. We would all be perfect beings. We'd be floating around with a harp.

S: This is very helpful, because if you don't know that it is your shadow, you will just go with it. Many people don't even have a notion of what the shadow does, how it works.

Anthony: You see, I don't like to call it the shadow, because that makes it seem that it's just a little part of you. I like to call it the ego, the whole of it. All of my ego is always inclined to disagree with higher ideals. It will always fight them. And I don't see why I should select a little part of it and say, that's the shadow, and the rest is nice. It all stinks. The ego, by its very definition, always seeks to satisfy itself and no one else. I mean, what does the ego worship? *Itself.*

S: Could you say that the ego is ignorance?

Anthony: The ego is smarter than all of us here put together. It will outwit you at every turn.

S: But it is the opposite to knowledge or insight.

Anthony: But I'm not interested in that. You're asking me about the ego and I'm telling you he's very, very smart. As a matter of fact, like Paul just said, if you say that every night at eight o'clock you are going to sit down and study, at eight o'clock the bell will ring, and your friends will come in. The ego set it up beautifully. Don't have any illusions that it's stupid, that it doesn't know.

S: No, I don't mean that the ego is stupid, but that the ego is there because of our spiritual ignorance, if you could put it that way.

Anthony: Well no, that's a much more complicated question. Because the ego is part of us in a way. It's that part of us which I spoke to you about before, that part of the soul which always seeks earthly embodiment. And that thing, that principle of the soul which has been embodied so many times and has such a storehouse of experience, is so rich in experience that it knows every trick in the book. You will need a lot of acute understanding to see when it's trying to pull the wool over your eyes. You've got to really be all attention. And it's *always* trying to pull the wool over your eyes. It's always interested in satisfying its own desires. Now it's true that as you get older a lot of the desires weaken in intensity, but they are not gone. For example, a man gets older, or a woman gets older, and the instinct for sex weakens. Maybe by the time you are sixty or seventy it even becomes a bore. But when you come back again in the next incarnation and you have the vitality, that instinct is right there. If you haven't conquered it before, it will be right there saying, "Let's go look for that girl with the goo-goo eyes."

S: So the soul's striving for embodiment is a striving away from the source?

Anthony: Well, you see, the short cut, the best way to work at it, is to understand the nature of mentalism and then try to implement that understanding actually in your own consciousness, so you know that everything is an idea in your mind, and you experience it. Then that desire for embodiment gets considerably weakened. Now, if a person reaches a stage in meditation where he goes into the void mind, that principle we call the reproductive soul that always wants earthly embodiment dies. When you come out you still have an ego, but the function of egotism is gone—no longer there. And you are now at what the Sufis call the first of three stations. Now you have realized that the ego is absolute emptiness, it's nothing, there is nothing there. It's a matrix of thoughts and possibilities which revolve around an imaginary center. You have realized this in the void. After you have realized the emptiness of your own ego, then begins a long training. It's like the higher soul starts instructing you. And when you go through that training, that's the second station. The third is when the soul permanently takes possession, and that's the stage of the sage and the philosopher. They no longer have an ego like you and I have. Their "ego" is dead. And that is a very, very highly spiritual stage.

S: What did you say the first was?

Anthony: The first station is the annihilation of egotism, the death of the ego as we know it. First of all, I can assure you, you are not going to put the ego aside. There will come a time when a person achieves the highest state, sagehood, and that means that the ego, or egotism, gets destroyed. But he still has the vehicle through which he can operate, the body and his mind. The death of the ego, or the crucifixion, can only take place at the level of the void mind, when you reach that level of consciousness and the mind becomes absolutely void. That is where the ego can be destroyed. Anything below that—you won't succeed. The most you will be able to do is to train it to do what you want it to do.

S: So you mean that the ego must discipline itself and you use the ego to do that? But so often you hear that you should try to put the ego aside, or anyway weaken the ego's influence as much as possible.

Then more of the higher power will come through, and you can let things happen more by themselves.

Anthony: It is true that the less there is of the ego, the more of the higher self can come through. That is true.

S: So on one hand you discipline yourself with the ego, and at the same time you diminish your ego to let more of the higher power come through? You do the two at the same time?

Anthony: Yes. We spoke a little bit about the philosophic aspect of this teaching. That was one approach. The meditational techniques that will have to be used are another approach. And then there is a third approach that has to considered and that is the ethical application and the morality needed to bring this doctrine to fruition. That, too, is involved. So it is not only that we have to have the correct ideas, the correct understanding. We also have to implement those ideas, we have to actualize them in our everyday life. To have the correct ideas and not to implement them is useless. So all these things, all these different aspects, are going to be brought together. It is a tremendous goal that is planned for mankind's future. It is up to us to try to cooperate with that World-Idea instead of fighting it all the time.

S: What is this goal?

Anthony: To become a philosophic, spiritual person. Not to become gods or anything like that, but all that is implied when you say "human being." Because we are a strange mixture. There is a part of us that is angelic. That is the highest part of the soul. There is a part of us that is devilish. That is the ego and the animal body. And there is a part in between, the human being—the rational human being. We are constituted of these three different sectors: an angelic part, a human part, and an animal part. And the evolution has to take place at the two lower parts. We have to become human beings.

S: Do we have to become angelic?

Anthony: Well, you first have to become human before you worry about that. To speak about becoming a sage, a man of wisdom, without having first succeeded in becoming a human being is really to talk nonsense. And a human being is not necessarily to be confused with a creature that has two arms and two legs and a head.

That doesn't make you human. Look around the world and you can see that there are many, many millions of people like that, but they are not humans. It is wrong to say they are human.

S: *Where does it stop? It sounds like there is an end to this evolution, as you said we are not going to become gods or anything beyond human.*

Anthony: Why should it stop? There is a point where we can speak profitably about becoming a Buddha, and that is the goal that we are working towards. But that does not mean that it stops there. As far as we are concerned that is far enough. Where does this evolution stop? There is no stop. There is no beginning, there is no end. When did the universe begin? When will it end? All this is nonsense. There has never been a beginning and there will never be an end.

S: *But the world's manifestation, doesn't that have an end?*

Anthony: Look up into the sky at night. I think the astronomers have counted ten to the eleventh power of stars just in our galaxy. Some are a billion years old, some are ten billion years old. How can you talk about a beginning or an end to all this? In the same way, there is no beginning to your soul, no end to it. It wasn't made at a certain time.

If you understand mentalism, you understand that there is no such thing as matter, so what in the world are you talking about? I'm trying to point out the immensity of what we are talking about. To speak about the end, *finis*, the end of the book—that's for children.

S: *So what is the third station then?*

Anthony: When the soul has united with the ego, with the individual consciousness, permanently. This is not a glimpse, this is for good.

S: *But then the ego must be dead.*

Anthony: The ego is dead. The way we should say it is that *egotism* is dead. But not the ego, not the psycho-somatic organism.

S: *But you had three stations.*

Anthony: Yes, the first station is the result of this long process. You learn to meditate, you achieve in meditation the state of the void. When you enter into the state of the void there's no place for the ego to hide. You have to encounter it there. And if you encounter it there, in the void, the ego no longer has the support of thinking or feeling the emotions. So there you encounter it in its nakedness and you see it for what it is. It's absolutely nothing. No, I shouldn't say nothing. It is a matrix of tendencies, this totality of tendencies which all together constitute what we call our ego. That dies there. That doesn't come out. When you come out now you are free of that egotism.

S: *You are already free of it in the first station?*

Anthony: Yes. First of all, you must understand what I am saying when I say that the function of egotism dies, not the ego. If I go into the mystical death, if I go into the void and I succeed in killing the ego, I come out, right? I am still alive, the body is still living, but "mine-ness" is dead. No longer will I say, "This is mine, that is mine, she is mine." That is gone. The feeling of possessing anything, the feeling of grasping, that this is mine, is gone. That is no longer there. That is the first station.

Next, now that you recognize the emptiness of the nature of the ego, you can be instructed. Here is where the soul starts instructing you. When the training is completed, that's the second station. Now you are ready for the soul to combine with that individual consciousness permanently and make you a sage. You will then always be identified with the soul, you will always be soul, you will never think of yourself as anything but soul. You will not think of your body as you. That's the third station. They also call that the three initiations. Those are very advanced. It could happen and it does happen to people, but we are talking about very, very advanced spiritual matters.

S: *You said evolution will not ever happen automatically. Do you mean that souls could forever stay on a primitive level? You also say that life will always teach you.*

Anthony: Well, some people are intractable. They need many, many, many, many lessons. In a sense, the World-Idea has already decided the goal that mankind will reach. But it hasn't fixed the time. So you can take a long, long time or you can hurry things up. That is left up to you. But inevitably and ultimately everyone must move towards that goal. The whole world and the totality of circumstances are moving in such a way that all of mankind is being pushed, whether they like it or not.

It isn't a question, for example, that we had a choice of whether or not to discover the atom bomb. If you investigate the history of the period in which that weapon was developed, you will see there is a kind of guiding thread behind the World-Idea. If you read that period of history, you can see that there were circumstances at work that were greater than any individual—and individual doesn't even count here. Nonetheless, all these individuals were brought together to do that work. It's amazing to read those stories of Fermi, Szilard, Oppenheimer, to see the way the weapon was finally produced. You say, "What's that got to do with the subject?" Well, that weapon has now put us in a situation where we either grow up and become adults, no longer adolescents, or we will destroy ourselves. The choice is being given to us. Which way do you want to do it? So it isn't that the individual counts anymore. The World-Idea is pushing these ideas to the foreground and we have to confront the fact that it's not going to allow us to live like animals any longer. You can feel the force of that World-Idea. It doesn't matter who you are. This is the way it is now. It's saying, "Are you people going to get your heads together and come up with a sensible solution or destroy yourselves?" If you can discern it and see it, then after a while, you begin to see how events are falling into place with that guiding idea.

S: If you are ill, if you have psychological problems, if you are neurotic and cannot turn to meditation . . .

Anthony: If you are neurotic then go and see a psychologist. Get professional help. If you're sick, you go to a doctor, right? If your car breaks down, you go to a mechanic. Well, why not go to a professional therapist? Find a good one and go there for help.

Meditation requires that you're at least normal. Abnormal people can't practice meditation. It will do them a lot of damage. They will get a little vision and they'll think that they are the new Messiahs. You've seen them on 42nd Street. They have a big sign, they say, "The world is coming to an end. I found out personally, I was given the message." No, we have to be normal to meditate. If we are not normal we must try to become normal. We must learn to accept normalcy. You know, do the things that are required. Eat, sleep, work. Take care of your family. All the duties you are supposed to do, do them. The people who run away from that and say, "I want to spend my time meditating," you'll see that they never meditate. "Oh, I have no time to take care of my family, I've got to go meditate." I used to find them hanging out in the bar. So we first become normal, all right? And then when you become normal you start wondering, "What am I doing all this for? I go to work every day, my life is slipping away. What am I doing all this for?" You're normal. Now the questions come up. What am I living for? What is the meaning of my life? Now you could start meditating. Now meditation is going to mean something because you want to find out, from within, what it's all about. And if someone comes over and tells you that you are living for the state, or you're living for a football team, or you're living for this, living for that—it is not going to mean anything to you.

A person who has gone through normal life and has begun to realize how unsatisfying it is starts asking himself real questions. And they mean something to him, because they are not conceptual. He's asking them from within. Sometimes it happens in a heart-breaking way. You go through grief or you go through pain and you ask yourself, "Why? Why is this happening to me?" And you will turn inward, because there's nowhere else to go. Then that person will meditate and it will be meaningful. Most of us have to be driven into it, unless you love truth and beauty so much that you do it naturally. That's another way. But don't expect neurotic people to be interested in truth. The very definition of being a neurotic is that you are preoccupied with your ego. That's what it means to be neurotic. There is only one thing you worry about, me, me, me, me, me. And if it gets worse he becomes psychotic. Are you sure you want to talk about practical ethics?

S: So it is suffering that brings you to the quest?

Anthony: One man by the name of Meister Eckhart said, "The horse that will bear us quickest to perfection is suffering." Nothing will open your eyes like when you suffer. When you are having a good time, everything is going smoothly, you're enjoying it, life is a breeze, there's a balmy wind. You are back there drinking beer and looking at your girl with the goo-goo eyes. Who is interested in the truth? Everything is all right. Along comes a little misfortune, and you start saying, "Why did this happen to me?" It's as if somebody is saying, "Hey you, wake up!" No, I don't want to talk about ethics.

S: What you have said is very helpful. We tricked you into it after all!

Anthony: I don't think there is anyone here who hasn't been put through it one way or another, everyone has been put through it some way or another. And I think you will see the reason for yourself. People who study truth, the philosophy of truth, will always be just a tiny little number. Very, very few. And if you go to the stadium where they are playing a football game there will be a hundred thousand. If you go to a political rally there will be a million. But the people who are interested in truth, in their soul, you can count them. Five, ten, fifteen, twenty, you can count them. I remember once PB was smiling, he was almost laughing, and someone asked him what was it all about. He said, "I'll have to look into it." And then, about a minute or so later he said, "Oh yes, questers are very peculiar people."

That's why the sages keep coming back. To help us get a step ahead, another step and another step. Because it is so difficult. And it is so subtle. To find your way to the truth is really going to require all the brains you've got, all the will you've got, all the sensitivity you've got. And not only for a short while—like my friend who wanted to do it in one summer—but in many, many lives. Nobody is going to succeed in trying to understand the vastness of this thing by a couple of years' work. So one of the first things you have to realize—and it will be absolutely important to realize—is that the adventure that you're trying to get into is an infinite adventure. It's not going to end. When you find your soul, it's not the end. Now you've just begun to live. Until then we are animals. We think we are human beings, but if you read your history you would have to say, this can't be a race of people, of humans, they've got to be animals. You look at the history of the world, especially the past fifty years.

So we have a lot ahead to do. Everyone has to do it for himself, too. That is what makes it difficult.

SIX
The Reality of Mind

Anthony: Let's get a little deeper into mentalism by exploring part of an essay on mentalism by PB.

Only those who have not grasped mentalism can assert that it denies the existence of the objects of experience. It only questions the nature of the content of such experience. It only denies their materiality and unquestioningly affirms their existence.

"I clearly see matter confronting my eyes and experience it all around me at every moment." This is the naïve belief of the man who has not investigated the subject to its fullest extent.

Mentalism does not deny the independence of the world any more than a materialist does. It admits it. Only it points out that the character of this independence has to be interpreted in a wholly different manner from that in which the materialist interprets it. The latter makes the mistake of concluding that the world is independent of any experience altogether. Mentalism declares that the world exists not as a material thing but as a construction of the mind. The world's presence is not refuted but its materiality.

That the mind alone is, that the world does not exist outside Mind, that everything which unenlightened men regard as material is really mental—these are among the most essential tenets of our teaching.

What the modern psychologists call association of ideas, what the ancient philosophers called remembrance habits (*vasanas*) partly account for the mind's construction of the world. It is the influence of associating certain ideas together and remembrance tendencies out of past births which in part accounts for the construction of the mind. The mind lends objectivity to its own constructions.

But it doesn't matter how many hundreds of births it took to create these mental pictures and tendencies. It doesn't matter how long they have been forming. They can be dispelled in a short time if the right way is found. And that way is discrimination between what is eternal and what is transitory. But we succeed only in fooling ourselves if we imagine it will ever be possible for man to eliminate this fundamental process of birth, decay, and death that holds sway throughout the universe. Man can never master it, but will always be mastered by it. Through learning to understand it he may modify its workings in various ways, and thus improve his position, but he can never outwit a process which carries the very planet on which he dwells along with it. Why he cannot do so is revealed by metaphysical enquiry which shows its value by saving him from time-wasting and fruitless effort. *(unpublished)*

Anthony: That's an easy one, right?

S: The way to dispel the old tendencies and vasanas would be to discriminate between what is real and what is unreal. That is the main point, isn't it?

Anthony: Yes, it certainly is a main point. I think we ought to try to list the main points. If we start again:

Only those who have not grasped mentalism can assert that it denies the existence of the objects of experience.

Anthony: That's an important point. Mentalism doesn't deny the existence of the objects of experience just because it says that they are ideas. A lot of people think that when you say a thing is an idea, you've gotten rid of it. And that's the first point you have to get clear. I told you that a man like Einstein misunderstood one of these tenets. You remember I told you the story, he said to James Jeans, "Why are you bothering to study the stars? They don't exist for you. You're a mentalist." PB is saying: "No, mentalism does not deny the existence of the object of experience. It's trying to understand and clarify what is the *nature* of that object." So it's not denying the object. That star is going to stay there. The tree is going to stay there. Everything is going to stay the way it is. When I understand its nature I'm not going to make it dissolve. So the first thing he's pointing out is that understanding mentalism, understanding that the world is an idea, does not dissolve the world. It leaves it where it is.

It only questions the nature of the content of such experience. It only denies their materiality and unquestioningly affirms their existence.

Anthony: So it affirms the existence of the object of experience but denies that it is something material.

"I clearly see matter confronting my eyes and experience it all around me at every moment." This is the naïve belief of the man who has not investigated the subject to its fullest extent.

Anthony: So you look around and say, "But I see matter all around me. What are you trying to tell me? It's all around, it's all matter. This here and this here. How do you know about it?" And we go through the process of analyzing how you know something and you find out that all you could know is ideas. You say, "Wait a minute, wait a minute!" And you get uncomfortable. Yes, these are all ideas, everything that you experience is idea. "This cup?" Yes, that too. It's hard. Hardness is a sensation. It's round. Round is an intelligible meaning. What kind of taste? Can I bite it? That, too, it's an idea. If you go through the analysis of anything in your experience, you can't get away from it—that it's an idea. Hardness, roundness, color, everything you could think about is an idea. But you have to investigate. Everyone is born with the notion that it's a real thing out there. I mean the dog goes out and chases a rabbit because he thinks it's real. Well, sure, it's real, but it's still an idea.

Mentalism does not deny the independence of the world any more than a materialist does. It admits it. Only it points out that the character of this independence has to be interpreted in a wholly different manner from that in which the materialist interprets it.

S: Independent, but not from the one who experiences it?

Anthony: No, not from the one who experiences it. I don't think he's denying that but he alludes to the fact that the World-Idea has a kind of continuity and a persistence. Even for the individual perceiver the World-Idea does have continuity, does have persistence. It does have a kind of objectivity in the sense that you're not going to turn a tree into a cloud.

S: I only wanted to know what was meant by the word "independence" here.

Anthony: I would have to agree with you. It doesn't mean independent of a knower but independent in the sense that it has its own continuity. When a mind perceives a world, that world is given to it. It doesn't bring about any world and it doesn't change it from day to day or from moment to moment. So the world that is given to the mind has a sort of independent objectivity in the sense that it does have the laws and rules and everything else of its own.

> The latter makes the mistake of concluding that the world is independent of any experience altogether. Mentalism declares that the world exists not as a material thing but as a construction of the mind. The world's presence is not refuted but its materiality.
>
> That the mind alone is, that the world does not exist outside Mind, that everything which unenlightened men regard as material is really mental—these are among the most essential tenets of our teaching.
>
> What the modern psychologists call association of ideas, what the ancient philosophers called remembrance habits (*vasanas*) partly account for the mind's construction of the world. It is the influence of associating certain ideas together and remembrance tendencies out of past births which in part accounts for the construction of the mind. The mind lends objectivity to its own constructions.

S: What does he mean by "the mind lends objectivity to its own constructions"?

Paul: I think what he is referring to is that the mind, through the habit structures that have been built up, imputes the belief in the object's reality. Through the habits of the mind, the constructions are invested with reality as if they are independent.

Anthony: It's like saying that when the mind produces a dream, it also believes in what it did, and by believing in what it made, it has to take it to be real. So the mind lends or superimposes or gives the feeling of objectivity to what it makes. The mind is giving it reality. It lends objectivity to the idea. The mind gives objectivity to what it creates.

S: Would you say duality too?

Anthony: Naturally.

Paul: I think this is more specific, though. A couple of schools within Buddhism concentrate on analyzing this belief in inherent existence that the mind is always imputing into its images. If the mind doesn't invest the images with a sense of reality and externality, you don't take them as real. And through the reverse process, when you are trying to meditate, you divest the images of reality, you're trying to pull that back into the mind.

S: Would that include space and time too? The vasanas?

Anthony: Yes, that would be included. If you go back to the example of the dream, the dreaming mind has to project the images, one after the other. That gives you a sense of time. It has to project them in space and that gives you the feeling that the idea is out there in space. Kant would say that the first two things that you could say really and truly belong to the mind are these abilities to spatialize and to temporalize. So he says the mind has the function of sensibility. He says that the first characteristic that we could ascribe to the mind is that it could pictorialize things as well as put them in space. PB refers to it in *The Wisdom of the Overself* as the image-making faculty of the mind. Insofar as the mind can make images, that's what gives reality to the ideas that are being projected. That tendency to spatialize and temporalize could be stopped in meditation, when you cut it off. The point there is to cut off the image-making faculty, to stop it from working, to try to get an idea of what the mind is when it doesn't make pictures. That's the purpose of meditation, to stop that activity and try to see what the mind is like in itself.

S: What is the image-making faculty without the vasanas?

Anthony: Well, that's a vasana, too. The image-making faculty is a habit. It's not the natural state of mind. The natural state of mind is quiescence.

S: Is the world nothing but vasanas and mind?

Anthony: Well, it's going to be more than just vasanas. We'll leave that aside for now, because that's a little more complicated.

Paul: You see, that's why he says, "They *partly* account for the mind's construction of the world."

S: If you cut off the image-making faculty, do you then get to the Witness-I?

Anthony: Yes, it's possible that you might get the experience of yourself as consciousness and not as thoughts.

S: Could you still live in the world then?

Anthony: Well, we won't worry about that. You won't be missing much. Don't worry. [laughter]

S: But this is the mind's way to get an understanding of its own nature.

Anthony: Again, let's stick to the point. As soon as you deviate, back to the point. You see, what is happening is that we keep picking up one subject at a time. Little by little you're going around in a circle, picking up all the points. And it's not that your questions aren't questions. They're questions. But you want to get to that point, and you're over here. Wait until you get over there. That notion of vasanas, for instance: there's a very nice write-up on it in a work by Eliade called *Yoga: Immortality and Freedom*. If you could read the chapter on that, it's very illuminating. It's one of the best chapters I have ever read on the nature of memory, vasanas. The Hindus call them vasanas, or *samskaras*. We could call them habit-energies. You can get information about them in psychology textbooks or in the Hindu texts, which talk a lot about samskaras. Your mentality is dominated by your habit-energies. Yoga goes into it in minute detail because you have to try to destroy all of them. There is one book, *The Path to Liberation*. It is an ancient text, written by a sage called Vidyaranya, and all it deals with is the vasanas. When you get to a certain level of development you start destroying them all. You can't do it prematurely because they are very powerful. Everybody thinks that he can overcome his habits. That's not true. If you toss a baby up in the air, for example, he will instinctively react with fear. That's a built-in vasana. If you hold him, he will suck your breast. That's built in. Those habit-energies are built in. And without them we wouldn't be able to exist.

> But it doesn't matter how long they have been forming, they can be dispelled in a short time if the right way is found.

Anthony: There he's talking about what Jung would call the phylogenetic and ontogenetic development of the psyche. In other words, through hundreds and hundreds of incarnations you learn to put certain sensations together and they become like pictures. And then these pictures are part of your psyche and they can keep coming up. But he's saying here that it doesn't matter that it took so long and that they are part of the psyche, you could still destroy them.

> And that way is discrimination between what is eternal and what is transitory.

Anthony: That's the technique they all use. And that's the hardest one. Let's say you're on the path and a situation comes up where this young woman offers to make love to you and you have to discriminate, "What do I really want? What is really of ultimate value, this momentary pleasure or the real, the eternal, the true?" And a person has to learn little by little to cut off those things that have only a temporal pleasure. Cut them off. Little by little he has to cut them off and keep saying, "I want only that which is eternal. I want that which, no matter what happens, I'll always be that." In other words, he wants the truth. And if he wants the truth, he has to give up, to some extent, the temporal pleasures, to deny them any foothold. And that's very difficult. But after all, all we're doing now is investigating. As we go along, maybe we'll do some of these things a little at a time.

S: What about food, for example?

Anthony: No, it doesn't apply to the natural things like the food you need for the body, the warmth you need, not to live in the snow.

Paul: But the fourth helping of cake?

Anthony: That it applies to! It's just an application of rationality. When they say discriminate between the temporal and the eternal, they're not saying that you shouldn't eat. They're just saying, "Think of what it is that you really want. Do you really want the eternal?" But you have to keep your body strong. You have to keep the body healthy. You don't eat mud. That doesn't mean that you go out and turn yourself into a gourmet. Just use common sense.

S: What about music, for instance?

Anthony: Music is all right. There's no objection to the arts. Don't become a misanthrope.

Paul: All the forms of art are different ways of trying to appreciate the Beautiful, which is also an aspect of the eternal. Plotinus speaks of the Idea of the Beautiful. And in that sense Beauty is tending toward the eternal too.

Anthony: PB has some very nice notes on that. He points out that in a lot of the traditions, like in certain schools of Buddhism and in some of the Vedantic schools, they don't permit any art or music. And he says: We don't have to be like them. We could admit art into our lives. Look at the ascetic who lives in a dirty filthy house. He doesn't take care of anything and he thinks he is spiritual. The man actually thinks that ugliness and dirt is spirituality. There's no need for that. You could live in a decent home, you could have art in your life. There are no objections to that.

S: Where do you draw the line?

Anthony: Yes, that's what you have to watch for. If it becomes an obsession, then you're in trouble.

S: But you can be obsessed by philosophy, too.

Anthony: That is all right. You're allowed. You're allowed. If that happens I'll even send you a telegram of congratulations! [laughter]

S: What about obsession with beauty?

Anthony: Ah, that's wonderful. Because the ultimate beauty is the World-Mind. Did you ever read the *Symposium* by Plato? Do you remember how Diotima had to teach Socrates? She tells him that there may not be enough love in his nature to reach all the way up to that ultimate Beauty. Don't worry about it. Beauty is all right, you're allowed that—the *real* stuff, not the imitation stuff. But I can't give you a step-by-step of your lifestyle. You've got to evolve that. For instance, look at a lot of art today—I don't call it art, I call it an insult to my intelligence. But that's my evolution. Someone presents me with a painting and says, "The essence of it is that it is unintelligible." I say, "Good, go ahead, you go your way, I go mine." But you have to evolve yourself. Don't forget what I told you. When you get obsessed with philosophy, you let me know!

> But we succeed only in fooling ourselves if we imagine it will ever be possible for man to eliminate this fundamental process of birth, decay, and death which holds sway throughout the universe. Man can never master it but will always be mastered by it. Through learning to understand it he may modify its workings in various ways and thus improve his position. But he can never outwit a process which carries the very planet on which he dwells along with it. Why he cannot do so is revealed by metaphysical enquiry

which shows its value by saving him from time-wasting and fruitless effort.

Anthony: There are people who are preoccupied with longevity, with living as long as possible, 500 years, 1000 years, forever. In India there was a man by the name of Aurobindo who was developing the yoga of immortality, physical immortality. Anybody could have told him, "Look, you are going to die just like me," and he did. When your time comes, you'll go. And when your time comes to come back, you'll come back. And you'll be complaining on both sides.

[continuation of same essay—ed.] What are the elements involved in every act of knowing an object? A simple analysis reveals that they are three: the object, the awareness which enables us to distinguish one thing from another, that is, the thought which has itself come into existence only because it has an object as its content, and the knower. When a table is seen, you are aware that it is you who see it, and that it exists for you. Hence we say that in every act of knowing, in every sensation that reports the world, there must be a mind present. The bodily senses could not report independently of the mind what they see hear taste smell or touch, nor could there be any other mind to which to report. They testify to the apparent existence of a material world only because they interact with mind. The body itself is a mental sensation. It is an object the same as any other. Mind is more generalized than our finite intellects, but it is essentially related and continuous with them.

We can trace the communication of the sense report from organ to nerve, and from nerve to brain, but what of its passage from brain to consciousness? The brain is just as physical as the eye and ear. When we come to consider the final process of knowing the existence of things we face a startling fact. A nervous function, a structural process, suddenly ceases to be such and literally changes into a psychological experience. How has the gap from matter to mind been crossed? How can a contradictory activity, this physical disturbance, suddenly change its nature and appear as idea? How can material substance—an antagonistic element—enter into union with intangible mind? Do what it will, expend its utmost ingenuity as it has already done, physiological science is unable to fill in satisfactorily the hiatus between physical vibration and the conscious perception. The movements of certain molecules in the gray matter of a man's brain can never be brought into the same order as his imaged thoughts or logical reflections. The two belong to totally different worlds of experience. Those who ascribe the thoughts to the kernel of the skull instead of to Thought itself, who would make mental experience solely a product of the physical brain as bile is a product of the liver, fail to grasp this fact. The problem of constructing a bridge over the gap between the end of the physical series and the beginning of the mental series solves itself easily when it is reconstructed in this way, by denying any difference in the character of both series. This links both ends neatly together by placing them both in mind. It does not start with any distinction between them.

But after we have done this, what becomes of the impression on the eyes, the eyes themselves, the sensory nerves and the brain? What else can become of them except to be turned into ideas themselves? The gap never has existed save in the self-deception of thought. Science has viewed a single unity under two different aspects, and in setting up such a strange problem for solution, science set up a problem which was utterly irrational and wholly unintelligible.

Those who would set up the body as a standard of reality, who make the knowledge of matter the knowledge of truth, set up a definition whose terms exclude both reality and truth. For they leave no room for mind, which cannot be felt with the palm of one's hand as one can feel the body.

All things are mental things; this alone do we know indubitably. Yet nobody will repudiate realism and accept such doctrine with confidence until he has previously prepared himself for it by inquiry and reflection, and unless he has been led to it by the sheer rational force of what he has thus ascertained. For the innermost beliefs of the masses will always be outraged by such a fact because their primary instinct is impulsively and prematurely to take things as they appear to be, whereas the philosopher can only arrive at his truth as the final step in a long journey.

That the percept is an idea, we know; that a material thing is the basis of this idea is mere conjecture. That there is a material object apart from and outside of the perceived mental image of it or corresponding to the idea formed of it, is only an inference. Its independent existence cannot be proved and cannot be established.

We may search through every part of space even the most

distant stars of the universe and still find no trace of this impalpable and ghostlike matter. No one through any of the five senses has ever seen or felt, tasted, smelled, or heard this mysterious substance called matter which is supposed to be stuffed somehow into the wall. If this substance is so imperceptible are we not justified in denying its existence?

If by matter people mean only the direct experience and conscious sensation aroused by any object one could not criticize their acceptance. But we know that they do not mean this. They mean always that there is a separate and independent substance quite apart from the experience and the sensation of an object. Matter in itself possesses neither color nor shape nor size nor feel nor visibility, nor tangibility. The credulous masses do not even know whether it is a solid or a liquid or a gas. The truth is nobody has ever seen matter, and hence the total ignorance concerning it of those who use the word. To deny matter is one thing, but to deny the feeling and the perception of external objects is another and would be a totally unreasonable and inexcusable act.

We "think" our object. All external objects are known only as mental objects. Mankind naturally and normally assumes that it possesses a firsthand knowledge of an outward, non-mental object. But that this is a mere assumption is quickly proved. For we know a thing by knowing our own perception of it. All that we know at first hand of a thing is the thought of it. All that we know at first hand of an event is its occurrence in our own mind. Our direct awareness is of our percept of the outward thing, not of the physical thing itself. The thing is not to be confounded with our personal perception of it. The latter is indubitable, but the former is established by an act of inference.

The act of knowing and the thing that is known are identical, and the thought that your mind holds is nothing less and nothing else than the thing itself, so that the thing and the percept is identical. All that we need to grasp this is to re-interpret our experience of things by the light of mentalism. As all our sensations are known to some mind, the ultimate reference involved in the existence of everything is mind. Even when we think a thing is outside the mind, the very act of thinking makes it mental.

The sensory process itself can be no less an idea than the things which exist and the events which occur outside it. We must not only make mind the stuff of all experience, but we must also make it prior to the first sensation of the first thing in experience. *(unpublished)*

Anthony: We can stop there. It's a marvelous summary. Could you give me a summary in a couple of sentences of what he did?

S: Well, he gave the background of the unresolved gap. And now by understanding that there are not two series of different kinds but that they are identical, the gap is bridged, as I understand it.

Anthony: Yes, when the scientists give a description of the physiological process that they claim brings about perception, the explanation fails because the act of perception or the act of knowing is so different from the process. You can't bridge the gap, you can't leap over it, you haven't explained anything. So then he goes on and says: now, the solution is very very easy. Just make both the same kind—the description of the so-called physical process by which we know something and the knowing itself—make them both thought. In other words, make the thought first, and then you won't have that problem. How do you see it, Paul?

Paul: Physiological sciences are using thought to talk about or describe what they think the world-thought is. So the whole series is thought.

Anthony: Let's reread parts of this and talk about them as we go along.

> This links both ends neatly together by placing them both in mind. It does not start with any distinction between them.

Anthony: It does not start with any distinction between the so-called physiological processes and the so-called mental product. If it's all thought, there won't be any gap. And actually, when you think about it, if you speak about an electromagnetic disturbance going up to the brain, that's a thought. You speak about the brain, that's a thought too. When you describe this process you're as much in the world of thought as when you claim that the process results in thought. You've never left thought at any time. If we start by saying in our analysis, well this is mental, this is mental, then how could you examine the physiological process and think that it's something other than mental? You start out with the premise that it's mental. You start out with the notion, here's an idea. If you understand that, then you can see that all you can have is idea from beginning to end.

S: How could there be any new discoveries, any new thoughts which aren't just re-creations of old stuff?

Anthony: Your question reminds me of a story about Brahms and Mahler. The two of them were standing on a bridge and they were looking at the Danube, the water, the waves. Brahms turned to Mahler and said, "You know, there are no more inspired melodies." And Mahler said, "Take a look over there, Johannes. You see, there's the last wave!" There's no end to the novelty of creation. I mean, I give you seven notes in one scale, and you can go on creating melodies endlessly.

S: But this is all just re-creation. Are there really new ideas which have never been thought before, which are not just combinations of old stuff?

Paul: All the galaxies and solar systems are visible manifestations of the Infinite Mind's contemplation. In a sense, there's creation going on every moment. But each solar system is employing its previous history to recreate. You're not looking at the vastness of this process. You're putting boundaries around it.

Anthony: Don't worry, you're not going to exhaust the profundity, the fecundity, and the meaningfulness of ideas. That will never happen.

S: But you said before that there is only vasanas.

Paul: No, he said that vasanas partly account for the construction of the world.

Anthony: Try to remember the story about Brahms and Mahler. Mahler said jokingly, "There's the last wave, the end of creation, no more waves!" And then within a short time Mahler came out with a second symphony and a third which are such magnificent creations that you would think Brahms would get the point. There's no end, don't worry. You people keep thinking that there's an end. You have to remember that when you trace back all these things you trace them to the ideas that are within the Intellectual Principle. There's no possibility of ever exhausting the wisdom of God.

But let's get back to the article we were discussing. It is very straightforward. If you read *The Hidden Teaching* and had difficulty, this article lays out, in a couple of pages, the whole mentalistic doctrine. Read a little bit more.

This links both ends neatly together by placing them both in mind. It does not start with any distinction between them.

But after we have done this, what becomes of the impression from the eyes, the eyes themselves, the sensory nerves and the brain? What else can become of them except to be turned into ideas themselves? The gap has never existed save in the self-deception of thought. Science has viewed a single unity under two different aspects, and in setting up such a strange problem for solution, science set up a problem which was utterly irrational and wholly unintelligible.

Paul: What he is driving at here is that the gap is a false problem. He is saying that if you start from mind, the whole series is a process that is occurring for mind and in mind. Then there is no gap. The only reason the gap developed was because of the way science had bifurcated experience.

S: I saw a program on TV called "The Brain." A scientist put a brain on a table and asked, "Well, where is the I?" Then he went through an analysis and concluded that the "I" is the sum of all the information that comes up to the brain. But he didn't confront the problem of the gap.

Paul: They don't pursue it, because they don't relate their explanation back to your conscious experience. They make it seem like a cartoon strip—you know, where the thought is drawn above the character. There's a relationship of molecules and pop! . . . a thought appears. You move the molecules this way and you get this thought.

S: But there is some truth in the scientific explanation, because you can manipulate the brain with chemical stuff, like tranquilizers, and so on.

Anthony: Let's say that they give you some kind of drug, and it has a certain effect—any kind of effect you can think of. Who will experience the effect, the brain? Who knows that effect?

S: The mind.

Anthony: Yes. You haven't faced the problem and answered the question because it's the same thing as if I say, "Well, the hardness that I experience is where?" It's in my mind when I am squeezing this. The hallucinatory drug which I experience, is where? Same place. It's in the mind. If I experience the mind malfunctioning and I ask, "Well, who is the experiencer?"—it's the experience of a mind, it's not the experience of a brain. The brain doesn't experience. The brain is not the conscious subject.

The point to grasp here is that in any modification of the body—of any part of the body, including the brain—that which experiences the modification is a conscious subject. They can take an electrode and poke the brain and you get images. But the question is not a question of images. The question is, "Who is the perceiver?" It is not the brain that is perceiving the images, it is the mind that's perceiving the images. So the fact that you could modify the brain, or damage the brain, does not change the fact that the conscious subject of that pain is going to be the mind and not the brain.

S: But when the mind is identified with the body, then you will experience dizziness when you take a drug.

Anthony: You are missing the point. The point is that the awareness, the knower, is never the brain.

S: But you don't experience that awareness all the time.

Anthony: You can't experience the awareness, because you *are* the awareness. Any damage that you do to your brain, any alteration in the way you function does not affect that awareness. The scientist misses the point when he says, "I caused the contents in your mind to change by manipulating the brain." That's not the question! The question is: Who is the subject? The awareness is different from the contents of which it is aware. That's the point, and that's the problem. I know, I went through all the experiments of Jackson and Penfield. They miss the point, they miss the philosophic question that is involved here. The brain is *not* the conscious subject. The brain is as much a content of the conscious subject as any other part of the body. All these experiments about showing that images arise when you poke different parts of the brain are beside the point. The question is not the contents, not the images, but who perceives the images, who is the subject.

S: So there is really no difference between poking the brain and pinching the arm?

Anthony: No, there's no difference. Of course not. The gap is just thought deceiving itself. It is a man's inability to reason something out and follow his reasoning process. All they simply mean by the "gap" is that you have two orders or two levels of reality which cannot be brought together. The gap is in the physiological process of explaining perception.

S: *But the gap must be a thought in the mind, like the brain is a thought in the mind.*

Paul: That's being too general. The brain, and the whole physiological process that includes the eyes and the nerves and so on—those are all ideas in the mind, ideas that the mind is employing to gain experience. Now, we come up with a dilemma in the physiological explanation of the world, and we call it a gap in their reasoning. And PB is saying that you can't bridge this gap with concepts which are wrong. There is no gap, and this is the way it is: there is mind.

Anthony: You could think of the gap simply as a missing link in their reasoning process. If you have a series of numbers: 1, 2, 3, 4 . . . 6, 7, 8, you say that there's a gap in there. You're missing one of the prime numbers. In their thinking, in their attempt to show how perception arises, they start out with a reasoning process; they go 1, 2, then this, then that, then that, and then all of a sudden there's an abyss, and they come up on the other side. So a gap in this sense could mean a link in their reasoning process which is destructive of the whole reasoning process, which reduces it to incoherence and makes it self-contradictory. That's all the gap means.

S: *Now, may I ask something? The mind has a habit of experiencing through the help of the brain. That is a very old habit. If some part of the brain is damaged, can that person's mind then form a new habit of bypassing the brain in order to perceive directly?*

Anthony: Do you mean if the instrument through which the mind is transmitting and operating is defective? For example, if we have a radio, we know that it's receiving from a broadcasting station certain vibratory waves, and that if you select the right band, they'll come in through the radio. But if there's something wrong with the radio, then those vibrations coming from the broadcasting station are still coming, but the radio is not receiving them and transmitting them. By analogy, if the body is defective, it can't act as a medium through which the mind can operate.

S: *Yes, I can see that. But my question is: Is there a possibility for the mind to bypass the brain?*

Anthony: Well, if the mind is going to have experience of the sensible world, or whatever world that body is in, then the vehicle has to be in working order. But in itself, the mind is not affected if it can't have experience of that world through that body. The mind remains what it is.

An extremely highly evolved spiritual entity can develop new habits. But usually the new habits have to be developed when you're in the body. You can't learn to meditate outside the body in the sense that if you want to make a habit out of it you have to make the habit when you're in the body. Let me give you an example. If you persist in meditation, and it becomes an ingrained habit—you know, like a built-in—then if at the time you're used to meditating you're not sitting down, your mind automatically gets quiet anyway. It has become a habit. After a while the habit becomes so established that you could do it any time of the day. Right? Then, even if the person passes on or perishes, the habit of meditation will persist even though he no longer has a body.

Insofar as a very highly evolved person, like a Bodhisattva, has completely withdrawn that desire which wants to be always embodied, to fulfill its desires, when the time comes that he wants to reincarnate, he has to *will* it. It won't happen by itself, whereas for most of us, when that desire to be embodied comes upon us, we'll come right back into manifestation again. But in his case, he broke the habit *here*. So when he wants to come back, he has to re-employ the habit; he has to bring the will to bear on it in order for him to come into manifestation.

Now the point I'm trying to get at is that, yes, the mind is always what it is, but if it's the karma or the destiny of a person to inhabit a certain kind of body, there's no way around that. If it's a defective body, the person will have to experience the inaptitude of that body. He's getting a different kind of experience than we are. I don't think we know what that experience is. But there are no two ways about it, the entity is getting an experience which means something to him, otherwise karma wouldn't be working. In other words, his mind evidently is benefiting—let's say, exhausting or fulfilling its karma. Otherwise, it wouldn't make any sense. Do you see what I'm getting at?

There are mysteries in the world and we're not going to get rid of them. As a matter of fact, when you finish your studies, and when you've penetrated the deepest mystery of all, it'll still be a mystery. You're not going to take the mystery away.

Paul: Doesn't PB say somewhere in *The Wisdom of the Overself* that the real mystery and wonder is the miracle of existence itself?

Anthony: You have the same confrontation when you have the experience of the void. What you experience is an unfathomable mystery. But anyway, let's go back again to the points he's making here in the mentalistic doctrine.

> That the percept is an idea, we know; that a material thing is the basis of the idea, is mere conjecture.

Anthony: The important thing here is that the percept is an idea. And if you think there's anything underneath the percept, or behind it—in other words, that there is something else besides the appearance—he's saying: "That's a guess."

> That there is a material object apart from and outside of the perceived mental image of it or corresponding to the idea formed of it, is only inference. Its independent existence cannot be proved and cannot be established.

Anthony: You could never prove to me that there is something beyond all the sensible qualities that this object has, something beyond the taste, touch, smell, color, feel, all these things. And when you say there is, you're just making a big guess.

S: You said that there is no thing beyond the appearance of sensible qualities, but an eagle or other animal would see the object in a different way.

Anthony: But no matter which way the eagle sees it, it will always be in terms of sensible qualities. When you say, "I know an object," what you're saying is, "I know it is hard, I know it is white, I know it is tasteless, and so on." And that means you are saying, "I know just the idea of the object." Well, if you know only the idea of the object, why bring in something you cannot prove, something besides all these sensible qualities I just mentioned? Why say it's made of matter?

S: But if you change the senses you would perceive different sensible qualities. That means there must be something outside the sensible qualities that remains the same.

Anthony: The fact that you rearrange the way the object appears still does not give you the right to infer that there's something above and beyond those sensible qualities. Whether you're an eagle, a dog, or whatever you are, the object that you perceive is always going to be perceived in terms of sensible qualities. It doesn't matter that the dog, for example, will see this without color. The fact is, he will know only that object which sensation informs him is there. And if you changed me into a dog or a reindeer or an eagle, the only way that I could know an object is that it exists for me through a combination of various sensible qualities.

Therefore, if all you can deal with is mental qualities, why insist on speaking about a material world which is independent of you who know it? That's the whole point: that the knower and the known could never be sundered, divided from each other. If all that the knower has the right to speak about are the ideas that he is dealing with, then why bring in an extra idea? A material world?

You know what the problem really is? Most people are afraid that if all they are is an appearance, there won't be any reality behind them.

The point here is to recognize that all you can know about the object is always your mental constructs, your sensation. This is the point that has to be driven home, over and over again, because the point is an ancient one. For instance, some would say that there is a kind of matter, which is the support of all the different attributes. So you say, there's a table, it is green. And there is some thing, call it X instead of a table, on which you could superimpose all these qualities: color, size, shape, taste, feel, and all that. And they say that if you could get to the bedrock, to what underlies the sensations, you would be getting to the thing itself, the "matter" of the thing. But the point that PB keeps stressing is, you won't find any such thing! If you take away the taste, the color, the sound, the tangibility, the solidity—which are all sensations—what have you got left? You've got nothing left, if you could do it! All we could do is theoretically abstract these things; but if you could really do it, you wouldn't have anything there! So what you analyzed was an idea. And if you analyze the constituents of the idea, and take away all the constituents, there's nothing else there.

For instance, say I imagine very intensely this man in front of me, or this tree in front of me. I imagine it very intensely, and now it exists in front of me. So I start analyzing it: take this away, that away, that away, take all the sensible qualities. What am I going to have left? Nothing! There isn't any substratum underlying the appearance of an object. It's frightening, because we all like to think that underneath appearances there must be some reality. But the fun of it may be that there isn't any.

S: Well, we could say there is mind beneath everything.

Anthony: But mind is intangible, ungraspable, unthinkable. So what are you going to find there? To say you're going to find mind is, again, like saying, "I am going to find something there." No matter how you do it, no matter how you twist and turn, the fact remains that the very logic of our analysis shows you that there isn't anything there. And people will not accept this. Why? Because built into the very structure of their mentality is the notion that there is an object which is external to the thinking mind. It's built in. It's as if somebody opened you in the back and fixed all the dials and closed it up and from now on you have been programmed, that is the only way you can think. And if someone tells you, well, it's not that way, you'll have the man locked up!

You see, you never confronted the mystery of thinking. Everybody takes for granted that they know what thinking is. It's the one thing that you should never take for granted. What is thinking? It's really another one of these things that we have to investigate.

S: Are you saying that the tree we experience is made up of many different kinds of ideas, with no material tree behind it?

Anthony: Yes, the idea of the tree is a synthesis of a large number of mental constructs and sensations. And if you cut the tree in half and say, "You see, it has matter inside!" then I would go through the same analysis. I'd show you that anything you know about the inside of the tree is also more sensations, more ideas. If you try to get to what is the "stuff" that underlies the tree, there isn't any "stuff" underlying the tree. You'd end up just like the modern physicists who try to find out what is the nature of matter prior to its existence as a wave or a particle. They found that there isn't any substantial and independent thing there.

S: But when the physicists have accepted that there is no matter, how can the other branches of science go on believing in it?

Anthony: These scientists are subject to the same cultural mores and influences that you are. They're subject to the inherent ignorance that is built into every human being. The scientist is as much a human being as you and I, and his ignorance is just as pervasive as yours and mine. So you go to school and you learn a little bit about their tricks and you can be just as good as them. But it doesn't mean you can think yet. Thinking is a very difficult thing. It's very hard. As a matter of fact, one man, Nikhilananda, made the statement that man would rather die than think.

S: Is it the same with feelings?

Anthony: Well, no. We all like our feelings, although a few people do run away from them. But the analysis of cognition is a very strict rational activity. It requires the utmost and demands the utmost. But it will give you in return a real reward. If a person says, "Well, I see the sun rise, and you can't convince me that it doesn't rise," then there's no sense arguing, talking, because he wants me to prove something, but he won't accept reason as the guide. And if you don't accept reason as the guide, then there's no sense arguing or having a discussion.

S: Is it fear that makes him not want to accept it?

Anthony: Oh, it might be fear, but I prefer to refer to it as what it is, our inherent built-in ignorance.

S: But I don't understand. There must be an idea of a tree behind the tree?

Anthony: Yes, of course. But we are not discussing that there is a true idea—in the Intellectual Principle—of what a tree is. We're discussing the sensible tree here. There *is* a real idea of any object in the universe. But we're not discussing that, because that's ontology and I don't want to get you into ontology when you don't understand epistemology.

S: Can you say that the objects are created, or thought out, in two ways: from the World-Mind directly, and from the World-Mind through us?

Anthony: Well, through us. Each individual mind manifests for itself the World-Idea. Now, you could say: "Well, the World-Idea is the product of the World-Mind's thinking." Yes. But all that we know directly, indubitably, without any hesitation, is the fact that anything I experience is within my mind. I don't care whether you're talking about Sirius, the stars, or the tree in front of me. They all fall under the same category of "known." *I-know-that.* As soon as you analyze the experience, you have the knower and you have what is known. Nobody can get around that. No one. So if I say there is a World-Mind which has thought the idea into my mind, that discussion comes later on. What you first have to understand, without any doubt, without any hesitation—you have to understand it because you reasoned it out over and over again—is that what you experience all the time is your mind. That has to come first before we worry about anything beyond that. You have to actually get the feeling of that.

There are times—when a person is under bereavement or extreme grief, for example—that the world is so devaluated that he sees it's a ghost, it's a shadow, it's not a reality, it's a thought. He devaluates the world immediately. And then he sees it for what it really is. But you can get the same thing by constantly reflecting and trying to understand the very nature of the world, just like you can understand that the sun does not rise even though you see it rise. You can actually come to that by constant reflection and analytical analysis. And then you can come to that again if you go into meditation, and you succeed in getting your mind absolutely still. You will see that everything is an idea. You'll not only see it, you'll feel it. You'll know it. And then the next moment, when thoughts are agitating the mind, you'll be back in the ego again and you'll say: "That object is a material thing."

S: *Why do we so stubbornly want to think that there is something out there?*

Anthony: Well, that is the nature of any habit.

S: *Isn't what we're after to know the idea of a tree in the World-Mind?*

Anthony: No, what we are after is to experience that tree as a mental phenomenon. That's what we're after first. Until a person has gotten himself to that level, to speak about understanding the idea—the "Idea" in the Platonic sense—is a waste of time. There's no way anyone, including any of the great mystics, could try to convey to you what the nature of an Idea is in itself. You know, that's out of the question. To speak about the Idea as an eternal presence, immutable and powerful enough to manifest itself yet always remaining identical with itself—these will be words that you'll memorize, you won't understand what they mean. You have no experience of that kind of a world. So let's stay where we are and learn what we have to learn first.

You have to go through the process of reasoning, where you finally get to the point where you can obliterate, stamp out any objection. And when I say "stamp out," I don't mean that you *deny* it, but that you *answer* every question that your doubting mind brings up to you. Until you can do that, you're not free yet. So the technique that we employ is that the question has to be answered, providing it's a legitimate question. Questions keep coming up as to the nature of mentalism. They must be answered, because until they are answered, you won't be satisfied. But once you have answered every question as to the nature of the objects that we experience—whenever the question comes up, you can answer it no matter what, no matter where it's attacking you from—now you're in a position to understand mentalism. But you have to go through this lengthy, difficult, annoying, irksome process of reasoning out what the nature of mentalism is.

It's the same as when a person has a glimpse, and he experiences for a few moments the divine, or the bliss of his own soul. When that experience is over, within a few minutes the ego comes in and takes over completely and starts saying: "It was my experience, I'm the one who had it, I'm the one who got the benefit," this, that, that, it goes on and on and on. It takes over completely, it gets inflated. "Ain't I great? Ain't I wonderful? You should worship me. Why aren't you adoring me?" And it goes on and on. You can't believe the power it has. But that's the nature of habit; that's the nature of mental energies which have, literally for many incarnations, had their way.

It is scary, because I've seen it in myself, I've seen it in others. They get a real glimpse of the soul, and a week later they're involved in some new love affair. It shows you how strong the ego is. It'll completely throw you out. It says, "Uh-uh, I better make sure that doesn't happen any more. You stay right down here with the rest of us." I know the power of those vasanas. If you get a little *kundalini* the first thing you will think of is sex. It has nothing to do with sex. Nothing. But right away you'll think, "Wow. What is that? Oh, ecstasy—sex." The mind interprets the world of experience according to the understanding that it operates with. And if you have a limited understanding, you are going to interpret the world with that limited understanding.

You have to remember that the sage is no fool. The sage is one who has reached the flower of intelligence. Usually they're very refined, sensitive, aesthetic men who have a tremendous sensitivity to all life, who appreciate and have a reverence for life. But they are not fools. When I listen to some of the stuff that goes on, when I read things like "Kill the Buddha" in some of the books that are being published, I can't believe how stupid people are.

Those of us who are a little older remember when the Zen people first came into the West back in 1945, 1955. Then carloads of Indian gurus started coming in during the late 1950s and the 1960s. And now the lamas are being shipped in carloads at a time. But no matter how many of these traditions come in and get established here, when all is said and done, you're going to have to reason out all of this for yourself. Nobody can do it for you.

S: But you don't object to these traditions?

Anthony: No, I don't object to them. I'm just pointing out that no matter how many traditions you go into and study, you're going to have to, sooner or later, reason the whole thing out. You're going to have to think for yourself. If not today, if not tomorrow, then the day after—but you're going to have to think for yourself. In the beginning you need a little help, but after a while you're going to have to do it for yourself. There are no two ways about it. When you understand why even the sages themselves—when they come out of the void—disagree in their statements, you'll see what I am talking about. Let's re-read one more part of that article.

> Those who would set up the body as a standard of reality, who make the knowledge of matter the knowledge of truth, set up a definition whose terms exclude both reality and truth. For they leave no room for mind, which cannot be felt with the palm of one's hand as one can feel the body.
>
> All things are mental things; this alone do we know indubitably. Yet nobody will repudiate realism and accept such doctrine with confidence until he has previously prepared himself for it by in-

quiry and reflection, and unless he has been led to it by the sheer rational force of what he has thus ascertained. For the innermost beliefs of the masses will always be outraged by such a fact because their primary instinct is impulsively and prematurely to take things as they appear to be, whereas the philosopher can only arrive at his truth as the final step in a long journey.

Anthony: Yes, these couple of pages are amazing. Every now and then he does that, every now and then I find these little gems scattered here, scattered there. But this is so fundamental, this is so important, that I feel that this is really worth all the effort, time, patience. It's worth everything. Understand this, then the other things start opening up. Because this is the key. Once you understand this, then you can understand other things. You can understand telepathy, telementation, teleportation, telekinesis, how these things are possible. But if you can't understand mentalism, then why bother talking about these other things? Not only does it give you an insight into them, but what's more important, this is the spiritual philosophy.

Now, there are some people who say that they are spiritual. They go to church on Sunday, or whatever. But these people go on believing in the existence of matter. From the point of view of the mentalist doctrine, no matter how religious or spiritual they think they are, we say that they're materialists. Because if you believe in the existence of matter, you are a materialist and no two ways about it. And I can't see how you're going to come back, body and soul, resurrected at a certain beautiful age that you decide on, and you're going to play on the harp for the rest of eternity.

People actually want to come back and have this experience of a material world, or what they call a material world, and this is the basic fallacy in almost all religions. But almost all religions have more esoteric teachings. If you study the Sufis, for example, you can see that they come to the same conclusion. You study Vedanta, all right, same conclusion. But at the religious level they tell people that there's God or gods and there's a heaven, and when you die you go there and you enjoy yourself for thirty-two million years, or whatever. And all this in our time is unnecessary. There's no reason why the depth and the truth of the doctrine shouldn't be drawn out and given to them.

S: Isn't it true that there are gods, different gods?

Anthony: Well, among the ancients, what they call the gods—like what the Platonists called the gods—are really principles, they're not beings. In other words, what's a god? Well, a god is characterized by a simple aseity. So, for instance, there's such a thing as a god of love. The only thing that characterizes that god is love. It can't have any other attributes or characteristics. Consequently, you can't think of it as any kind of individual being. And the ancients thought this way about almost all the forces and powers of nature. They gave them names and all that, but if you read these ancients—Anaxagoras, Anaximander, Thales, other ancient Greeks—they knew that these were just personifications.

S: If you have the experience of a god, what is happening?

Anthony: If you *see*, you're superimposing images from within yourself. You can't *see* a god. You may be able to feel the presence of what some call an angel or an archaangel, or things like that. Their presence is something that you could feel, and it is electrifying. But if you see anything, you've superimposed your own images on it.

S: What about heavens? Do different heavens really exist?

Anthony: Yes, they're different states of mind.

S: The Bible says, "In the beginning was the Word . . ." What does it mean?

Anthony: That's a mentalistic statement. In the beginning was the Idea, and the Idea was with God.

S: So then they dropped that?

Anthony: Oh, sure. As a matter of fact for four, five hundred years in the very beginning of the Christian era there were men who understood that. Origen, Clement of Alexandria, quite a few of the early Church Fathers had a very profound understanding of these things. But little by little, these teachings were shut out. And, as a matter of fact, anybody who believed in reincarnation was killed—outright. One emperor—was it Justinian?—killed over a million people in about the sixth century. So, little by little, as the Church became more and more powerful, they stamped out all teachings except what they wanted to teach.

In my mind there's no doubt that something like this could happen: Let us say you come back in four, five hundred years. There won't be

Vedanta. There won't be Buddhism. There won't be Platonism. All these traditional philosophies and religions will have disappeared. Nonetheless, if a person has taught himself to think deeply about these matters and reflect, and has understood them within himself, it won't matter to him. It won't matter, because he knows that God cannot be grasped through any graven images, whether it's a statue made of stone or a statue made of words. He knows that he's got to find Him within himself, in the impalpable Spirit that is his own mind.

SEVEN
Soul as Teacher

S: Ramana Maharshi pointed out to his disciples that the method that would take them to the end was to constantly repeat "Who am I?"

Anthony: Very few people are capable of asking the question "Who am I?" continuously, without break. That is very hard.

S: If you just hear someone tell you it is good to repeat "Who am I?" and it doesn't mean anything to you, it won't help.

Anthony: I figure this way. At that time if you went to see Ramana you were spiritually ripe.

S: I don't see the connection.

Anthony: If you understood enough to go all the way to India to see Ramana, you were ripe for the question "Who am I?" That was the technique used by Ramana.

Let me tell you this story. There was once a king who employed a pundit to teach him the doctrine. So the pundit taught him the doctrine and explained to him about liberation . . . this, that, and the other thing. Then the king told the pundit, "I want to be free tomorrow, I want you to free me." So the pundit went home and said to his daughter, "Ah, the king will have me killed if I don't free him. What am I going to do?" His daughter said, "I'll go tomorrow in your place."

So she went and spoke to the king. She told him, "I would like you to try something. Have your guards chain you to that pole and chain me to this pole." So the guards chained them both. Then she called out to the king: "King, please release me, help me, free me." And he says, "What are you talking about? How can I free you? I am chained myself!" And she says, "Well, that is the way my father is.

He is in the same position. You want to be freed by him. But he can't free himself."

Unless a teacher is a man of power, he can't do it. A teacher can come over and tell you to practice and do something, and if he is a man of power very often he gives you the initial impulse to do it. But if he is not a man of power, it's no good. It won't work.

If I were a king and you told my guards to put me in chains, they would not pay attention to you. But if I said, "Put *him* in chains," they would put you in chains. So a person has to have power. If a sage tells you to practice "Who am I?" he knows what he is talking about. If someone else tells you to practice "Who am I?" it is not going to help you.

S: I didn't mean to question that Ramana could give that advice. I didn't doubt that. I just meant that what is a good practice for me may not be a good practice for someone else.

Anthony: But generally if two of you go to a teacher it is very unlikely that he'll tell you both to practice the same thing. A teacher usually has a feeling for the differences. And according to those differences and their own intuitions, they tell you what to practice.

S: And a different kind of teacher may give me a different kind of advice?

Anthony: Oh yes, but the point is, once a teacher is accepted and you get certain recognitions from within yourself, then it is wise to follow him. But if you don't get internal recognition, within yourself, that he is the teacher you have been looking for, it is not going to help. There has to be a response in you.

And don't go over to the teacher and say, "Will you accept me as your student?" Because as soon as you say that, he'll ignore you. That is not the way it works.

S: I didn't really understand what you said.

Anthony: If you don't know in your heart whether you are a student of a certain teacher, there is no sense in telling you. It is not going to work. You have to know from within yourself, "He is my teacher, there is an affinity I have for him."

PB recognized Ramana as his teacher not because Ramana told him, but because the certification came from within himself. In other words, it is your soul informing you that this is your teacher. And if you have to go to a teacher to get that confirmation, it is not going to work. I mean, it is not going to be a substitute. When you have that kind of confirmation from within yourself that he is your teacher it doesn't matter, he could throw you off a bridge, you are not going to stop being his student.

S: Don't you have to be pretty well developed spiritually to have that intuition about a teacher?

Anthony: I don't know what the statistics are. If you are searching then you have some recognition and some sensitivity.

Well, you know, the quest is the greatest adventure you'll ever come across and there is no end to it. PB once told someone, "Well, if you don't intend to study, just go to church and forget about everything." Because if you mean it, you are going to have to study, you are going to have to reflect, you are going to have to meditate. You have to do all these things and you'll say, "Where am I going to get the willpower to do it?" You'll get it. A couple of times now and then something will hit you on the head and you'll begin to say, "Hey, I've got to get out of this situation." You'll do it. Life will teach us, little by little.

S: Is the reason to create these good habits so as not to have to be reborn?

Anthony: Well, I don't know about that part. I think it would simply be that you want to make things a little better for yourself. Because we are going to be incarnating for a long time, maybe longer than you think.

S: You say life will teach us. What life?

Anthony: You don't know? Well, I guess it is going to teach you.

S: Could you say mind will teach you instead of life?

Anthony: Yes, if you talk about life the same as talking about mind. I mean it is a living mind that we are talking about. It wouldn't be a dead mind. It has to be a living mind. And it will teach you. Life itself will teach you. The experiences that you get in life will eventually teach you everything that you have to know. It may take a little time, but it will do it.

S: Maybe we could understand mind as something that is everything yet is without characteristics. But how could this operate in such a personal way that it teaches you? In other words, there is this philosophic, very abstract knowing of mind, and then a more personal and religious way of thinking of it. There is a huge difference between them.

S: *No. Everything you experience is thought—and these thoughts teach you. It is mind teaching you in daily experience. It's not illogical.*

Anthony: I think what you just said is that it's mind that teaches and mind who is learning. Mind is what's teaching you and the one that's learning is the mind itself that is teaching. But that would be an incorrect way of stating it. There are differences between the mind which is the ultimate substance of your being and the mind which is always in the process of learning. It is a question of recognizing that mind has distinctions within it. The mind is a whole of parts. There are parts within it that have to be instructed and taught.

S: *Must some of this instruction, some of the techniques used, be kept secret?*

Anthony: Not any more, it's all out in the open now. Things may have had to be secret in the past, but those days are over. Today if you have something to say you must say it clearly, explicitly, and rationally or people will just laugh at you.

S: *I think there is a need for some sort of formal initiation by someone who has mastered the techniques.*

Anthony: No, the only one that could initiate you, now listen to this very carefully, is your soul. Nobody else could do that. I have known many people who have received the so-called initiation from their own soul. By their constant aspiration, prayer, meditation, their soul has revealed itself to the person. That's the only place where there is initiation. Everything else is man-made. Don't buy it. You're buying a technique or you're buying a bit of knowledge or something like that, but nobody could initiate you into the soul except the soul itself. That's the God within you. He decides. Sometimes he decides that the best way for you to get initiated is to go to a person who will make you aware of such a situation, such a technique. But ultimately it's always the soul within you that initiates you.

When I was a young man I used to read all these books on initiation, and the great Mahatmas and the great teachers, this and that. And I was getting very discouraged because I figured if anyone would never get initiated it would be me. I didn't have any of the qualifications that these people are talking about. I was an unregenerate, impatient. I knew all these good qualities, I . . .

S: But isn't initiation the same as getting grace?

Anthony: Yes.

S: But can't that come from your teacher?

Anthony: No, that comes from your soul.

S: But through your teacher?

Anthony: I love my teacher very much. And when the aspiration is there, the reverence, and I reach up to him in loving thought, then let's say a response takes place. It's from my soul.

S: But isn't the teacher a channel for the grace to come through?

Anthony: No! The teacher may be a guide, an influence, a direction, point out certain things to you. But if grace comes it comes from your soul. It couldn't come from anywhere else. You know what you want to do when you get an opportunity, if you get the chance? There's one man whom I respect and I always admired, who put me on the track a long time ago. His name is Ralph Waldo Emerson. Read him. There's an essay of his called "Self-Reliance." Read it. Self-reliance: rely on your own higher Self.

S: But I must rely on my teacher.

Anthony: First of all, if you meet a great teacher—a real teacher—and you tell him "I want to be a disciple," a real teacher will tell you, "I have no disciples." No, my dear, you'll see that the grace you experience comes from within yourself. For instance, I'm meditating on a picture of Krishna and I succeed in retaining the image, and in meditation the image of Krishna appears to me and I get overwhelmed by ecstasy. The great ecstasy, the rapture comes from my soul. The picture of Krishna comes from the outside world, but the ecstasy comes from within myself. It's my soul, not your soul. Each person's soul is his inviolable being. It's his true being. And the highest state of the philosopher-sage is that he's achieved complete union with his soul, not with Brahman, not with Tao, not with any of these things. His soul. Boy, I could sell you anything if you believe that it comes from somewhere else!

The teacher has a different role to play. A teacher could certainly send you his blessing, if he is authorized to do so. But wouldn't it be amazing if a teacher could enlighten you? Then we all would have been enlightened a long time ago! A man like Jesus would go around tapping people on the head, and as he went along they would all get enlightened.

All right, so then tonight, you'll all go home and you'll immediately sit down and practice meditation—one straight solid hour without a break. Have you meditated any considerable amount of time? Can you sit for an hour?

Do you see what I am interested in doing? I'm concerned that people should trust and look into their own soul and never mind expecting to find the solution by looking up theories, history, facts, things like that. This is a whole different kind of an approach to the problems of existence, to the problems which history has posed. You won't find this in the universities. There won't be any courses that say the best solution to the world's problem is that people become good. You won't find a course like that anywhere in the universities.

S: Have there been any spiritual philosophers who were women?

Anthony: Yes. There was a very remarkable and amazing woman you may have heard of, Madame Blavatsky. In ancient times in Alexandria, there was a woman named Hypatia. She was a foremost philosophic student of Platonism. She left no written works, but she did a lot of teaching. There was a woman who lived in India in this century, Anandamayi Ma, who was an extraordinarily gifted philosophic woman, a *jnani*. In her early life, she went through all kinds of tremendous mystical experiences. But when she got older, they stopped, and she became more and more established on the path of knowledge. She was able to give instruction on philosophic texts, higher than the yoga texts. She was a very holy woman and very advanced. However, it is not common to find a woman in these matters.

S: Why?

Anthony: Well, there could be many explanations. For one thing, the social mores—you know, I don't have to go into that. Women haven't been allowed to develop their potential like men have. They haven't had the freedom men have had. And also, they are more likely to have a problem with emotionality, although there are certainly exceptions. Emotionality always indicates a belief in materiality, so it makes it harder for a woman than for a man. On the other hand, a woman can more easily have the mystical experience than a man can, because she can be more passive to the Higher. She can remain passive to the spirit within her, whereas a man tends to be more aggressive.

It hasn't been the role of women, although I think that more are getting involved today than ever before. I don't think I have to explain that women have been put down all the time.

S: *At what level would you say that women are different, and that they have more emotions?*

Anthony: I don't want to get into that, because I am going to be called a chauvinist! But the fact remains that a woman's body is much more subject to nature than a man's body is. It is harder for women.

S: *But at what level will these differences come in? Mind doesn't have different sexes, does it?*

Anthony: That really depends on the evolution of the soul of the specific person, where they are in their understanding. The more mature a soul is, the less difficulty it will have with these things. Some of the women I spoke about were very mature even as children. Another example is Saint Teresa. She decided to leave home to go to the nunnery, and she had to walk a dozen miles or so to get there. She stole a penny because she was thinking, "With this, I can buy some bread on the way." But then she said, "That I should put my faith in a penny!" So she put it back and continued on her way.

Saint Catherine of Genoa could hardly wait for her husband to pass away so that she could go to the nunnery. But you can see, that is a mature soul. She had had her fill. She didn't want the world anymore. She wanted to find her own soul.

So there are exceptions. There have always been some extraordinary women. When I worked in the bookstore, I was amazed to see that the women used to outnumber the men in the interest in mystical subjects by five to one, or seven to one . . . something like that.

S: *There are some people who are very aware of their egos or of their lower natures and would be on the quest if they knew that there was such a thing as the soul. But they may lose hope because they see inside, they see their ego, or some of it, but don't know that there is something else, something higher. There are many people like that in our culture, because there is so little teaching about the soul.*

Anthony: You can rest assured that if someone is supposed to know or find out about his soul, he will. There is no getting away from that. When the time comes that you are supposed to know about the soul you'll find out. Period. There are no two ways about that. That is not left to chance. The soul will get you to be concerned about it when the time is ripe. But most people are not interested. It's a fact of life. They go to church and they go through the rituals and the ceremony, but I don't see how a priest or a preacher, or anybody could ever give you what you are looking for. If it doesn't come from within you, you are not going to find it.

S: But the choice of a teacher would come from within yourself. It might look like someone is teaching you, but actually it is you who chose that person.

Anthony: Yes, but let's say five of you accept me as your teacher, all right? You all go home now and you meditate very hard, and all five of you see me in your meditation. Do you think I'm there?

S: In some way.

Anthony: No.

S: Not you . . .

Anthony: No! It is your soul that is providing you with the image that you see of me. And it is your soul that provides you with, let's say, the feeling of ecstasy. What I'm trying to get across to you is that it is your soul that is teaching you. Now it may use me to turn the switch on. But the electric light is your soul, not mine. I'm not doing anything. For example, someone may ask me what I was doing at four o'clock in the morning, because they had to wake up then from their sleep. I had nothing to do with it. They got up. I didn't get up. I didn't do it. Someone else comes over and says, "In the dream you told me that I should clean my house." "Well, what are you blaming me for? It's your soul!"

The truth is that if you come across a sage, he can trigger your own soul and activate it. But it is your soul you experience. Here's an example that PB gives. You're meditating on a picture of Buddha or a picture of Christ. You meditate very intensely. And then whether your eyes are open or closed, he is right there in front of you. And then there is one instant where all of a sudden you come together and you experience unity and ecstasy. Now the ecstasy comes from your own soul. It doesn't come from the picture of Buddha or the picture of Christ. It comes from your soul. That's what is pouring into you, the ecstasy. The picture is something you picked up in your culture. Now the funny part is that the Buddhist is going to argue with the Christian and the Christian is going to argue with the Buddhist about who is God. "No, Christ is God." "No, Buddha is God." They are both wrong. It's their soul.

S: Everything that is happening to me, is that my soul teaching me? Is that true?

Anthony: Yes. It's your soul. The only little modification I would bring in is that the teacher, especially if he is a sage, triggers it off. Well, a sage could do more than that. But the ordinary teacher is a shoemaker. Don't get carried away with his importance and don't turn him into a tin God. He's just an older student than you are. But with a sage, it's entirely different. He could concentrate on you, imagine you in a certain way, and then the help comes in, gets you started. A sage is different. But the ordinary run of teachers, gurus, lamas, whatever you call them, they don't do these things. This is what your soul is doing to you. So a person might come to the Center and feel that I am responsible, that I brought him there. One fellow even told me, "Why don't you leave me alone in my dreams!" But I don't do these things, nor does any other teacher. It is the person's soul who is communicating to him and trying to do these things, wake him up to the fact that the soul exists.

S: But isn't it true that the teacher has a much stronger ability to concentrate?

Anthony: A little bit, a little bit. But the point again is that when the teacher sits and meditates, he doesn't do anything. He knows that the more he can keep quiet, the more still he can get, the better he can help you. But he doesn't *do* anything.

S: He acts like a channel?

Anthony: A channel. Yes, all right. But you have to remember, and remember this all the time, no one could initiate you except your soul. Only your soul could initiate you.

Maybe you feel a little disappointed, but you shouldn't. The truth is always better. But remember, I made the exception—with the sage, it's different, absolutely different. It's just that I have seen the difference between the sage and the gurus, lamas, teachers, whatever you want to call them. And the difference is too real. When a teacher is teaching students, there is an exchange of ideas, there's a kind of mental alchemy that's going on, and little by little the students' ideas are being changed. And that's the role of the teacher, hardly more than that. But that's important. Because unless your ideas are changed around, unless your basic understanding is altered, then the other things can't happen because of the very nature of our ignorance, which stops them from happening.

Once you begin to realize, "Now I understand, this is really what I am, I am the mind," you open yourself up inside to let things happen, whereas the other way you are closed. You don't let anything happen. You figure the world is hostile and so you put up all your defenses. But once the person understands, he says, "The whole world is a projection of my mind. No matter what I experience, I can only experience my own mind, my own thoughts, my own feelings. And when I say, 'This is hard,' the hardness is something that belongs to my mind. When I say, 'This is soft,' it's something that belongs to my mind. There's no such thing as hardness, softness, tangibility, without the mind."

So once I really begin to understand that, then I open myself up; I become receptive, and then the higher mind could start flowing in. But most of the time we believe that this lump of flesh is our mind and that we are made up of ten dollars' worth of chemicals and that when we die it gets broken down and we go back—dust goes back to dust and all that nonsense. And the very reality that we are . . . Remember that reality I was speaking about, that pure awareness, like when you are looking into the darkness and I tell you, ask who is looking? That's the reality, *what is looking* is the reality, not what you see. And then you begin to realize, then you open up inside. And once a person is opened up inside, his heart becomes sensitive. He can feel and be aware when the soul sends in promptings, intuition. And that's the work that the teacher has to do. That's the important work.

A guru or teacher has to have this interrelationship with the students, this clacking of skulls, mixing of ideas, changing of understanding. But the sage doesn't work like that at all.

S: How does he work?

Anthony: He works quite differently. He goes into the stillness, into the void mind. Then when he comes out, he holds your image in his mind and he imagines you or conceives you to be what you really are and then he dismisses the picture. And then for the next ten lives you may be struggling to become what you really are. And the very power and concentration of his thought is so intense that it will bring to pass what he imagines you to be. So he's quite different. He just has to see you once, that is enough.

S: But does he do that to anyone?

Anthony: No.

S: How do you know?

Anthony: Those are things that you know inside. You can't know with the head, but you can know in your heart. And for that you have to, again, get very deep into meditation. And when you get very deep into meditation, you can find out many of these things, many of which you will never speak about to anyone, because it's yours, it's very private. And some things you can speak about.

The sage is different. But he doesn't work this way with everybody, because the sage has an affinity only with certain people, and those are the people he is going to work with. Just because he goes to the post office and meets a man there, he is not going to worry about him. But those with whom there is an affinity, those whom destiny has brought together, he'll work with them. And once you know him to be your teacher, nothing in the universe could ever destroy that, no matter what happens. And that's something that has been going on for a long time. The sage is a mysterious thing. His state of being is hard for us to understand, because he not only sees the world the way we see—he knows this is a cup, this is a book, for example—but he also sees the invisible world. He perceives it directly. He doesn't use his eyes or anything. He doesn't see *with*, he perceives the intelligible world directly. Plotinus was such a man, Buddha was such a man, Christ—these men perceived the real world directly. And they're different.

S: And they were living in the world at the same time as they perceived the reality?

Anthony: Yes, the sage has the faculty to perceive the reality in the sensible object, whereas we can't. That's what we meant when we said that the sage has insight. He sees that everything is pure mind. He sees that directly but he sees the chair too. In other words the soul has, or the mind has, these two different faculties. On one hand, the substratum of the whole universe is mind, but on the other hand, there are many forms that the mind can take. We all see the forms that the mind can take, but we don't see the mind. The sage sees both.

S: But does he have to have a little bit of the ego left to do that?

Anthony: There has to be a little bit left. If there isn't a little bit left, he won't be here. Ramakrishna pointed out the same thing. The great sages point out there is a little bit left, otherwise they won't be here. But they are rare birds. Sages are very hard to find.

The sages are not limited to any religion. PB pulled out the best from all religions. If, for instance, he went to the Middle East and spoke with Sufi masters, he would extract the essence of the Sufi doctrine. And if he went further east and studied with Vedantists, he would distill the essence of their doctrine. He made extensive notes, and then later on all of this was incorporated into his own writings for our benefit. His notebooks are very extensive, and they show the work of a lifetime.

S: Did he compare different religions?

Anthony: Yes. He also investigated and wrote on many of the modern movements like New Thought and Christian Science. He knew personally many of the representatives of those movements and others similar to them. His correspondence was worldwide. He could put thirty-five secretaries to work and wear them out—I know, I used to be with him! He was regular dynamite. He worked constantly. He retired when he was over seventy-five and started working only twelve hours a day. So, such men are very rare.

S: Did PB meet people he considered to be sages?

Anthony: Yes, he speaks about them in some of his books. He considered Atmananda a sage, and Ramana Maharshi, Shankaracharya, and many others. He met these people, he knew them intimately. The only one of those three who is still living is Shankaracharya. He is the one who told PB to go to see Ramana—do you remember that story from *A Search in Secret India*? He is the head of Hinduism in South India, and he lives in Kanchipuram.

S: *PB liked traveling, didn't he? Is traveling helpful for spiritual development?*

Anthony: Well, let me tell you something about that. It's interesting. PB did travel a lot. He went to India, China, Siam, Burma, Mongolia, Japan, Egypt, Australia, New Zealand, and many countries in the West.

But then once when he was in Chicago, in a hotel room, he got the Cosmic Vision. Do you know what that is? The Cosmic Vision? It's the vision that God is everywhere, the whole universe is God, and that God's infinite intelligence is present throughout life, throughout the universe, and throughout history. It's a vision of the intelligent ordering of the whole cosmos. This is something that happens maybe once or twice in a century. You can read about it in the *Bhagavad Gita*, where Arjuna gets this vision and says, "Take it away, I can't bear it." PB said that it's the most humiliating thing that you could go through. You don't come out with a big ego, you come out utterly crushed, but you know that God is everywhere.

After that, PB realized that he didn't really have to go anywhere, he had never really had to go anywhere to find his soul. He realized that his traveling had been an expression of certain strong tendencies of his own from the past. After he had done all that work, he said, "I didn't have to do it. My soul is within me."

Let me tell you something else about PB. After he wrote *The Spiritual Crisis of Man*, he put his pen down because he knew inwardly that he wasn't supposed to write anymore—at least not for a while. Then after a certain time he got the inner prompting to start writing again. And he started writing the notes that we now have as his notebooks. But he wasn't interested in publishing them. A lot of people had the mistaken notion that he had died as an author, but that was when he really started working.

He got the final illumination sometime in 1963, and he became what they call in the East a *jivanmukti*. His mind became permanently established in the higher consciousness, and he was a sage from that day on.

What is most unusual about him is that he was not only a sage, but a philosopher-sage. Not only did he establish this consciousness but he also had the facility, the breadth of knowledge, the technique, and the wisdom to be able to communicate it. That is very, very rare. It is almost impossible to find in one man the combination of this ability to be a very proficient mystic with, at the same time, a background in almost any field within this realm. He was well-educated and had a tremendous knowledge of science. He was also capable of writing and communicating very clearly, very precisely, what he thought.

There are various levels of spiritual development. You have the ascetic, then the saint, the seer, and the prophet. Then you have the sage, and then you have the philosophic sage. The philosophic sage is a person who always lives in the reality and knows the reality—he never loses it—and at the same time is well aware of what is going on in the world and can communicate either side. They are down-to-earth, very practical people. I was washing dishes after dinner one day after I had been with PB for a while, and I asked him as he walked by, "Well, when are you going to teach me philosophy?" He answered, "I am."

S: How did you meet PB?

Anthony: It was in 1946, June 15. I wrote him a letter saying that I wanted to meet him. I thought he was in India, so I sent the letter to his publisher and figured they would forward it to India. Then I got a letter back telling me to meet him at the Café Paris on 63rd Street at 2:00 P.M. It saved me a trip to India! And he came. He had a little briefcase and he was dressed in a suit, a business suit, and I looked . . . you know, I figured he'd come with a dhoti and a flowing beard and a big turban! But then as soon as he said the first word—boom! it was all over. I knew who he was. But he had come looking like a regular businessman, with a business suit and a briefcase.

Don't be misled by that either—even then he was a most unusual man. One entry in his notebooks, for example, is about an experience with a cobra in India. PB was resting in the grass, and when he raised his head there was a cobra in front of him ready to strike. He realized in that instant that if he were to show any reaction, any kind of fear, the cobra would strike. So he immediately embraced it in his love—he sent out his love, and embraced everything that was around him in love, and the cobra went down and went away.

There is a similar story about Ramana. He'd be sitting in the cave and a tiger would come in and go out. It looked at Ramana and felt completely unafraid, no need to react. Because Ramana was radiating compassion in all directions, the tiger felt comfortable. As a matter of fact, the tiger would very often come and sit by him and just stay there with him.

EIGHT
Mind Beyond Images

> They form a mind-picture of the experience or enlightenment that they expect to get as a consequence of their practice, or of their discipleship, but in the end the expectation either proves illusory or imagination fabricates the fulfilment for them. *(V11, 16:14.100)*

Anthony: Very often, when people sit down to meditate, they have a picture in their mind of what it means to get a glimpse. And one of two things can happen. One is that when it does come they don't know that it has come because they have a different idea of what it should be. And the other possibility is that if it doesn't come they make an image, or their imagination provides them with an experience, and then they're deluded into thinking that they got a glimpse.

You read something in a book, for example, and then you think that this is the way enlightenment should be, or a glimpse should be. And then you imagine it. And if you imagine something hard enough you'll see it. That's why it's better to have no ideas of what a glimpse is like. You are usually better off with no idea. If it happens, then you'll find out what it's like.

S: PB never tries to describe it, does he?

Anthony: As a matter of fact, he does describe them. And you'll get a *feeling* from him of what the authentic glimpse is like. That's one of the things PB's books do. He's clearing this jungle. He's making a path in this jungle and he's making a map of the whole of mystical philosophy. As a matter of fact, when you read his notes on them you'll feel affected. And the right thing that we should do after we read them is to meditate.

S: So isn't it good to read things like that?

Anthony: Yes, if it's written by a sage.

S: It seems like a good way to use your imagination, that could inspire . . .

Anthony: I think the point he's making here is that unless you have had some experience of the glimpse or a glimpse of the soul, you have no idea of what it's like. But you will try to imagine what it's like, and then you'll be subject to the imagination producing that glimpse for you. So he's warning that when you meditate it's wiser to have no expectations. Just do the work.

S: But if you have had some glimpse, it's good to use your imagination.

Anthony: If you have had a glimpse, then that's another story. Then you try to recall what that glimpse felt like and it can provoke a glimpse again. That's if you had an authentic glimpse.

S: But isn't it possible that if you get a glimpse it can be too much, and you can become afraid?

Anthony: No, no, it's not possible, you can't get enough. If it lasted all day, all night or a week or a month, you wouldn't get enough.

S: But if you get it before you have been thinking about these things, you won't understand . . .

Anthony: You won't understand anyway, don't worry. Even if you're very informed about these things in philosophy, it will always remain mysterious. Don't worry about that.

> The man's own mind colours the truth which it receives or communicates. His personal tastes and private bias enter into the pattern. *(unpublished)*

> Mere chance happenings are made to hold deep esoteric significance. *(V11, 16:6.54)*

Anthony: What do you think that means? Do you remember the example about synchronicity of Jung? A chance happening is made to hold very deep esoteric significance. Or a trifling accident or incident happens in a person's life and he interprets it cosmically. Have you come across that? "Oh, this has vast cosmic significance."

S: You mean it's usually not like that?

Anthony: It usually isn't like that. Don't see the designs of the universe in that.

> It likes to create pleasing illusions for itself. *(unpublished)*

Anthony: What do you think the "it" here is?

S: The ego.

Anthony: Go on to the next one!

> It is hard for a foreigner entering a strange country for the first time to get true and correct impressions of it. They will necessarily be surface ones and may therefore be misleading ones. In the same way, without this previous instruction and training, it is hard for a mystic to get true and correct reception of the revelatory experience. This is because his mind will unconsciously reflect its personal limitations into the reception, so that what he gets is not the experience itself, but the experience in conjunction with those limitations, and therefore under them. He does not get direct reception at all. *(V11, 16:14.90)*

Anthony: Remember the example about how one man uses the image of Buddha and another one uses the image of Christ when they meditate. In both cases, the soul pours in ecstasy. And one man says, "Oh, Christ enlightened me." And the other one says, "Oh, the Buddha enlightened me." The point here is that simultaneously with the activity the mind interprets what's going on, and so the man will think that it was actually the Buddha or the Christ that did this. The very ideas, the very complexes in our minds are projected simultaneously when a mystical experience takes place, and then we have the problem of disentangling and distinguishing what is authentic and what you put into it.

> He can meditate safely when he's intellectually prepared and emotionally purified for meditation. *(unpublished)*

S: Emotionally purified?

Anthony: It's not wise to meditate if you're in a negative state of mind. If you're full of hate, anger, jealousy, you should not meditate. You should always try to remember that when you sit down to meditate, you should leave all that outside. On the other hand, if a person is like that all the time, psychologically he's sick. He shouldn't meditate.

S: Will it be disastrous if these emotions come up?

Anthony: Well, you can make a lot of trouble for yourself. It's always worthwhile to keep in mind that you should try to live the kind of life that is conducive to what you're seeking. You know, there was once a thief who saw some Sufis ecstatic, in rapture. When they came out of the rapture, this thief went over to the Sufi master and said, "I want to do what you're doing." The Sufi master said, "Sure, why not? But you have to return everything that you stole." The thief exclaimed, "Do I have to do that!" You can't kid yourself about these things. If a person does want the higher type of soul-experiences then he has to live that kind of a life.

> Such will be the shape of mysticism to come. It will not seek to keep the old traditions alive but rather to create new ones in conformity with twentieth-century needs. *(V11, 16:1.21)*

Anthony: Well, that's obvious. Mysticism has to be modernized. I don't see why I have to go to a monastery to practice mysticism. The demands that are made on our life are too great. We have to do what we have to do, but the fact that I have to be of the world, or busy about things in the world, doesn't mean that I should be denied the training and the understanding and the possibility of developing a mystical inner life. A lot of people believe that you should go into an ashram, a monastery, that you should renounce the world, do this, do that, and all that's nonsense. That's why I like Emerson so much. He threw all that out the window. You could be a mystic and go on living a normal life.

S: But not too extroverted.

Anthony: As you develop as a mystic you will know. You can't make theories ahead of time. If you're developing as a mystic there will be times when you'll get the inner call to go on retreat, to do this, to do that. And if you have a listening attitude and you're attentive to the life that's going on within you, you'll respond to that life. You have to stop thinking that it's some kind of a machine. It's a living process that goes on. And the guidance that comes from within your soul is real.

S: If I do something, there is always the possibility of doing it a different way. And if I do that thing differently then I think I should have done it the first way.

Anthony: That's because you got no guidance, no intuition. When guidance comes there are no two ways.

S: If you have no intuition, what do you do?

Anthony: If you have no money, what do you do? You go out and earn it. You go do something and get it. If you have no intuition, you start teaching yourself how to get it. You start learning to listen. You start meditating. We are not born as Buddhas. We're not Buddhas. A lot of people think that when they come into this world they're omnipotent. Anything they want, anything they think comes into existence for them. No. These are things that we all have to learn the hard way. Practice. You want to be a pianist? You have to practice. You want to be a writer, you have to practice a lot. You want to be a painter, a sculptor, you have to work. You don't get anything for nothing. Right? You pay for everything you get. One way or another, you're going to pay for it. So, you want intuition? Learn to shut the factory down.

It's not something you get for nothing. You have to sweat over it. You have to consider every possibility. You have to examine every position. You have to consider each pro and con. You have to think about it, to understand it in detail. Then if you can't come to a decision, you have to resign and wait for the guidance. And very often the guidance doesn't come until the last minute, because your ego is going to go through a little humiliation to realize that it doesn't know. The ego never likes to wait. "I want to know now, I don't want to wait for next week. I have to know right now."

One of you told me, "When I have a decision to make, I can't tell the guy to wait a half hour while I go into the other room and meditate for an answer." But when you have learned to meditate, you can get to the core of the problem immediately; you pierce through everything that's irrelevant and you go right to the point. If you learn to meditate you can do that. Let me give you an example. Let's say you're a good musician. A man comes over and says, "I want you to listen to my great composition." And he plays it. If you're a good musician, if you're a sensitive musician, you will know immediately, this is junk, throw it out! You don't have to say, "Let me go into the other room and meditate for half an hour and then I'll come out and tell you."

Here's an example. Way back in '39 or '38, I was sitting next to a famous music critic in Carnegie Hall during the first performance of

Sibelius' Violin Concerto. We're listening, and the critic is writing his criticism which will be in the *New York Times* the next day. And the man writes that this is a stupid piece, there's no musicianship, there's no inspiration, blah, blah. Then he turns and asks me, "What do you think?" And I told him, "The exact opposite of what you just wrote in your notebook." Why? As the violinist was playing the piece, I was immediately inspired. I knew it was great. I didn't have to step outside and meditate about it. Because of my training, my discipline, my concentration was right there. Now, when you begin to meditate, and you meditate for real, I don't mean for fun, you can keep an idea in front of your mind for ten minutes, twenty minutes, half an hour, and you don't let it go. That's concentration.

Say, for example, that you get very absorbed in a novel and I take the novel away and you stay self-absorbed. That's concentration. It's not concentration if someone reads a sentence to you and you start bringing in things away from the issue. Concentration means that you can get right to that point and you stay in that point and don't move from that point.

When I first started meditating, I would take an important text, read it, memorize a passage, close my eyes and think about that passage until I was blue in the face. Sometimes I didn't get up all night until I understood that. I wouldn't move. I wouldn't even get up and drink a glass of water. I said, listen, you're going to understand this or you drop dead here! It's for real, if it's not done that way you will not learn to concentrate. Sooner or later, you're going to take your ego and you're going to punch it in the nose and you're going to say: "Stay here until you understand this." No two ways about it. Now when you develop that, then when you hear someone talking you can see what they're saying. You can get right to the core.

S: Is it possible to get this experience without grace?

Anthony: Yes, you can get the concentration without grace. You simply have to make up your mind. Did you ever study an instrument, like the piano? A piano is a good instrument for learning concentration. Do you know why? First of all you have eighty-eight keys, and only ten fingers. The teacher puts a piece in front of you; as you're looking at the piece your fingers have to hit the notes, you have to keep time, and you have to be concentrated. If you do sight-reading, then if for one second your concentration isn't there, you stop, you can't move, you can't play the next note. If you take an instrument like the piano—or any instrument, the violin—you have to be totally present when you're doing it. Do you follow me? That's concentration. That's not even meditation yet, and that's not contemplation yet. Meditation is more involved, and contemplation is absolute self-absorption. That's how it is when a person learns, and there is no way to get around it. Don't wait for grace. I thought some day a miracle would happen, a revolution would take place and I would sit down and be able to concentrate. So I waited and I waited and I waited. This will never happen.

S: But it's possible to get grace without the ability to concentrate.

Anthony: Oh, yes. You could get grace. A person may be a good person, a loving person, or may love his soul. He doesn't have to be an intellectual, he doesn't even have to know how to concentrate, and he may get grace and a revelation from the soul. But you see, then that goes away and you want it back. Now, how do you get it back? You have to go through the process of learning to concentrate and meditate and then contemplate. Because you want this all the time.

Now, glimpses will come, but they go. And the one agony that I lived through was when it left me. I went into a dark night, I went into a pitch blackness, I didn't want to go on. How could I live without it? And then I had to go through these studies to find out that there are ways that you could develop your concentration and learn to meditate. You have to fight your ego every day in the week, every day in the year. It says, "You don't want that, you don't want that. What are we going to meditate for? Let's go out and play ball, let's go out and shoot pool, let's go and look for go-go girls." So every day was a fight, every day was a struggle. But little by little, and I mean little by little, you gradually begin to learn how to concentrate. Even today, after twenty-five years, I sit down with a text—very often I'm studying very intensely—all of a sudden: "Did you pay the telephone bill?" "Oh, shut up, you idiot!" I'm reading the text. What do I care about the telephone? But that's the way the ego is. It will bring up a scene, like all of a sudden you see a picture, a big fire engine, and firemen going up to the top of the building. Why is this image coming in? The ego can get your attention like that.

Want to try a nice exercise? This is a very good meditation exercise. You only have to do it one day for a half hour. You sit down, close your eyes, and every thought that comes up into your mind, trace it to its origin. Where did it come from? And it will have come from your ego, and it will be concerned about money, lust, greed, avarice, pride, and on and on. Every thought that comes up, that's all it will be concerned about. After a half hour you get so sick of it that you say, "Oh God, I've got to do something about this garbage can!" This is something I learned the hard way, you're going to learn the hard way. Everyone here is going to learn the hard way. You're going to have to learn to concentrate.

Here's something else you could try. Do you like music? Good. Sit back, turn the music on, and listen to it, five minutes worth. Count every intrusion. Within five minutes, you'll have 112 thoughts that came in and interrupted your listening. That's the way we are. That's why they call the mind a mad elephant. It's like a monkey, or better still, a grasshopper. Did you ever watch a grasshopper? It's everywhere. And you say, "I bet it's gonna go that way," and then the grasshopper goes off another way. You can't tell which way it's going to go. That's just like our mind. So every now and then you have to take out the whip. Bam!

> This exercise of emptying the mind of its thoughts begins as a negative one but must end as a positive one. For when all thoughts are gone, it will then be possible to affirm the pure principle of Thought itself. *(V15, 23:7.153)*

> We must move from consciousness to its hidden reality, the mind-essence which is alone true consciousness because it shines by its own and not by a borrowed light. When we cease to consider Mind as this or that particular mind but as all-Mind; when we cease to consider Thought as this thought or that but as the common power which makes thinking possible; and when we cease to consider this or that idea as such but as pure Idea, we apprehend the absolute existence through profound insight. Insight, at this stage, has no particular object to be conscious of. In this sense it is a Void. When the personal mind is stripped of its memories and anticipations, when all sense-impressions and thoughts entirely drop away from it, then it enters the realm of the empty unnameable Nothingness. It is really a kind of self-contemplation. But this self is not finite and individual, it is cosmic and infinite. *(V15, 23:8.8 and Perspectives, p. 325)*

> Reason tells us that pure Thought cannot know itself because that would set up a duality which would be false if pure thought is

> the only real existence. But this is only reason's inability to measure what transcends itself. Although all ordinary experience confirms it, extraordinary experience refutes it. *(V16, 28:2.132 and Perspectives, p. 385)*

Anthony: You know, it's not something far away from you. It's not out there. It's like I said, when you close your eyes and you look within and you see this blankness, ask yourself the question, "Who sees this blankness?" Try to understand the *who* who sees. Never mind *what* it sees. Just concentrate on *who* sees. After a while there develops the looking sensation, that you're just looking. Then after a while that drops away. The sensation of looking drops away and there's just looking. And then you begin to feel that you aren't any thing at all, but just this infinite consciousness, which has no limits to it but is right there when you close your eyes. You say, "Look, I see all these thoughts running around." Never mind the thoughts. Who sees the thoughts? "Oh, I'm disturbed today." Never mind the disturbance. Who sees the disturbance? Always go back to the *who*. It's that point of light within you that you have to go into and follow through all the way. And that's the Void that he's speaking about. That seer is consciousness. But if you *think* about consciousness then you'll be off the point. Because to think about consciousness is to put you outside of consciousness. So all you can do is to be attentive to that seeing. Never mind anything else. Who's looking, who sees this blackness in front of me? It's horrible. I keep looking, I keep hoping to find myself, but all I see is this blackness, this darkness. And you have to try to remember—go back to who sees it and stay with that. Don't let the contents usurp your attention.

S: This is not what you would call the Witness, this is beyond that.

Anthony: You go through the Witness-position too. The important point here is to try to understand by *being* that awareness. That's the only way that it could be understood, by being that awareness.

S: Are there any experiences which could be like that experience, but which are not that experience?

Anthony: You could imagine, if this is what you mean, you could imagine that you're having the experience. But whenever you imagine anything, it won't give you the feeling of being infinite awareness, boundless, uncircumscribed, empty of everything.

> At last he has entered the absolute stillness, the glorious liberating awareness of true being. *(unpublished)*

Anthony: Here he is speaking about a person who has practically entered into what Plotinus might call "the intellectual phase of the Soul," the highest phase of the Soul.

> There is here no form to be perceived, no image born of the senses to be worshipped, no oracular utterance to be listened for, and no emotional ecstasy to be revelled in. Hence the Chinese sage, Lao Tzu, said: "In eternal non-existence I look for the spirituality of things!" The philosopher perceives that there is no such thing as creation out of nothing for the simple reason that Mind is eternally and universally present. "Nothing" is merely an appearance. Here indeed there is neither time nor space. It is like a great silent boundless circle wherein no life seems to stir, no consciousness seems to be at work, and no activity is in sway. Yet the seer will know by a pure insight which will grip his consciousness as it has never been gripped before, that here indeed is the root of all life, all consciousness, and all activity. But how it is so is as inexplicable intellectually as what its nature is. With the Mind the last word of human comprehension is uttered. With the Mind the last world of possible being is explored. But whereas the utterance is comprehensible by his consciousness, the speaker is not. It is a Silence which speaks but what it says is only that it IS; more than that none can hear. *(V16, 28:1.115 and Perspectives, p. 382)*

Anthony: That's a long quote, so maybe you have to listen to it again. But it's a very beautiful one. He's talking about the Void. You get a feeling for that? That's a very beautiful passage. It comes from personal experience, you can see that. When you make contact with what Plotinus calls the Intellectual Principle, that's what the Intellectual Principle is. The Void. The Void Mind.

S: Is it above the soul?

Anthony: It's above the soul. The individual soul is receptive to it, or what you call the individual mind is receptive to it. [Quote is reread.] He's talking about your mind, the essence of your mind.

S: There's nothing like that that's similar?

Anthony: It's the highest experience that's open to a human. I say human, because I don't know of more, nor can we know more than that.

S: That experience can only occur in a deep trance?

Anthony: Yes, basically that's true. He's speaking about the perception of the Intellectual Principle, where you experience universal existence. And you experience your mind as that universal existence. Generally it's a very deep trance, but a sage like PB doesn't have to go into a deep trance. As a matter of fact, he could be sitting quietly and it's there for him. In the beginning he had to learn to go into a deep trance and train himself, but PB pointed out that after that he could do it in a minute, go right into it.

S: Does the ego usually get crazy after that experience?

Anthony: Usually for those who go into that, when they come back there is no more ego. The whole function of egotism dies. You no longer have the feeling, this is mine, this is my body, this is my house, this is my wife. That's gone. That result won't come through a glimpse. A very sustained effort is required. The glimpse is usually a glimpse of the soul. This is when a person is established in the soul and has a glimpse of the Intellectual Principle. So it's a little different.

S: What is the difference between a glimpse of the soul and a glimpse of the Intellectual Principle?

Anthony: The sage unites with his soul and he's permanently soul. He can get a glimpse of the Intellectual Principle but he cannot become or be the Intellectual Principle. He must return and be soul. He will always be soul. You, I, and everyone else. So the higher glimpse is not your glimpse of the soul, but the soul's experience of the Intellectual Principle. When you achieve identity with the soul, you can get a glimpse of that Void. You can call it the Intellectual Principle or you can call it the Absolute Soul in the Intellectual Principle. It doesn't matter what you call it, because the One, the Intellectual Principle, and the Absolute Soul of Plotinus—those three Primal Hypostases together—can be considered as the Void Mind. But this higher glimpse is distinct from the unity with the soul, the identity with your soul. It is a different kind of experience. You could know many things when you achieve identity with the soul, but when you have the glimpse of the Intellectual Principle, the only thing you could know is that it is. Nothing else. So in other words, you could know that God *is* after you have achieved union with the soul. Before that, all that you could know are the contents of the soul, and the soul itself.

Paul: In the Buddhist tradition where they direct their meditations toward the void and not toward the nature of the soul, can one get that insight of the void first?

Anthony: No. The whole issue is a little confusing. First of all, because the very nature of the Absolute Soul is Void, the individual soul as absolute is also void. PB points out that when the experience of the union with the soul takes place, one recognizes that his soul or his mind is of a void nature. That nature is similar to but not identical with the Intellectual Principle or the World-Mind. When one is in that position, that union with the soul, then he can receive the aura which is emanating from the World-Mind. And he knows—that is, his soul knows—that that principle is.

If we say that the experience of the Intellectual Principle can't exist, then the most that we could know is the existence of our soul as the absolute individual; and we would never know what Plotinus refers to as the three Primal Hypostases, or even what PB refers to as the World-Mind. You couldn't know it. But because the very nature of the soul is similar to the Intellectual Principle, it can receive the aura which is emanating from the Intellectual Principle. And in that emanation the soul receives the fact or the revelation that God is, the existence of God.

Now, this may not sound important; but when you understand the teachings in some depth, and you realize that the most we could know is our own soul, then you begin to realize something utterly astounding: the individual soul as absolute can actually be receptive to the emanation or the aura of the Intellectual Principle and that individual soul, that sage, can even be directed by the Intellectual Principle. But its direction wouldn't be like any kind of message or anything of that nature. When a person, for instance, is on the path of mysticism and he's developing his interior life, there comes a time when he starts hearing what they call the Interior Word. Your soul actually talks to you, gives you advice, tells you what to do. It may be difficult to believe this, but it's an exquisite experience when anyone comes into contact with it. There you're actually guided and told what to do, and your development takes place that way. But when we speak about the silent utterance of the Intellectual Principle, you don't even have that kind of guidance. It's absolute silence. The reception of the Void, that Intellectual Principle coming into your soul, is utter silence. It's so silent that it's deafening.

Paul: In the Buddhist meditational approach, can you directly pursue the Void Mind?

Anthony: No, you must go through the soul.

Paul: In many of the actual methods in the Zen tradition or Chinese tradition you don't find them speaking about the soul.

Anthony: They speak about it as mind. They speak about the direct transmission of the doctrine of No-Mind, and things like that. When Hui Neng, for instance, speaks about "from the first not a thing is," he's speaking about the principle of his absolute mind, his individual mind. That's where he's coming from then. He's not coming from the Intellectual Principle, the principle of Emptiness. This is the position that all you could know is your own mind and that if you could experience it in its profoundest level it would be void.

Paul: When you speak of that mind, you speak of its void nature and you speak of its aspect as consciousness. My question is, can the consciousness pierce into the emptiness, is there a meditational approach?

Anthony: Your question is, can the individual consciousness, my individual consciousness, go directly to and receive the aura from the Intellectual Principle? Isn't that your question?

Paul: I don't know if I want to say the Intellectual Principle, because that's beyond my understanding.

Anthony: Then call it the Void. What void are they coming into contact with? Of course, the Buddhist will tell me, "Well, you are making conceptual distinctions."

Paul: I'm not trying to say that. But the tradition of the void or emptiness is the core of the Buddhist tradition, the void mind.

Anthony: Yes. But what mind are they talking about? That's the question I'm asking. Are they talking about the Intellectual Principle or are they talking about the individual mind? Now it will vary according to the texts that you read. Among individual Zen teachers, some have been quite mistaken, and others have been quite accurate. So I have to know which ones you are referring to. I went through that difficulty quite a few times and I got very confused, because these distinctions do not exist in a great deal of their literature. Nonetheless, I'm quite sure that the great Buddhists have had authentic experiences. Hui Neng and Bodhidharma knew what they were talking about, it's just that they haven't left it behind in written works. It wasn't that I found that they were useless. I found that what I wanted to know wasn't in there.

Paul: I'm trying to remember that quote where PB speaks of how the two approaches do not contradict each other but can both be used . . . where he speaks of experiencing your own consciousness and then the void.

Anthony: Let me try this way. Let's say that you're in some sense proficient in meditation. You reach what they call identity with your soul as absolute, and you keep going and get a glimpse of the Intellectual Principle. That could happen in one hour. You could go through that whole process, but you must go through the soul. When you come back and examine every step, you can see that you first achieved identity with your soul and then at that moment you were also receptive to the emanations coming from the Intellectual Principle. In other words, your individual consciousness, as it is here and now, even if distinguished from your ego, cannot directly go into the Intellectual Principle, cannot be receptive of the Intellectual Principle. It must do so through the unity of the soul, through the unity of your mind.

The available Zen literature has many instructive anecdotes, much beautiful stuff. But I couldn't find this teaching there. I did find it in PB, in Plotinus, and in some of the other Buddhists. Many of the Buddhist texts bring it out. Tucci's *Religions of Tibet*, for example, lays it out very carefully. And in the system of the four Tantras, the last Tantra is concerned with this.

With the others, though, I found too much confusion. And that's to be expected, it can't be helped. Because very often the people who write about these things have not had the experience themselves—they're writing about someone else's experience. When you write about these things, you should make clear whether this is something you know from your experience or if you're quoting someone else. The latter is very frequent today.

Paul: I always felt that PB brought together in his own way, with the notion of the Overself and the notion of the Void, the emphases in the different traditions of the Orient. The Hindus rejected the notion of the Void and the Buddhists rejected the notion of the Overself. Neither one worked with the other concept.

Anthony: Yes, but you remember PB points out that each and every one of us has an Overself, and then there is the universal principle of Overself. Let's say there is the Universal Self, and from it come all these individual Overselves. Each one of these individual Overselves is made of the very stuff of awareness, of which this is the universal principle. In other words, there's the mother Overself, the universal consciousness, the principle of awareness, and then each individual Overself is a unit of awareness, an absolute individual. And each one of these units of awareness he refers to as an Overself. I have an Overself, you have an Overself. Now if that's so, wouldn't it make sense to you that in order to make contact with the Universal Overself, the principle itself, you would have to do so through the intermediary of your Overself?

This would be the same as when Plotinus says that the Absolute Soul is the Soul Essence undivided and integral to the Intellectual Principle, and from it emanate individual souls. He calls them units of life. Now wouldn't it stand to reason that each one of these souls that emanates—or each one of these minds that emanates—has to be of the very essence, of the very nature of that Absolute Soul, that Universal Overself? Your Overself comes from there, my Overself comes from there, her Overself comes from there. And the nature of her Overself, my Overself, your Overself is similar to the nature of that Universal Overself, pure awareness. Now in order for me to become receptive of that Universal Overself, I first have to become the Overself itself, my individual Overself.

The individual Overself is similar but not identical in essence with the Universal Overself. PB makes this point quite often: there is a difference between every individual Overself and the source from which it comes. The individual Overselves that emanate from the Universal Overself are somewhat less in essence than the universal. But the important thing is this, that the only way that you can receive or perceive the Void is to become that pure awareness that your Overself is, because it's that pure awareness of what your Overself is which is receptive to the Universal Overself. There can't be any admixture in that awareness because it would interfere with the reception of the Void. So there can't be any kind of individual consciousness that receives the emanation from the Void. It's a cosmic consciousness, your absolute mind, that receives that. Now this is the way I understand Plotinus, PB, a few of the others.

In order to get a mystical perception of the Intellectual Principle, you have to reach the essence of your own mind, and through that essence of your own mind you can enjoy what they call the mystic identity with the Intellectual Principle—whether for a day, a week, or a month, it doesn't matter. The point is that when it's over, you return and remain soul. That's the point. Even though a person could go through all the levels of his inner consciousness and reach right up to the top and then get a perception of the Void itself, it would have to follow that route, even if it all happened within a couple of hours.

S: When you have a glimpse of the individual mind, it would have to be void too, wouldn't it?

Anthony: Yes.

S: Could what in the Zen tradition is called a satori experience be a glimpse of the individual mind?

Anthony: It depends, because they could call even the perception of the Intellectual Principle a satori, too. So the word satori isn't going to help us.

S: They don't make any distinctions?

Anthony: They don't have texts available on these things. When PB speaks about what a philosopher sage is, he points out that the philosopher sage is a person who has achieved permanent union with his soul. He doesn't say that the philosopher sage is one who has achieved permanent union with the Intellectual Principle or with the Absolute Soul, but one who has achieved permanent identity with his soul. This soul that he speaks about, this is what he refers to as made in the image of God—in other words, the image of Intellectual Principle. And this is what the philosopher or the jnani is, he's that soul. He knows that his essence comes from the Intellectual Principle. He knows it, not intellectually, he knows it because his soul is a direct emanation from that, and the soul's self-cognition automatically includes the recognition of its principle—where it came from.

So it's true that the glimpse into your soul is of the nature of the Void. It's true. But it's also true that the essence of your soul, even though it is void, and the essence of the Intellectual Principle, which is also void, are distinct. Now what is the distinction between these two? When the philosopher sage says to you, "God is," he's not saying that my soul, even though it is cosmic and infinite, is God. He's speaking about the Intellectual Principle, and that's the experience that comes to the philosopher sage, whether we speak about this sage or that one. PB even says that if that's all they can communicate, it is enough. When the individual soul or individual mind has the authentic experience of the Intellectual Principle, that is the announcement he makes, by referring that experience to God. He says that's God. Plotinus goes further and says that in that identity he even achieved mystic identity with the One itself, Mind itself, Absolute Mind, that which is beyond the Intellectual Principle. And he goes on and describes it. But I don't want to get into that now because that's too complicated.

S: *The void of the individual mind, is that experienced when the chakra on top of the skull is released?*

Anthony: No, that's all psychic, far away from these things.

S: *Would you say that experience of the Overself begins when the mind has completely left the chain of the chakras or has been released from them?*

Anthony: We can't put it that way because not only is the gross body in the Overself, but also the subtle is in the Overself, and the causal bodies are there too. They're all in it.

When you think of the Overself, the Soul *per se*, in itself, then think of it as pure awareness, which has intrinsic self-knowing. Intrinsic self-knowing means that there's no other object for it. It's just that. And then also think of the soul, that it can have understanding of everything within it. It can understand the World-Idea within it. And if you keep these two things in mind, that it can be this way or that way, then questions like where does it begin are not rightly put.

S: *No, I don't mean where does it begin. I mean in experience, when do you awaken to the Overself? Is that when you have been released from the ladder of the chakras?*

Anthony: The glimpse is something that happens within the absolute silence and that means there's no physical body, there's no subtle body, all these things are gone. Otherwise you are not in the silence, there's still some kind of thought going on. So I don't know that I could answer the question the way you put it.

S: One could get released from the physical and subtle bodies. When they are left behind, is that when you awaken to the Overself?

Anthony: Do you mean that when every form of thought is no longer present, then is the experience of the Overself available? Yes. When any form, all forms are gone, then one could have the experience of the Overself. Any functioning at all comes to a halt, ceases. And that happens in almost any glimpse, even if it's a momentary glimpse. For a second, for a minute, for an hour, all form of thought is gone.

What we are speaking about now is far beyond the psyche and the subtle world. Anything that has to do with the psyche, anything that has to do with the chakras, all that's in the realm of the psyche; that's not at all spiritual, in the way that we're talking about spiritual.

S: Could you have a glimpse of your Overself or your soul without having to go through the chakras?

Anthony: Yes. During the glimpse there is no time-space continuum. There is no form of thought. You are in utter and absolute silence. If you bring in the slightest breath, the least preference, then you have heaven and earth all over again. It calls for absolute silence.

A lot of people who have experiences of the psyche think it's the soul. I made that mistake quite a few times. The psyche is not the soul. The psyche is not emptiness. The psyche is the living form of the organism, whether it's endowed or embodied or whether it's in the realm of the psyche itself, in the subtle realm. It's not the spirit at all. It's not the Overself.

But I think we are getting away from the point. What he's trying to communicate here is what the nature of a spiritual experience is. And to get sidetracked into what a psychic experience is, is beside the point. You will always recognize a psychic experience because there is some form involved—no matter how subtle, no matter how angelic it appears, it's a form. In a spiritual experience of the Overself, none of that is there. So if you get the feeling, for instance, that some divine being has come down and placed a kiss on your forehead while you're meditating, it is psychical, not spiritual. And there is no end to the different kinds of psychical experiences you can have. There are at least a billion and five hundred million different kinds. It's not the Overself. It's almost impossible to convince people. When they go through it they say, "That is the soul, don't tell me otherwise." I won't tell you, let's talk about the weather. These are things we are going to learn the hard way if we don't listen to someone who already knows.

S: *But if the experience is more real than the experience of this world, then you will know it's genuine.*

Anthony: It is the authentic experience if it's an experience of the soul. And your interpretation of that won't dissolve the authenticity. But you have to remember that many people, many mystics who get involved in these things, when they come out and talk about them, they don't know what they are talking about. It takes a mastermind, a master sage, to be able to distinguish all the various components, all the various aspects of the mystical development. Anyone less than a sage is playing with fire.

> Philosophical mysticism keeps and contains all that is best in ordinary mysticism but reinforces and balances it with reason, culture, shrewdness, and practicality, expresses it through service or art. *(V13, 20:4.53)*

Anthony: That's philosophic mysticism. The other kind of mystic can go crazy. Some of them go and live in caves, in dirt and filth. They're ascetics, they don't eat right, they don't do anything right, and they tell you that this is the highest teaching. They make dirt and squalor spiritual.

You know, in some traditions no music is permitted. Now, I personally have found music very spiritual, and some of my finest spiritual experiences came through music. If I had listened to those other people, I would never have had them. Even Beethoven testified to the spiritual quality of music. He said that the gods up there is the music down here. In other words, music is a personification of the gods. And he had the experience of samadhi, he had nirvikalpa. But some religions tell you, do not draw, you can't make any images, we don't permit it. Every one has its peculiarities. If you go to Islam, no image is made of man, so they have everything in mosaic patterns.

You go to Christianity, medieval religion, and they paint God in a million different ways. So each religion has these peculiarities. But PB points out that philosophy could include all that. It could include culture, it could include the finer feelings, it doesn't have to deny these things.

S: But how can these feelings take form through music?

Anthony: It isn't that the highest spiritual feeling is the music. Remember the example we discussed before? You're concentrating on a novel. You get very, very concentrated. The literature is so beautiful that you feel elevated. You feel expanded, you feel that there's a beauty that's inconceivable. At that moment, forget the novel, and remain in that state of mind: you are self-absorbed. From there on it's a short-cut to the mind itself. You have to try these things. Now it's very hard for me to turn on a piece of music and then all of a sudden to cut it off and just remain self-absorbed. It's very hard, and I think it's hard for anyone else. But the same thing could happen if you're reading a beautiful poem and it has carried you away. Let us say that you are so sensitive to the nobility and grandeur that the form of these words has captured, that at the moment you assimilate it, you *are* that . . . and then you drop the poem, the words, from your mind . . . the form now is gone, there's only this rapt self-absorption. You are next door to the mind, the void mind. It's too bad that people don't try to simply see and have the experience of these things.

One day my son Anthony came downstairs—he had been listening to the late quartets of Beethoven. He was overwhelmed and he said, "They are so beautiful." I told him, "Anthony, don't listen. Stay like that." But he went upstairs and listened. He had momentarily perceived beauty itself. Then after that, of course, chaos. You can get that experience. It's not that hard, because for many of us music is such a beautiful thing that it's a very easy way to meditate.

The first time I heard Bach's *Saint Matthew Passion*, I swooned from the beauty, I went out. You people keep thinking it's something up there, a hundred billion light years away.

NINE
Reconciling Thoughts and Mind

> This is the paradox: that *both* the capacity to think deeply and the capacity to withdraw from thinking are needed to attain this goal. *(V13, 20:4.68 and Perspectives, p. 263)*

Anthony: PB once told me that Plotinus had this ability to concentrate, to achieve tremendous concentration, with thought or without thought, either way. He would contemplate for hours and then sit down and write out a whole tractate. And once he wrote it, that was it. He'd never look at it again. Porphyry had to do the editing—Plotinus' eyes were very bad. Plotinus thought the whole thing out in his mind and it was there like a statue, the whole thing. He also had the capacity to withdraw completely.

Basically, we have to learn to do the same thing: to think deeply, penetratively, and also to be able to be absorbed but have no thoughts. We have to develop both these things. Most of the yoga schools are preoccupied with just learning to block all thinking out, but that's not going to bring them to the higher philosophy. Because the mind will think, and when you come out of a trance, the mind starts working again. So thinking is always there, and you're going to have to deal with it.

> Nevertheless, the endeavour to grasp what is beyond its reach is not a wasted one, for it carries the intellect to the very limits of its own being and then invokes its higher counterpart to come to the rescue. *(V5, 7:1.128)*

Anthony: That happens a lot. I think up to a certain point, and then I can't think any farther. I can't see the solution. I don't know what to do. I just stay there and wait. And if I don't get help it just stays there. That's it. That's as far as I can go. But very often what does happen is that because of the willingness to wait and to be receptive, I get an intuition of how to solve this, and then boom! I go to work.

> The philosophic student knows that the same thoughts which rear their heads and obstruct the mystic from attaining Thought can be turned round and used to help him attain it. But to achieve this successfully there must be metaphysical knowledge. *(V5, 7:7.124)*

Anthony: What he's saying there is to turn thought back upon itself, to turn thought on itself and make it try to understand itself. The other path that the yogis use is to try to obliterate thought, to have no thought. That's one way. And through that way you have moments when there's no thought at all. But the philosophic way is to take the thought and make thought think about its own nature. You reverse its role. Then it has to go back into its own self and it has to understand itself.

When you have thoughts and you ask yourself, "Where's the thought coming from?" and you trace it back to its origin, you are using thoughts to *understand* thought; whereas the other way you are just trying to *abolish* thought. You won't understand it, you'll just abolish it temporarily. You get what can be called the vacuum mind, the mind of vacuity, where you have no thought. Of course, that's a very advanced state. But a state that's even higher is where thought investigates its own nature and then recognizes the fact that all thought is mind and as such comes from mind, is mind. In the higher state you can reconcile thought and mind, whereas a lot of yogis think that you have to be with a blank mind all the time to be enlightened.

> When he has climbed to the peak of a series of abstract thoughts, they may end abruptly and the higher faculty of intuition may then become active. *(V5, 7:1.68)*

Anthony: That's what we just spoke about. When you think a thing out to the end and you can't go any further, then you have to depend on intuition. The rational mind just can't go any further. It reaches its limit. And if intuition doesn't come and help, we're in trouble.

> Accurate ideas about the nature of the soul he is seeking to unite with—that is, right thinking—will not only not hinder his venture in meditation but actually promote its success. *(V11, 16:2.176)*

Anthony: Yes, I think you can see that the better you understand what you are doing, the more likely you will succeed.

Let's say you are going to meditate on Aum. That's all, you're just going to meditate on Aum. Now your first thought is Aum. Let's call that A. I'll use a diagram similar to one Taimni used in *The Science of Yoga*. Think of the circle as the field of consciousness, and think of what's in it as the content. So you are concentrating on A. You sit down and you say, I'm going to meditate. The next thought is B, it's not A. The next thought is C. And you say, "Wait a minute, I'm supposed to be meditating on Aum." And you come back to A. The next thought is E, and the next thought is F. This goes on for the first month.

Ⓐ Ⓑ Ⓒ Ⓐ Ⓔ Ⓕ

The second month you say, "Well, now I'm going to try to do better." So you concentrate on A and now for two minutes you can concentrate on it. The next minute you're off somewhere else again, but you recall it, you bring it right back. "No, no, no, you're supposed to concentrate on A." And you're concentrating on A. The next moment B, F—no, wait a minute!—you're off again.

Ⓐ Ⓐ Ⓐ Ⓑ Ⓐ Ⓐ Ⓑ Ⓕ

The third month comes along—or the third year. [laughter] Now you have made up your mind, "I'm going to concentrate on A, Aum, Aum, Aum." And then, just momentarily, there's only Aum. You forget about yourself completely, there's only this Aum right there shining at you. But then the next minute, the ego comes in with B, C. All right, you go back again, Aum, Aum.

Ⓐ Ⓐ Ⓐ Ⓐ Ⓐ Ⓑ Ⓒ Ⓐ Ⓐ

Then the fourth month, or the fourth year, you say, "I've got to do it." So, you're saying "Aum, Aum, Aum, Aum," and every now and then you forget yourself completely.

Ⓐ Ⓐ Ⓐ A Ⓐ A A Ⓐ A A

Then finally you get into meditation—you're saying, "Aum, Aum, Aum," and now, only the content of consciousness is there. You forget about yourself and there's just this thought persisting, remaining there constantly. Every thought that you have—even though you don't see it, but they keep coming—you keep to the subject that you're concentrating on. Now you're starting to get somewhere. This would correspond to the example where you're reading a novel and when we take the book away there's just this pure self-absorption.

A A A A A A A A A A

When you really get to that state where you're just self-absorbed, there's only the subject that you're concentrating on. Then you have achieved concentration. You just keep saying the same thing over and over again or you keep thinking the same thing over and over again. When you do this for a while, the ability will show up in other areas. For example, if you read a book your mind will get concentrated and you can get right to the subject matter, the point that the book or the paragraph is making.

So this is a rough idea of what we're talking about when we say that you want to learn concentration. That's all there is. There's only the thing that you're concentrating on, you're not even aware that you are there. That's why the circle in the diagram drops out. There's only the content shining pure.

> The faculty of attention is interiorized and turned back upon itself. *(V15, 23:7.216)*

Anthony: This says in one sentence what you have to do. Take the example again of reading a novel. You are very interested, you're absorbed. Then take the novel away and stay like that, very absorbed. Your attention is at a peak. Now you take that attention and you turn it upon itself. Do you follow that? That is very difficult, but it can be done, and you could do it.

Certain exercises will help. I recommend the Hua T'ou exercise because it is the quickest way to get to the attention. Close your eyes, look at your mind. It is dark, just pitch black. There is nothing there. You say, "What am I supposed to be looking at? There is nothing there." You keep looking, and a thought comes up. As soon as the thought comes up, you have a big sword, and you cut the thought right off. You stay there, you keep doing that. You have to be at attention, constantly. Every instant. Like when you're playing the piano. As soon as your attention backs off, the exercise is over, and you have to start again.

So, you are looking into your mind. Try to do this for a half hour, because it is really very strenuous. Every time a thought comes up, you cut it right off and you keep looking, constantly looking into your mind. As soon as a thought comes up, chop off its head, hang it, strangle it, anything you want to do—just get rid of it. It's that simple. Get rid of it. If you could do that for a few weeks I guarantee you results. I guarantee them. Maybe I shouldn't talk like that. But it is impossible not to get results, because your attention gets so intense that you become like a statue of attention, a mass of attention.

I myself would get so stiff that I was like a board. If you kicked me I would have just gone down like a board. That's how stiff you get when you're working at it, but that means you haven't succeeded yet. You have to get so intensely attentive that suddenly something snaps, and it is over. You are no longer tense, you are very relaxed. But you are at attention. Until that happens the exercise isn't completed. Assuming that happens, assuming that you finally get there, then the attention which is so alert, now you turn that attention on itself. That is like trying to see your own face, but it can be done. You can be focused, you can be reflectively self-attentive. You can have the attention looking at itself constantly. That is when the separation between your consciousness and your body starts taking place. You begin to feel that you are no longer your body, you begin to feel that you are distinct from anything and everything. So this is a very nice one.

> It is an error to say that mysticism and metaphysics are on equal levels. The first is more important than the second. There is no way to realize the Self which does not include going inside consciousness. Thinking, however metaphysical, cannot do it. Action, however self-denying, cannot do it. It must be found inside in the heart. The other things are needful but secondary. Without the inner consciousness, action becomes at best humanitarianism, and thinking a photographic copy of the Real. *(V11, 16:1.66)*

Anthony: What he is saying there is something like this, if I could use a vulgar analogy. No matter how many times you read the menu in a restaurant, your belly isn't going to get filled. You have to eat something. No matter how many times you read about these things, unless you actually have the experience in *your mind*, you are not going to be satisfied.

So, as we said before, you are practicing attention. Your attention gets interiorized, then you turn the attention upon itself. These are states of consciousness that you actually experience, when you experience yourself free from all thoughts, all objects. You have to experience that. My talking about it, and your talking about it—I read, you read—that is not going to give it to us. The experience, the actuality, is a living, vital experience, whereas the talking about it is like dead concepts, corpses walking around. And also when you get to the higher states of contemplation, the experience of the void is a real experience, it is not another concept. A lot of people think that a conceptual understanding in their imagination is equivalent to having the actual experience. And you have to be careful there. So metaphysics is important, to be able to understand these things is important. But it is more important for a person to have the actual experience that he *is* this mind. Because he experiences it in a living vital way through being that, rather than thinking about that.

> Like the two sides of the same coin, so it is that a thing thought of is thought of always by comparison with something not itself, that all our thinking is therefore always and necessarily dualistic, and that it cannot hope to grasp Oneness correctly. Hence the logical completion of these thoughts demands that it must give up the struggle, commit voluntary suicide, *and let the Oneness itself speak to it out of the Silence*. But this must not be done prematurely or the voice which shall come will be the voice of our own personal feelings, not of That out of which feeling itself arises. Thinking must first fulfil, and fulfil to the utmost, its own special office of bringing man to reflective self-awareness, before it may rightly vacate its seat. And this means that it must first put itself on the widest possible stretch of abstract consideration about its own self. That is, it must attempt a metaphysical job and then be done with it. This is what the average mystic rarely comprehends. He is rightly eager to slay his refractory thoughts, but he is wrongly eager to slay them *before* they have served him effectively on his quest. *(V5, 7:1.135 and Perspectives, p. 85)*

Anthony: I guess you know what he is talking about here. There is a sort of tradition in a lot of mystical groups that the most important thing to do is to destroy all thinking so that we can reach a mind of vacuity, a mind without thought. Many mystics believe that this is the right thing to do. I don't know if it's different in the East than in the West, but I have noticed that for Westerners it doesn't work like that. They have to actually exhaust the mind's capacity to think. They have got to use it. And only when they fulfill it in that way, when they take this potential power of thinking and employ it to the uttermost limits, only then will they give it up and put it down. In the East there is a tradition that in order to get to the vacuum mind, the wise thing to do is immediately stop thinking, cease thinking, destroy it some way or another, and get to the empty mind.

Now, PB in this passage is pointing out that it is necessary for us to employ thinking to the utmost. We should exhaust the function of thinking through using it to understand in depth the philosophy that we are speaking about, and then *after that* start trying to develop the empty mind. Let me give an example. Sometimes we have a very intensive seminar, think real hard for a couple of hours. And then we go and meditate. Then your mind is just willing to drop everything, and it becomes so much easier to get a quiet mind. But that doesn't work for everybody, because some people get so stimulated that they can't stop thinking. So people have to experiment and find out which way is better for them. At any rate, it is not wise to get rid of the thinking mind until you've developed it, because you have to apply intelligence, you have to use intelligence to know what you are doing.

The goal, the ideal should not be to obliterate the thinking mind. The goal should be to develop and fulfill the thinking mind. Once you have thought out and understood the basic implications of metaphysics, then if you go ahead and proceed to acquire the vacuum mind, you already have that knowledge, you know how to operate, you know what you are doing when you are in contemplation or meditation. So basically what he is saying is that the way of obliterating the mind isn't the correct way.

Let's take, for example, a man who has a very meager intelligence. He decides that he wants to be a mystic and he doesn't develop his mind, he just develops the faculty to meditate. And let's say he succeeds to some extent in bringing about a quiet mind. In his case he could have a quiet mind, but he would also be a stupid man. You wouldn't be able to get much out of him.

You first understand and then you do. To first understand means you have to develop, you have to use your brains. But you can still meditate. You don't have to wait until you fully develop your mind to get started in meditation, because then you may have to wait a long time!

S: Is meditation a way of developing the mind?

Anthony: You develop the ability to concentrate with thought and you develop the ability to concentrate without thought. Both things have to be developed. A sage, like I told you, is not a fool. Ramana Maharshi seldom talked, but don't ever think he was a fool. He was very, very perceptive.

Paul: He answered many technical questions when he was asked about Vedanta philosophy.

Anthony: Really difficult questions, and he never even read the books. He had a developed rational mind when he came in. That wasn't something he had to acquire. You have to remember that the development of a mystic or a soul seeking God is a development that takes many, many incarnations.

S: Couldn't you also take concentration on different jobs, or sports, as a first step in meditation exercise?

Anthony: Yes, you could do it if you want. You could go out and play tennis and tell me you are practicing concentration. Sure, you could do that. But I won't believe you. Because the kind of concentration we are talking about is abstract. We all concentrate on things we like. If I am making money I can get very concentrated on making money, or if I am a sportsman I can get very concentrated on the game I am playing. But to get someone to concentrate on attention itself? "I'll go play tennis, I'll get concentrated there." Or another friend told me, "Bridge requires tremendous concentration, so I am taking your advice, I am learning to concentrate."

> Continued and constant pondering over the ideas presented herein is itself a part of the yoga of philosophical discernment. Such reflection will as naturally lead the student towards realization of his goal as will the companion and equally necessary activity of suppressing all ideas altogether in mental quiet. This is because these ideas are not mere speculations but themselves the outcome of a translation from inner experience. While such ideas as are here presented grow under the water of their reflection and the sunshine of their love into fruitful branches of thought, they gradually begin to foster intuition. *(V13, 20:4.66 and Perspectives, p. 262)*

Anthony: That is pretty obvious, straightforward. Obviously the more you understand about these teachings, the more fertilization occurs, the more intuitions and ideas of what to do come to you. So the repetition of these ideas in your mind, reflecting upon them, will be a considerable source of understanding. Intuitive ideas will come to you. Very often you'll do an exercise and while you are doing it you will get an intuition about how to modify it or change it a little bit. It's an obvious thing. The more you know about what you are doing, the more equipped you will be to be able to do it. It isn't a useless expenditure of energy and thought to master the theoretical doctrine so that it will support the practical work. Theory and practice have to go together. The more you understand of theory, the better your practice can be. The more involved your practice becomes, the more you understand the theory. It is like the two legs. We need two legs to walk.

> In this exercise the eyes are fixed on the sinking sun, the mind lost in its beauty, and the body kept still on its seat. *(V3, 3:7.42)*

Anthony: That is all. You sit outside, you watch the sun setting. And you just watch it set. You just look. Sit still. Don't move. Watch it set. The experience is inevitable. Do that for about forty-five minutes, especially when the light is beginning to fade, and it's getting dimmer and dimmer. Do that for forty-five minutes and then when you get up and walk away and start getting thoughts, it sounds like someone is in there with a cymbal. It gets so noisy. But the quiet is something you can experience with every sunset.

> Imagination is likely to run away with his attention during this early period. At first it will be occupied with worldly matters already being thought about, but later it may involve psychical matters, producing visions or hallucinations of an unreliable kind. *(V4, 4:3.56)*

Anthony: That is why they tell you to stick to the theme that you are meditating on. Don't be preoccupied with other ideas. If you are going to concentrate on Aum or you are going to look at an image in front of you, stick to it. And very often people say, for example, "Do you know, I had this sensation that someone was hovering . . ." "Yes, concentrate." They say, "But what does it mean?" "Yes, concentrate." And after three times, they still don't see the point I am getting at. You are deviating, you are forgetting about your exercise. The next thing you'll be doing is wondering about whether they have wings and what is the horsepower of the engine that they fly with.

Come on! Just do what you are supposed to be doing. When the real thing comes, you will know it. When that sweetness comes you know that you have to surrender yourself. But if you start looking for pictures, get up and go look at the television.

> A flower is as good an object to concentrate on as any other. Indeed it is better, for he may also try to make his own heart one with the flower's heart. *(Perspectives, p. 49)*

Anthony: That's a beautiful one. The Zen people like to use that—take one flower, put it in a vase, and concentrate on it.

> Press your consciousness inwards. *(unpublished)*

Anthony: You know it is always going out—to the go-go girl. He's saying, "Press it inward, press the consciousness inward." It's very hard to do the two of them together.

> In the early stage, when concentration is needed, he will succeed best by giving his attention strong forcible commands, by directing his mind toward the chosen topic with positive phrases. *(V4, 4:6.178)*

Anthony: "*You* are going to look at that image, do you understand? Now, *look*." Give yourself positive commands. Of course your mind will say, "Who are you to tell me what to do?"

> The head, the neck line, and the shoulders should first be pushed up and then kept straight and still. *(V4, 4:2.197)*

Anthony: It is always wise to keep this part of your body up, although there are other techniques. PB, for example, often used to like to meditate lying down. But if *we* do that we fall asleep. Probably within two minutes. That is what I found to be the cure for insomnia! When I say, "I can't sleep tonight—I am going to lie down and meditate," there is the sleep.

S: Wouldn't it sometimes be good to lie down and meditate?

Anthony: Some people can do it. They find it easier to lie down. You have to experiment. Some people have a back problem or something and can't sit up. So then they can try to meditate lying down. Some people have succeeded in doing that.

You lie down flat with your palms up, your feet spread just a couple of inches. You start by breathing in and out very slowly. As you are breathing in, imagine the breath going throughout your body, relaxing every part of your body. After you do that for a couple of minutes, then you start meditation. You select a topic and stay with the topic.

Also, Christians have been known to meditate on their knees. They get on their knees and can meditate for hours. If I do it for ten minutes, I get two big bumps! But some people can do that marvelously.

What I am trying to say is that this is not a dogma. A person really has to experiment and find out which way is good for him. One person likes to sit up, another person likes to lie down. Whichever way you feel you can do it, then do it, use it. Start with the exercise that you feel you like the most. Experiment a little bit. Once you find out which way you want to do it, then stay with it for a few months. You have to give it a few months.

In any case, you have to give your attention to what you are meditating on—whether it be a mantra, a scriptural name of God, or whatever. Let's say you are a Christian and you decide to try saying "Lord Jesus Christ, Son of God, have mercy on me a poor sinner. Amen." You have to keep saying it and your attention has to be on every phrase that you are saying. As soon as it becomes mechanical your meditation is over. In other words, if it is mechanical, you are not meditating. You have to put some feeling into it and you have to be attentive all the time. And just that exercise alone will take you right up to the void. Just saying that, with concentration and attention. The Hesychasts use that over and over and over until their consciousness drops into the heart. Then they are in the heart and they come into contact with the light.

S: But what about meditating with a mantra then? I mean, there you don't have to pay attention.

Anthony: If you do it without attention, you are not going to get anywhere.

S: But how can you have your attention on a mantra, when you don't understand what it means?

Anthony: First of all, you can understand what it means. You can go look up what it means. Secondly, you *can* be attentive to something that you don't understand. Like if you said, "*Aum mani padme hum.*" You don't know what it means and even if I told you in

English, "The jewel within the lotus," you still don't know what it means. But that doesn't mean you can't concentrate on it. Concentration is a question of gripping your attention and putting it where you want and keeping it there. *It is hard work.* It's very hard work until you get the habit. Once you get the habit then it gets easier, but it takes hard work.

Here's one where PB quotes from Julius Clausen:

> Concentration on the "within us" is the first necessity. And then one asks oneself the first questions, "Who are you?" "What is this body which belongs to you, and you to it?" "How have you become what you are—what have you inherited from your forebears, what part has your environment played, and what have you yourself contributed?" It is obvious that such self-questioning will not be answered in one brief meditation, but must be considered again and again, and deeper layers thoroughly explored. [The actual simile Clausen uses is of "coal-mining"—PB]
>
> But you will be rewarded for your effort, for in this way you will come to understand fully what is ephemeral and what is of lasting value, your spiritual "I," which Brunton calls the "Overself." When you have got so far, you can, in your "quiet time," consider other problems which are on your mind. Shall I in this matter do this or that? Or shall I give the matter up? And the inner Voice will always give you the right answer—but only if you have mastered the art of meditation. For it is an art, a difficult and demanding Art, which presupposes so strong an inner concentration that no thoughts or images can break in upon the meditation. It is hard work and demands constant practice. But those who only partially succeed will find the deepest satisfaction in seeing "across and through" and so become able to distinguish the true from the false values.—Julius Clausen on the Art of Meditation *(unpublished)*

Anthony: We have to go into ourselves step by step. Many of us have gone through experiences that are very painful. We cry and then the next day we forget about it. But the experience is in our mind. It is there. It is like when they brand a cow with a branding iron. A lot of times the experiences that we go through are like branding irons. They just sear into our soul. And for years and years we carry that pain with us, but buried. We don't want to think about it.

But one of the things I have found out that we can do is this. You meditate and you think about it, and you think very intensely about it. You don't run away from it. You go over the whole thing in your mind. You try to bring it up to the surface. You try to understand what the meaning was. Was there a lesson in there for you? Did it mean something special for you? Because nothing will happen to you except that it is ordained.

You can say this is an opinion, but it is an honest opinion. You may say it is not ordained. That's all right. You can believe your version. I am telling you mine. I feel that anything that happens in my life is ordained. What happens was going to happen. There were no two ways about it. When I was born. Who I married. How many children I had. The illnesses I received, whatever I had to go through. The heart attack, getting into an accident. Those things were ordained. So if these things are ordained in my life, then they have a meaning for me. They don't happen to somebody else, they happen to me. Therefore they have to mean something to me. What do they mean? So I take them into my meditation. I think about them, sometimes for weeks. I try to understand them, and then, after a while, I feel them dissolve, just leave me, go away. Any problem I had with them isn't there any more. I accepted, resigned myself to what happened. I tried to learn the lesson from it and then it didn't bother me any more.

So meditation could be used instead of going to a psychoanalyst and paying a hundred bucks an hour. Stay home and do it yourself. Self-help! Try it, it works. Take some experience that you have gone through, good or bad. Make it a topic of your meditation and try to understand that experience—what lessons were in it, what meaning was there for you. For each and every one of you here, there's no exception, life has a meaning for you, which is *your* life and *your* meaning. Nothing will happen to you except what was ordained to happen. Here is the picture of the world, which is in the mind of God, the World-Mind. Everything in that picture is already ordained, so anything that happens has a very specific meaning for you. That is what I am trying to get at. And sometimes the best way to try to get to what that means for you is to meditate on it. Let's say that when I'm eighteen years old I get my legs broken. I think about it, and I concentrate on it, and I try to understand what it means. "Well, you dope, obviously you shouldn't be playing football. You are not a football player." It's like the Higher Power is trying to say, "Get out of that, that is not for you. What are you doing there? You want to learn the hard way? All right. We'll teach you the hard way."

S: But you can find a lot of explanations for why things happen to you.

Anthony: Yes, but not if you are meditating. When you are meditating, just hold in your mind's eye the experience. Just hold it. Wait until you are told what it means. There is a difference between you talking to yourself and your inner being telling you what it means. You'll know, because the conviction comes with it. It's not like when you say, "I think it means that," and then the next minute you say, "No, I think it means this," and then the third minute you say, "No, it meant that." When you get it from within yourself there is no doubt, because it comes with its own conviction and authenticity.

S: Can you also do that if you don't know which step to take next?

Anthony: Yes, but here you first have to be able to be very quiet, have no thoughts. That is the prerequisite. Your mind has to be still, then you could ask the question. Usually it is wise to ask for advice when you are coming out of meditation. Not when you are going in, but when you are coming out. Let's say you have been sitting for forty to fifty minutes and you finally get quiet. Your mind is quiet. Now, when you come out of meditation you ask for guidance. You may have to do it once, maybe ten times. I don't know, but don't expect an answer right away. Very often the answer doesn't come until the last minute.

S: Is that way rather advanced?

Anthony: Well, how long do you want to stay an infant? It will not work unless you can keep your mind still. But you will notice that towards the end of meditation your mind starts getting a little quiet, if you have been doing it regularly.

First, though, you have to do everything you can to understand the problem, to work it out as well as you can. If you can manage it on your own, in terms of your own understanding and rationality, you are supposed to do so. You are only supposed to ask for help when it is impossible for you to see a solution, a way out. You shouldn't be always asking for help because, after all, the soul wants you to develop your own powers. It doesn't want to come in and keep taking care of you. You have to do what you can. But sometimes there are problems in life that you feel totally inadequate to solve. That is the time to call on help. But don't ask, "Should I get this apartment or that apartment?"

You should try to see the problem, why things happen. When something happens you try to understand it. It can be done. But like I said, you have to get the mind quiet and then go over, in your mind, what happened. Very carefully go over it. The other exercise you can use is to review the problem in your mind just before you go to sleep at night. Review it for a few nights. The first night, second night, third night, and then one morning the first instant you are awake you may get an answer about what to do, or what it means. But it has to be the very first instant you are awake, that is when you may get the answer. If you don't get it there, then the ego comes in and it starts all over again. Very often, I go over the problem and try to fall asleep with it in my mind and ask for guidance. Then the first instant of awakening I sometimes get an answer. But you have to remember, these things don't always work because we are not proficients, we are beginners. Here's a note about one exercise we already discussed:

> When wholly absorbed in watching a cinema picture or a stage drama or in reading a book with complete interest, you are unconsciously in the first stage of meditation. Drop the seed of this attention, that is, the story, suddenly, but try to retain the pure concentrated awareness. If successful, that will be its second stage. *(V4, 4:3.80)*

Anthony: When someone asked a great Sufi master how he learned to meditate he said, "By watching a cat watch a mouse. Just by watching them I learned how to meditate."

S: Some Zen masters say that the only way to get enlightened is by paying attention.

Anthony: Yes, that is one of my favorites. People ask me, "What shall I do?" Be attentive.

S: In that way you could go about your daily life and still be somehow rooted in your Self?

Anthony: After a while it becomes very natural to be in an alert, attentive, concentrated state of mind, just like it used to be very natural to be in a sleepy, vague, ambiguous state of mind. It becomes very natural. I remember many years ago there was a lecture being given at Columbia University. Several teachers were sitting around a big table, and D.T. Suzuki was among the speakers, and it looked like he was half asleep. The window was open and all of a sudden the wind blew in, and papers started flying. But before the wind ever got to his papers, Suzuki put his hand over them. They thought he was sleeping but he was right there, all the time. To be concentrated doesn't mean that you have to be like that statue, *The Thinker*, where you see all the wrinkles.

S: When you say your mantra can you engage in activity?

Anthony: Yes, you could do that. It is a question of practice. Just try it. I know people who practice a mantra while they are working. Some of them are clerks, working at a cash register, and all the time, under their breath, they are saying their mantra.

S: But then is it without feeling, automatic?

Anthony: Their attention is on their work and their attention is on their mantra. And they try to say it very intensely. There is only one way you are going to find out and it is: Do it.

Do you know the Plato edition by Professor Jowett, the man who translated the complete works of Plato? Did you ever hear of him? Well, this man was a professor at Oxford. He was a don, a very learned man. He translated a lot of Greek literature, including the complete works of Plato. This man was always muttering under his breath the Lord Jesus prayer. Whether he was teaching, whether he was at a party, whether he was in the administrative office, whether he was out talking to people, he was always practicing it.

You are coming from the point of view of someone who hasn't tried. I know myself, personally, I was a manager of a big bookstore, and I was saying my mantra every day from the time I got up to the time I went to sleep. It goes on by itself after a while. Mentally it keeps going on all the time. But if someone says, "Well, you can't be doing both things," all I could tell them is, "Try it." Don't tell me what I can't do and can do. Try it and then you'll find out. A beautiful story you could read is that of Brother Lawrence. It's in the introduction to a book called *The Practice of the Presence of God*. He was always practicing the Presence of God, even in the kitchen where he had to cook for 300 people every day. But he didn't accomplish it in one day, it took him time.

S: Is there a difference in quality in the two kinds of thinking? Do you think and talk on one level with your surface mind and say the mantra on another level?

Anthony: We could think of an actress or an actor. There are two levels there. The actress is completely identified with the role, acting out the role, but then she knows herself distinct from what she is doing. There are two levels of being operating simultaneously.

> "Like a caged lion, our mind is always restless," said an ancient yoga master to his pupil. *(unpublished)*

Anthony: Somewhere else PB calls it a wild elephant. I call it a grasshopper. But I can see why he calls it a wild elephant. The restless mind is really very difficult to overcome and it is very powerful.

> It is useful only in the most elementary stage to let thoughts drift hazily or haphazardly during the allotted period. For at that stage, he needs more to make the idea of sitting perfectly still for some time quite acceptable in practice than he needs to begin withdrawal from the body's sense. *(V4, 4:3.6)*

Anthony: So he says in the beginning it is all right to let the thoughts go and come, because the first thing you have to learn is to be able to sit quietly for a certain amount of time and keep the body still. So in the beginning it is all right that your thoughts drift around. They play hide and seek and all that.

S: Don't the thoughts have anything meaningful to say also—like dreams?

Anthony: They probably are very important thoughts you are having, I am sure!

> [continuation of previous quote] He must first gain command of his body before he can gain command of his thoughts. But in the next stage, he must forcibly direct attention to a single subject and forcibly sustain it there. He must begin to practise mental mastery, for this will not only bring him the spiritual profits of meditation but also will ward off some of its psychic dangers. *(V4, 4:3.6)*

Anthony: So in the second stage when you learn to sit for forty minutes and concentrate on a topic—whatever the topic is—that very concentration prevents any entities from coming into you. If your mind is blank and passive, and if there are any stray entities flying around, they say, "Hey look, there is a vacant apartment!" But if you are concentrated, they see the sign, "No Rooms to Let," and they keep going.

You could experiment right now. You can take an object and resolve that you are going to look at that object. As you are looking very intensely at that object you can see that thoughts are trying to come in, but your stare, your gaze, your attention just blocks them, they can't come in. As soon as you drop your attention, boom!—they come right in. So in the same way when a person is meditating and sticks to the topic, these impulses can't come in. They are just kept out. So the thought wants to come in, "Hey, you have to pay the telephone bill." No, it stays out there.

S: But you can be saying a mantra, and still all these thoughts come and go.

Anthony: You are telling me that you are really saying the mantra, but thoughts are coming in all the time. And I am saying to you, you are lying. Yes, you are! I think what we should do with you is to give you a quadratic equation to work out, a problem in algebra! If there is a lack of intense attention, you could be saying a mantra but your mind isn't there. That is what I mean when I say you are not saying it.

Think of your mind as an ice cube. As the ice cube melts, it must turn into water. In the same way, if you are saying the mantra, every thought is always the mantra. Your mind as it is melting is becoming the mantra all the time. The mind functioning is nothing but the mantra. It's not enough just to say it. You could always be talking with your mouth and be thinking about something else, but your thought processes have to be directed into the mantra.

The mantra also has a different kind of effect. It is not always the meaning that's important. Very often it is the intonation of the mantra that's important. When one says, "*Aum amida bitsu, Aum amida bitsu*," for example, and keeps saying that, there is a kind of intonation and gradually the rhythm builds up. So you keep saying, "*Aum amida bitsu, Aum amida bitsu . . .*" and after a while it starts having an effect of paralyzing the mind. That's the whole point. So it isn't necessary that you know what it means, but you have to be concentrated. If you say it, it'll have its effect anyway. Sometimes they'll give you a very long one or a short one. "*Aum mani padme hum. Aum mani padme hum.*" You keep saying that. After a while the mind is put to sleep, the thoughts stop.

I used to study with a teacher who was a Jesuit. Do you know what he would tell you? Go and sit over there and do the mantra. And he would stay with you for hours. But I can't do that with you. You are going to have to do it. Some teachers will sit with you until you learn to do it the right way. They have infinite patience.

> The difference between the first stage, concentration, and the second stage, meditation, is like the difference between a still photograph and a cinema film. In the first stage, you centre your attention upon an object, just to note what it is, in its details, parts, and qualities, whereas in the second stage, you go on to think all around and about the object in its functional state. In concentration, you merely observe the object; in meditation, you reflect upon it. The difference between meditation and ordinary thinking is that ordinary thinking does not go beyond its own level nor intend to stop itself, whereas meditation seeks to issue forth on an intuitional and ecstatic level whereon the thinking process will itself cease to function. *(V4, 4:4.29)*

Anthony: I think about a thing and I keep my mind on it and I have to wait until I get so wrapped up in the thinking that then the intuition starts working. And out of the blue it will come out—this is what that means. Basically what he is saying here is that thought gets so interested in itself that it becomes paralyzed. And when that paralysis sets in, when thought becomes so abstracted that it is no longer there, that is when the intuition comes in. It becomes ecstatic at that minute and you feel very exalted: the thinking processes themselves have come to a halt, and in that moment the intuition could arise. The mind is exalted.

Many great thinkers do that. They don't know it, but they get so wrapped up in their thinking that there comes a moment when their thinking ceases and intuition pours in, just flashes down into their mind. Remember the example I gave you about Archimedes and the gold? That is an example of thinking becoming ecstatic. And when it becomes ecstatic then you are wide open to intuition.

S: You are concentrating on a mantra. If you reach a state where you are absolutely concentrated, do you leave that mantra behind then?

Anthony: Yes. When you get very concentrated on a mantra, it is like a train, it will take you to where you want to go. When you get there you get off the train, you don't stay on. In the same way, when you use a mantra you can get very concentrated. When you get very concentrated you forget the mantra and there is just the concentration.

S: After you have achieved concentration, is that when you can really begin to reflect on metaphysical matters?

Anthony: Yes. Unless a person has learned to concentrate, most of the philosophical problems are unavailable—the problems, let alone the answers.

> If the mental life is disciplined and trained along these lines, if for a chosen period each day the sense-experience is suppressed and the emotional life quieted, he will reach a point where a real spiritual experience may be within easy reach. *(unpublished)*

S: What happens to this person's emotions in his daily life? Will he be able to feel as intensely as before or will his emotions be more subdued?

Anthony: Generally when you sit down to meditate and you try to quiet the emotions or suppress them, if you have some success in doing so, then when you come out of meditation it will take a few minutes for the emotions to come back and start asserting themselves. But they will come back, they will be there. It isn't that you got rid of them.

The question that I think you are really asking is, "Will there come a time when the intensity of the compulsive power of emotions can be broken off?" I would say yes. There comes a time when a person feels a release from the compulsive intensity that emotions operate with. That is like being initiated. Because once you are released from the compulsive tendencies of the psyche, the emotional nature is considerably lessened. If you get an impulse to strike someone, if you get angry or something, that impulse can't effectuate itself, can't actualize itself. The way we are in the ordinary state, when an impulse arises we immediately do it. But after this initiation, when the impulse arises you don't do it. To some extent now you have disassociated yourself from thinking or feeling.

S: You don't experience the emotions as strongly?

Anthony: You don't experience them intensely, but in compensation for that they are very clearly delineated, they are very objective. In other words, if a person is talking to you and certain emotions are going through him, you can very clearly perceive what those emotions are. They are very objective to you. But to the other person they are not objective. He is identified with the emotions as they come and they go. At each moment that they come he identifies with them, he lives them out, and then they go.

Consider the point of view of a true artist. He knows precisely the emotions he has to portray and he can do so. If he gets caught up in the emotion he can't portray it. Let's say I am learning to play a piece on the piano. I love the piece very much. The intense feeling for the piece will prevent me from playing it properly. Whereas, when I have sufficient control over those feelings and I know that this should rise, this should fall, this should be spread out, this should be a *rubato*, now I can do it properly. I have such command that I can, through my playing, transmit what the composer wanted to say. I am not going to interfere. I can portray it perfectly without interfering.

S: That means you could also be a very good actor then.

Anthony: But if an acting coach doesn't understand this, he is going to think that if a person is detached he will not be able to portray an emotional quality significantly. This is not true. The great actors and actresses have a perfect command of what they are going to do. It isn't that the emotion comes in and takes over. They have a perfect command. They can portray that emotion, they can live that emotion and yet be behind it and see it very objectively and say, "Uh-uh, I didn't do that right." Whereas if you are identified with that emotion you can't see that.

So when the pianist is detached enough from the piece of music, he can objectively see very clearly what he has to do. It is the same thing for a writer. If he gets completely caught up in what he is writing, then the objectivity is gone and he can't actually portray what he sees in his mind's eye. He gets caught up in the writing, and you can see the writing get murky and unobjective. But as soon as he can step back, look at the idea, and only then try to portray the idea in the words, he'll find the right words for the idea he has. So you have to be in a position of command. But that doesn't mean you are not absorbed. You are quite concentrated in these situations. I never would try to practice a piece that I love too much. I knew I couldn't play it. I think a lot of musicians know that, and great painters as well. I have noticed it with quite a few artists. The greater the artist, the more there is something in him that stands behind it all.

It is certain that if he perseveres in this practice, if he does not lose hope but continues to strive with unbeatable patience, the thoughts will in the end give up their resistance and retreat like a besieged and beaten enemy. *(unpublished)*

S: If you start concentrating on your first thought and you find that your thoughts start wandering, could you just stop there or is it better to go back to the first thought?

Anthony: You have to stop when you find out that your mind is moving away from the thought. You have to do that, but the second thing you have to do is to bring your mind back to the original thought. You have to *keep* doing that. It is like when the cow keeps going over there and you have to keep bringing it back over here. You have to do it so many times that finally the cow gives up going over there.

So, you have to stop at that moment that you recognize it and then bring the mind back to the topic. It is not good just to stop there. It's wise to bring your mind back to the point. Then after many, many attempts, the mind begins little by little to get tired of running away.

S: I've found it somewhat helpful to try to concentrate just for a second. [laughter] Wait, it's better than it sounds! If I have to concentrate now for half an hour, the whole thing will kind of blur. But if I try to drop my thoughts just right now, I might succeed in doing that just for a split second. And then maybe I could repeat that and repeat it again.

Anthony: Yes, but don't do that in meditation, do it during various times of the day. In other words, that is a very good exercise. During the day, while you are about your business, every now and then stop, drop your thoughts. Stop it right there and then. When you see thoughts come in you say, "I don't want you. Out." That is very good. But not in meditation. In meditation it has to be persistent.

The nice thing about doing that exercise is that after a while you could learn that every time you get a negative thought you can drop it. When some negative thought—a thought of hate or dislike or animosity—comes up, you drop it right then and there. Every time you think about it, stop! But not during meditation. During meditation the whole thing is to learn to be able to persist for a half hour, forty minutes.

S: It resembles some advice I heard about how to stop smoking. Don't ever think, I will never smoke again, of the years ahead trying not to smoke. Just think, I won't take the next cigarette.

Anthony: Yes, it is a good technique. Don't think too far ahead. You know, like when you start working and you are twenty-five years old and you say, "Gee, I have another forty years before I retire." You will get tired the next day. One day at a time is enough.

But during the actual period of meditation you should try to acquire the ability so that eventually the time will come when after ten minutes or so you can get into a very concentrated state and stay like that for half an hour.

S: Would you say more about the exercise of watching your thoughts in meditation? Could you watch in different ways?

Anthony: Well, you could look at it like a child looks at it. Every time a thought comes, "Ooh!" Or you could watch it like a coach and say, "You are not properly dressed. You have the wrong words on you." Or you could look at it like a participator and say, "Hmmm." Or you could do the exercise.

You are supposed to be doing the exercise, right? When the thought comes, you don't care how it is dressed or how you are going to look at it. All you are going to do . . . you have this big sword in your hand. And as soon as a thought comes, off with the head. No thoughts here. That is all you have to do. You don't have to sit there and look at the picture. You don't have to say, look at that stupid thought, the wrong words, the wrong phrasing, it doesn't even have a comma.

> No matter how limited the period available may be, whether five or fifty minutes, approach it with the deliberate induced feeling of complete leisureliness. Bring no attitude of haste into the work, or it will thwart your efforts from the start. *(Perspectives, p. 39)*

Anthony: Never sit down with anxiety or haste. Always approach it slowly, gracefully. Don't run and say, "I've got to sit down now . . ." Don't do that.

S: What about the will? Sometimes when I try to use a lot of will in meditation, I worry that I might be strengthening my aggressiveness in some way.

Anthony: That is all right. You have no choice but to use the will. A lot of the training in the beginning is a purgation of the will. It is really how you apply it that matters. In meditation you have to use your will to some extent. It can't be helped.

S: It is hard to be a very nice person and then use all this will at the same time.

Anthony: It is all right to be a nice person to others, not to yourself.

S: But to the higher principle I have to be nice.

Anthony: Yes, but to the lower principle, don't be nice. You give him commands: "You are going to concentrate."

> The ancient manuals of yoga say that meditation is not to be attempted where the people around are wicked, when the body is tired or sick, or when the mind is unhappy and depressed. The reason for these prohibitions is simply that these undesirable conditions will render the practice of meditation much more difficult and hence much more likely to end in failure. *(V4, 4:2.106)*

Anthony: It is not wise to meditate when you are sick. It is more likely that you will fail than succeed.

S: Unhappy?

Anthony: Well, in a depressed state of mind very often what happens is that you exaggerate the depression, you magnify it. Now, what are you going to do, get depressed every day so you won't have to meditate? [laughter]

S: Couldn't you try to overcome the depression or aggression by replacing the feeling of aggression with a meditative feeling?

Anthony: Well, you are welcome to try. But I think most people would find out that if they are really upset about something when they sit down to meditate, they will be meditating about what they are upset about.

S: You could be depressed for days.

Anthony: Yes, if we are talking about a depression we are not talking about a passing moment. Say, for example, someone loses someone that they love, and they feel depressed. It is better not to meditate then. Wait a while. Don't get rid of your common sense.

Every good quality of character becomes a safeguard to his travels in this mysterious realm of meditation. *(V4, 4:1.45)*

Anthony: Yes, that of course we spoke about. It is important that you remember that morality, ethics, is a real safeguard. It is the only protection we really have. When a man is faced with a situation where he can choose to do something which is immoral and materially gain by it, the only protection he has is the kind of person he is, the kind of character he is. That is the only protection you have. In the same way, when you are meditating you sometimes might get a tempting vision coming through. If you have learned to have respect for these moral principles, you will ignore that temptation, you just won't pay attention to it. Something that happens with most of us when we start meditating, very often an impulse arises, an erotic impulse, a sexual impulse, a fantasy, and we look at it, we are strangled. But if you recognize the nature of what that is, you say, "I know. No! Out!" Because you have already learned that this is the kind of life you want to live. So morality is really the ultimate protection that we have.

S: But when you are weak for some reason, physically weak, doesn't that make it much more difficult to stop this thought?

Anthony: Yes, that is true. Remember when they told Gandhi that his wife had to eat beef soup, and he said, "No, she will not eat beef soup." They said she would die. He said, "No, she is not going to eat beef soup." You'll see that many of these people have certain rules that they live by. And if someone tells them, "If you don't alter it, this will happen," they say, "No, this doesn't change." PB was very strict about that. When he was told he had to take medicine that contained an animal product, he said, "No. If I can't get synthetic, I won't take it." And here you are talking about the life and death of the man. When I came out of my heart attack, the doctor said, "I want you to have some chicken soup." I said, "No, no, no, doctor, don't tell me what to eat." There are some things that apply all the time. You say, "These are the principles I am going to live by," and you stick to them. It is hard, sure, and very often we break down. But little by little we build certain ideals that we want to live by, and we want to hold on to them. You know, like the British say, "Every man has his price." And they tried to bribe Gandhi; it didn't work. You can't buy some people, no matter what you give them. They have achieved a level where that is their morality and that is the way they live. So little by little we have to imitate the life of the greater.

S: *But we can't just imitate, we have to come to that point where we really realize that that is the only way.*

Anthony: It has to be your own inward realization. Sure. You say it is good to be honest. Well, you have to come to that of your own free will. It is not something that comes easily, because it is our very nature to see if we can get something for nothing, any time and every time. And little by little we have to learn that there are certain ways of living that we have to try to live. If you read the lives of many of the great men, saints, heroes, they have ideals and they live by those ideals. You can't bribe them.

S: *But isn't it that they have gone through so many hard times that they truly realize in their hearts that that's the only way? I mean, you could talk to some people about how reasonable something is but they couldn't do it because they haven't gotten the understanding from their own experience. That's why so few people are doing these things—they haven't gone through that kind of experience.*

Anthony: Yes, there are many ways that we'll learn. That is why one of the greatest things that could happen to Western society would be if it could accept what the Easterners call the law of karma and what Jesus spoke about when he said, "As you sow, you shall reap." And the Buddha said, "You are the heir to the deeds that you perform." Everything you think, everything you do, everything you say, all these things will come back in one fashion or another. What you give out, you are going to get back. But we don't believe that it applies in the mental realm. We do believe it applies to the physical realm. No one denies that the law of cause and effect works in the physical realm, but they don't think it works in the mental realm—in the realm of feeling, thinking, and willing. They don't believe that at one time you did something and now it is being done to you—that there is a law of causality that applies in the mental realm.

Once you really begin to understand that, then you can much more understandingly accept the things that happen to you in life. You realize that if the law of karma, if the law of cause and effect really works, then what I have done has come back to me. If I have mistreated a child, then in turn I get mistreated. If I have loved a child, then in turn I get loved. There is no way around that. And that is why when we plant corn, we figure corn is going to come up. We don't figure potatoes are going to come up. We plant love in the world, then we will get it back. We plant hatred, we are going to get that too. That is very hard for people to accept.

S: People don't think the thoughts are so important, but they are even more important than words.

Anthony: But you see, that is because they have such an emphasis on the physical. They think that the physical is the reality and that our emotional and our mental life is not real. But the fact of the matter is that the emotional, the mental life is more real than the physical life. That is the one you are living in. That is why the Buddha said that we are the heirs to the deeds we perform.

The law of karma is something that has always been accepted in the East. They never doubted that. Emerson has a very beautiful essay, "On Compensation." You see, he didn't call it karma. He tried to sneak it in. He called it compensation. Emerson is quite a sage, an extraordinary man. Why do you think I tell you to read him? When PB was young, he read Emerson and recognized immediately that this man was a giant.

I try to learn from my mistakes. I don't always succeed. But I think we all have to accept the fact that we have to make mistakes and that we're only human beings. So don't worry about ethics too much, but do worry about this. Try to understand the principles, like the law of karma. Know in your heart the truth of what Jesus said, "As you sow, you shall reap." Once you know that in your heart, then you wouldn't want to hurt someone, because you know that it's going to come back to you. If the situation arises where you get angry and you're about to hurt someone, you think about it, you say, "No, I'm not going to do it." You have to apply it. And we're all in that situation. You know, very often people ask me for advice and I have to refuse. I don't want to give them advice. I want them to think it out for themselves. If they make a mistake, fine, and if they do the right thing, that's fine too.

The important thing is to learn the principles and then you will find out how to apply them. And you will see that if you can develop concentration, when you're in a situation that demands an immediate answer, all you have to do is pause, get still for one minute, and very often you'll know what to do. But very often you won't. There are no guarantees. None. Life is always full of surprises. Always. There's always one around waiting for you.

S: What can you do if you meet a person who is really negative?

Anthony: Run!

S: But if you feel you have to stay?

Anthony: Don't react.

S: Is that the only thing you could do?

Anthony: That is everything. Don't react.

S: You mean, you see the feelings coming out, but you don't do anything?

Anthony: If the feelings come up, it is too late, it is over. You have done it. Look, it is the same thing as with the Hua T'ou exercise. Once the thought comes into your mind, it becomes your state of consciousness. And you have to prevent the thought from doing that. That is why an exercise like the Hua T'ou is so good. Because before you could react, you have already cut the thought out. So in any situation like this, I immediately cut off any possibility of reacting by stopping the thought.

S: So you're not listening to the person?

Anthony: I'm listening to the person.

S: But you don't see his or her feelings? You cut them off?

Anthony: No, I'm not saying that. He talks. He tells me what is going on and this, that, and the other thing. All I am concerned about is that I do not react. And that means that I prevent any thoughts from arising within me that are reactive to what he is saying.

Paul: You have to observe without any reaction on your part.

S: Yes, but as soon as you see the feeling you are reacting.

Paul: No, then you haven't experienced your meditation exercise yet. You don't know what the Hua T'ou exercise is yet. That is what you want to employ. You do that exercise right then and there.

Anthony: If you have practiced the Hua T'ou exercise, you know immediately what I mean. Think of it like this: think of a pot of water and the water is starting to boil. When the heat reaches a certain point, a bubble comes up. At that moment where the heat reaches a certain point and the water starts to become a bubble, you have to prevent it. You can't let it become a bubble. In the same way when someone is speaking to me, I am listening to him, but at the same time I have the sword in my hand to make sure that no thought comes into my mind. If a thought comes into my mind, it will be in response and reaction to what he is saying. If that thought comes into my mind and takes possession of my mind, then I will be in the same place he is. I have to stop it before it happens. I can be listening, I can be observant, I can understand what he is saying, but I am preventing any reaction on my part.

That is one of the valuable things about the Hua T'ou exercise. When you do it you develop a kind of feeling, a sixth sense about when a thought is about to arise. You can almost feel it tiptoeing in, coming in a little. You can almost see it. Boom, you stop it right then and there. Because if you don't, it becomes your conscious state for that moment. Then the next thought comes in, becomes your conscious state. It is what we spoke about as the vasanas. Once the vasanas explode, they become your state of consciousness, you are reacting to that situation. That's why the exercise is so good.

Do you remember the word-association test Jung used? He says "black" and then you say "white"; "man" and you say "woman"; "life" then you say "misery." The reaction comes right out. You have to cut the reaction off before it takes place. When the person says "black," the instinctual response is to say "white." You have to cut it off before it happens. That means you have to be inwardly alert. It's as if one of your eyes is turned in, looking in, and the other one is turned out, looking out. In the beginning it is hard but after a while you learn to do it.

S: *Sometimes you say that we have to see the source of the thought. But you mean only the source in yourself and not the source of another person's reaction, right?*

Anthony: In this case, I am interested in myself—to prevent a reaction. Sometimes you could see what is going on in the other person. You could perceive it very clearly. But that is assuming that your mind is clear. And it is easier to see what is going on in the other person if you are not reacting to him.

To acquire a consciousness that could remain impersonal while it is in personal activity is not an easy thing, but once you get the knack of it you start doing it more and more. It is very good. You begin to live with a little peace. As you are now, if you are walking along the street and meet someone who doesn't like you and he insults you, then you go home and for a half hour you are in a state of agitation. But if you can cut it off right then and there . . . no bother. No bother.

S: Isn't there a difference between a thought and a thought with a feeling added to it? Isn't it possible to have pure thought that stays neutral?

Anthony: The very nature of vasanas, or instinctual responses, is that they are emotionally laden. That is their very nature. There is no such thing as having an instinctual response that isn't emotionally toned. I don't know what you are talking about.

S: Is there such a thing as a thought without a feeling on top of it?

Anthony: Yes, but then we are not talking about instinctual responses, vasanas, habit traces, memory traces. Yes, you can have thoughts that are neutral. But what we are talking about is something very deadly. A man comes over, he is full of hate. And the tendency is for your lower self to respond exactly like that and be an animal like him. If you want to be a human being, you have to learn how to stop that. If he wants to go on doing it, that is his business. My business is, I have to stop it. And that is one of the techniques that can be used.

A person can come over to me and threaten me, but now my instinctual reaction has been cut off. All I can feel is pity for him. I don't know if he will succeed in hurting me or not. I am not discussing that. I am just saying that I have trained myself not to react that way and all I can feel for him is pity or compassion, and that probably has saved me a lot of pain.

The Buddhist monks, for instance, put themselves through a course of training to respond always with a feeling of kindliness towards anyone, regardless of who that person is and what that person does. When they come out of meditation, whether they are just beginners or very advanced monks, the last thing they do is to send out compassion to the east, to the north, to the west, to the south. This is something that they learned, and they trained themselves to be this way.

But what we have been talking about is just ordinary common

sense. Every psychologist says, "If you take a rat and you do this, he will do that." Sure, he is a rat, he is not a human being. A human being is supposed to know better and is supposed to act better.

I am simply pointing out that you could take an exercise that you have practiced in meditation and apply what you learned in that meditation exercise directly to your life. In applying this discipline that you have acquired, you can even re-educate your instincts. Instead of a response of hostility, a response of compassion or of kindness could take place. You can directly apply what you learn in meditation to everyday living and you can start molding your character to a higher ideal.

> A vital point that is often overlooked through ignorance is the proper re-adjustment to ordinary routine activities just after each time a meditation exercise is successfully practised or an intuition-withdrawal is genuinely felt. The student should try to carry over into the outer life as much as he can of the delicately relaxed and serenely detached feeling that he got during those vivid experiences of the inner life. The passage from one state to another must be made with care, and slowly; for if it is not, some of the benefits gained will be lost altogether and some of the fruits will be crushed or mangled. It is the work done in the beginning of this after-period that is creative of visible progress and causative for demonstrable results. *(V4, 4:2.415)*

Anthony: Do you follow that? You can do some of your best work right after meditation. Some of your most creative work, creative ideas, can arise after you come out of being silent. If the stillness or the peace is very deep, then usually the first thoughts you have when you come out are very important. You don't try to think them, but the thoughts that arise naturally are very important when you come out of a deep trance.

S: When inspiration comes to an artist, what state of mind is he in?

Anthony: Usually the artist has experienced a period where he is very introverted, thinking about the matter at hand. When he gets extremely quiet, then as he is coming out of that, that's when he gets the inspiration. It is not when the mind is still that he gets the inspiration. Because then it is still, it is quiet. But upon coming out—or let's say there is a shift of attention from an inner to an outer—it is at that time that he will get inspired. Having plunged the mind into deeper waters, then when he comes out it brings some of that with it and illuminates the difficulties that the egotistical intellect was working with. It actually sheds light on it. It is when you're coming out, when you are shifting attention from the inner to the outer, that an illuminating thought, an inspiration, a creative idea can happen.

That is why even when you get up from deep sleep it is a good idea not to jump up out of bed and get going, but to get up slowly, give yourself a minute. Just see what the mind is bringing to you. Keep it very still, see what the thoughts are then—assuming that the night before you didn't go to see a horror movie or you didn't go get drunk or something! I'm assuming that the night before was meaningful. I make a point of when I go to sleep—if I am not going to do an exercise—I try to go to sleep with things that are worthwhile, a noble thought or some thought that is lovely and holy. I try to fall asleep with that. I try not to bring anxieties or my problems into my sleep. And when I wake up in the morning, the first thing I try to do after my mind starts working—after a couple of minutes—I direct my attention to my teacher. But each one has to find what he personally considers holy and meaningful and noble and think about that before starting the day. Or think about your soul for a couple of minutes and then start your day. I do that both before I go to sleep and when I wake up.

Often I do practice an exercise when I go to sleep at night and so I have to wait for the results in the morning. But, sometimes I don't do an exercise and simply try to fall asleep with a quiet mind. Generally I try to fall asleep with my mind thinking about something very specific in relation to the quest, the path, philosophy, something like that. I don't like my mind to wander around.

S: *When I try to meditate and get to the point when I feel a little peace of mind, then I sometimes get inspiration for writing poetry, and so on. That makes it hard for me to drop my thoughts, because at times like that there may be something valuable in the thoughts, some glimmers of truth coming out. I wonder how to choose, how to discriminate thought from thought? Maybe I could drop these thoughts and they would come back, but I'm afraid of losing them.*

Anthony: Of course you want to baby these nice little thoughts. "This is *my* thought. Come here, sweetheart!" Don't you understand what I have been saying? When you sit down to meditate you have to be ruthless, actually ruthless. Because your ego will start playing on the lyre and you'll say, "Oh, I hear such divine music, I'll forget about meditation today. Let me hear more." Or an angel will come by and say, "Look at me, I am flying." When you sit down to meditate, come hell or come high water, that is all you are going to do.

Otherwise, the thoughts will come by and say, "Look how pretty I am." I could almost call that a sickness. And in Zen literature they do call that, at a certain stage, the Zen sickness. A lot of the Zen monks would meditate and then start writing verses endlessly; that is the Zen sickness. You have to try to understand. If you recognize the value of meditation, if you penetrate somewhat into the meaning of what this could get for you, then when you sit down to meditate there is only one thing to do and that is to meditate. Any deviation after a while becomes a habit, and after a while the habit gets strong. Any time you are going to sit down, some interruption is going to come, you can rest assured. And if you don't cut it right off in the beginning, it'll go on and on and on for years and years. There is no end to it.

The inspirations will come to you, don't worry. If they come to you when you're meditating, they'll come to you later on as well.

S: Being compassionate, or thinking noble thoughts—this has its value in itself, but it's not meditation, is it?

Anthony: It's not meditation. And you have to remember that meditation also has a value, which if ever you should pursue it to the end, would make a galaxy a terrestrial incident in your consciousness. Do you understand? The whole of the galaxy would be like a terrestrial incident in your consciousness if you could pursue meditation to the end. Every event that you might look up to—you know, the fulfillment of any ambition, whether as an artist or world-conqueror or whatever—is absolute trivia in comparison to that. If you can pursue it far enough.

And it's also a habit that gets stronger once you establish it. In the next reincarnation you just automatically meditate and think it's the natural thing to do, and then in the next incarnation it builds up, it gets momentum, becomes more and more powerful in you. The power of these great men, whether it's the Buddha or anyone of this ilk, comes from their ability to contemplate.

S: You could say the reverse, also. If you learn to meditate, then when you want to write or do art work, that ability to meditate will help to bring the inspiration out while you're working, right?

Anthony: Sure, and also at odd times of the day. Very often, at haphazard times, you will get inspired ideas coming in and you can write them down. PB was like that all the time.

S: But for that you also need some peaceful moments.

S: But if you learn to meditate, you will get those moments. When you start to work you will get concentrated and peaceful, and it will come at the right time.

Anthony: That was why I thought that the best we could do in the time I was here was to concentrate on mentalism and meditation. I would like to get into more things, but if I can get across the sublime value of meditation and the perspective of mentalism, then it will open the door and from there on you can go on your own.

But these two things have to be understood. First, the nature of the world and of myself is of an idea. We are basically the nature of mind. Second, we are that mind.

Now how do I get to prove, in my own experience, that I AM, that the I AM or the greater consciousness includes within itself the whole World-Idea? I have to practice meditation in order to get the experimental proof that this is so. The other way is still theory. Until you can experience the Witness-I yourself, until you can actually experience that your consciousness includes everything, until you can actually experience the transformation of your being into thought, this is all theory.

You could talk to me about the great idea you have for your next book, and I'd say, yes, it's valuable, it's important, whatever, but not in comparison to once you say, "I'm going to start meditating." Then you have to be honest with yourself: *keep your appointment—meditate!* You have just as much an obligation to find your spiritual self as you have to society and other people. We all have an obligation to our own higher self.

They talk a lot about repression. Now, it may sound strange to you, but I think the trouble with the world today is the fact of spiritual repression. People have repressed the desire to find their own spirit, and now they speak about sexual repression, repression of aggression, this repression, that repression. The only repression I know that people are suffering from is *spiritual* repression, denying the spirit within themselves. You can call it the Christ within you, you can call it the Soul, the God, whatever. But this is what they have been denying for the past fifty years, with vehemence!

> It is a blessed purpose of this daily meditation to regain inner contact with the higher mind. With a successful result, there is a temporary disappearance of disagreeable or irritated moods, emotional hurts, or mental anxieties. *(V4, 4:1.294)*

Anthony: That's very poignant, because a lot of times when you go into meditation and get very deep into the stillness, you get very quiet. And I've seen something happen in my case and that of a few others whom I know. Sometimes when you come out of that stillness, there's a scene brought back into your life, something that happened to you which has tragic or sorrowful overtones. Let's say you hurt someone or someone hurt you, it doesn't matter. When you come out, there's a feeling of resignation and forgiveness. You actually forgive yourself. The rebellion is over, you feel there's no need to rebel any more against God. It just falls away. And then that incident that was brought up to mind melts away, just melts away. And it leaves you alone. From then on it doesn't bother you any more.

S: You mean right after meditation?

Anthony: Yes. Right after you've come out of it, you sometimes catch this scene. It's part of your own psyche that's come to the surface.

> As he sinks deeper after many relapses towards the undivided mind, as he calls on all the powers of his will and concentration to keep within focus the inner work of this spiritual exercise, he may get a sense of leading, of being directed by something within. *(V15, 23:7.201)*

Anthony: That's very pronounced. Let's say you're meditating, you're saying, *Aum bitsu, Aum bitsu, Aum bitsu.* You get very deeply into the mantra, and you feel something pulling you down into your heart. Then you drop everything you're doing and you follow the lead. Let it lead you. That's a guidance from within: the soul is telling you from within, "Follow me, come with me." Then you have to drop everything and just follow it.

So very often in meditation you can get intuitive guidance, as though someone is telling you what to do. Some mystics get so deep into these matters that their soul practically talks to them in meditation. They actually *hear* an audible voice telling them what to do. It's a phenomenon I mentioned before which is known as the Interior Word. It actually guides your life. And sometimes that might go on for a year or two. It doesn't go on and on and on, but for a period of time it actually takes over and tells you how to live, what to do. It nourishes your growth.

> An intuition comes into the mind suddenly. But so does an impulse. Therefore it is not enough to take this mark alone to identify it. It is strong; so is an impulse. It is clear; so is an impulse. To separate the deceptive appearance from the genuine reality of an intuition, look for the trail of assurance, relief, and peace to follow in its wake. *(V14, 22:1.216)*

Anthony: If you've accepted its guidance, there is assurance, relief, and peace.

S: How do I know when I know?

Anthony: Well, again, it isn't that you will know. He is trying to point out here that you could tell you had a genuine intuition if upon observing the intuition and following its dictates there comes, so to speak, the assurance, the certainty, and the peace. And if these things aren't there, then it wasn't an intuition to begin with.

It's not a simple thing. The word has been used to the point where everyone thinks they know what an intuition is, and most of us probably have had some experience with intuition. But there is a very definite way of cultivating the intuition, and one of the prerequisites is that the mind be kept somewhat still. Because it's only in the stillness of the mind that an intuition can arise.

Here's another one on intuition.

> Intuition will not mislead you but your conscious mentality, which is its receiving agent, may do so. For our consciousness may partially deviate from its message, or even wholly pervert it, in giving deliverance to exaggerations or extravagances, impossibilities or delusions, thus filling you with useless hopes or groundless fears. Consequently, at the very time when you suppose that you are being infallibly guided by intuition you may in fact be strongly guided by pseudo-intuition—which is something quite different. You may believe that you are honouring higher guidance when actually you are dishonouring it. The situation is therefore much less simple and much more complex than most people know. To get intuitive direction when, for example, two or more conflicting courses of action confront you is not so easy as it seems and less easy still during a time of trouble. For during such a time you will naturally catch at anything already knowingly or unknowingly

predetermined by some complex to be the best way out of it. The very desire for a particular thing, event, or action may put a pseudo-intuition into your mind. If you want to be wary of this you should seek corroboration from other sources and especially from right reason. Again, the first thought which enters your consciousness after you have decided to seek such direction and have committed your affair to the deeper mind, is not necessarily an authentic intuition. Nor is the second thought such a one, nor the third, and so on. If the impression is to be rightly received, it must be patiently received, and that quite often means that you must sleep on it, and sleep on it perhaps for several days, sometimes weeks. The trustworthy intuition is really there during all this time but the obstacles to knowing it are also there in yourself. Do not, therefore, lose the inner direction through haste nor set up a stone image to be worshipped by mistake in its place. Nor is it enough to say that intuitive truths are self-evident ones. What appeared to be self-evident to you twenty years ago may now appear self-delusive to you. Edit your intuitions with your reason. *(V14, 22:1.193)*

Anthony: So it's quite a complicated affair.

TEN
Developing a Philosophic Perspective

S: Do you have any advice for us on how to conduct our studies together as a group?

Anthony: I think the most important thing is complete concentration on the ideas. But that requires that, when you are about to talk in a group discussion, you should introspect into yourself and see that you are concerned with the idea specifically under discussion. If there's any doubt, then you should ruthlessly restrain yourself. Now it's a hard thing to do, but it can be done. Let the ideas be the all-important thing, and try to understand to the best of your ability what is being read or discussed. Another thing, of course, is that there must be a certain sympathetic kindness, to try to understand what the other person is saying. That's important. That has to be there.

A third thing that may at times be necessary is to have some kind of procedure. If people are interrupting one another, for example, make a rule: you have to raise your hand, and you'll be called on, and then you can talk.

Sometimes it's useful for a person to take a very specific assignment: he has to do it, he has to present it, he has to get all the work ready. And then the next week someone else does it, and this way it goes around. Very often, when a person is called upon to to write up a couple of pages or present his understanding of something, he works much harder and tries to understand it for himself. He knows that if he can understand it for himself, then he can deliver it, but if he doesn't understand it himself it's going to be a bad delivery. Those things are very useful.

Another thing that is useful is to spend ten or fifteen minutes in quiet prayer, asking for guidance and help before you start a serious discussion. That's always very good. I don't like to undertake any really serious study unless I spend five minutes quietly and ask to be guided, and then I start.

S: Do you think it is a good idea to take turns reading and explaining in your own words what is read?

Anthony: Yes. We often do that with Plotinus. Read one paragraph, or one tractate, and explain it. Then the next person reads the next paragraph or tractate and explains it. In the beginning it's difficult because we have a tendency to just repeat the words in the text, but very often what happens is that a person little by little begins to understand it well enough to say it in his own words. When you start saying things in your own words, then you've gotten it. If you can't say it in your own words, then either you're giving me back my words that you memorized or, the next thing, which is subtler, you memorized my understanding and now you're giving that back to me. So very often I have to break through that. It's not yours yet. I know you're using these words with some understanding, but until you've put it into your own words with your own peculiarities, it's not yours yet. So it's always a nice thing to put it in your own words.

S: Sometimes we can't understand these writers.

Anthony: There will be times when something cannot be understood. There will be those times. Then you put it aside, go back to it another time. Work with the ones that you feel you have a grasp of, that you have some understanding of, that your inner being responds to. Let's say you're reading a page. You read the first paragraph, and it doesn't make sense. Then you read the second paragraph, and something in you lights up. Stay there, go over that, bring it out, then continue. But first stay there as long as it's necessary. Don't feel any compulsion to finish a page, or a chapter. Don't work that way. What you're trying to acquire is understanding and meaning. And there's no organized systematic approach like, "Today I'm going to get eighteen units of meaning, tomorrow I'm going to get eighteen units." It doesn't work like that. You know, you plant a tree and you keep watering it; the sun shines and it grows its own way. You can't determine it.

But there's something that I think is noticeable when you are studying some of these difficult texts. You will see that parts of it seem opaque, you can't make any sense out of them; and then there's a part where a flash of light comes, or something in you responds. Stay with it, like when you eat an orange and you keep sucking all the juice until it's dry as a bone. You have to do the same with the passage. And then go on to the next one, then the next one. Later you go back and start all over again. I know this from experience, because we had to do this with Plotinus. At first you can understand only so much. If I try to bring in more, then you won't follow. So we just keep going. Then a year later we go back, we're doing it again. Now, all of a sudden you understand those things. You wonder, how come? Well, during that time your understanding was growing, if you kept doing it. The response I'm referring to is not something that comes from your head. It comes from your heart. Can you tell the difference? If it comes from the inner being, if it comes from your heart, it's there! Then it's a question of formulating it, verbalizing it, articulating it. But it's there.

S: But it can be very hard?

Anthony: Hey, look, when you were born, they didn't give you a ticket with a list of guarantees! Of course it's hard. Why do you think so few people are interested in these matters? They can go and do the most complicated computations if they know they're going to make money, but what's this going to get them? So their ego isn't invested in this. Most of the time you have to do this without ego investment. The ego says, "Hey, there's nothing in here for me. As a matter of fact, this is *definitely* not for me. Let's get out of it!"

If I could exaggerate the example: you go to college and you're working for an electronics or an engineering degree or something. You work real hard, and your ego is right alongside saying, "Good, good, let's do it, let's do it. Get a good job, then we'll make $60,000 a year and we can have a good time!" But when you're reading a tractate by Plotinus on the Intellectual Principle, the ego isn't going to come over and say, "Let's do it." The ego is going to say, "What's the matter with you? You sick? You crazy? What are you doing this for?" So you're not going to get help from your ego. Half the time you'll be doing it out of sheer soul-power. There's something in you that wants to know, and that something is what's driving you to do it. In the beginning, of course, there's a certain amount of ego. You want to show the other guy you know as much as he does, or more, and all that. But that doesn't last too long.

S: Often when there is a question, then the egos come in and there is a battle. I'd like to know how to avoid that.

Anthony: The thing to remember is that sincerity is the foundation for real personality. If I read a passage, I have to be sincere and say I do understand it or I don't. If you don't understand it, then drop away from the discussion. If everyone actually tries to do this, you'll see that very seldom will everybody know what the passage means. Sometimes this person, sometimes that person will understand it. But it's very seldom that all ten or twelve or twenty or forty will know what the passage means. Fundamentally, you need some kind of psychological understanding to try to see the tricks that the ego is playing and try to weed them out from the value of the ideas. All we can do is to try to be a little courteous towards ourselves and towards others and recognize that unless we are a little compassionate, the ego can take over and turn a discussion into a tennis match. In no way should it be undertaken in a competitive way—never.

I have very often experienced this, for example, with reading a passage. I don't know what it means, and no one around me knows what it means. Then someone will say, "Well, do you think it might mean . . ." Boom! They got it! So keep in mind that there are no sages here, but read the passage until something in you lights up. Then you know there's some meaning there for you and work with that. Most of us think that we'd like to start at the beginning of the book and as we go along we understand everything we are reading. It doesn't work like that. Just because this is page two and this is page one, it doesn't mean that you understand page one because you're reading page two. You're reading page one, you don't know what it means, and two and three, but you suddenly know what page four means.

S: Would you say that intelligence or knowledge is more something that comes with the right attitude than something you are born with, like a talent?

Anthony: I wouldn't say more or less. I'd say certainly a right attitude is a necessary prerequisite to understanding many of these teachings. A right attitude is very important. But it's only one of the ingredients. There are many other things. What I'm trying to say is that no matter how we twist and turn, we're not going to put life into a formula—you know: H_2SO_4, ah! I've got everything right here in a formula. Well, you can't do that with life. It always has corners that are spilling, other corners that are ragged, some that are straight. It's not organized.

S: *Apart from studying PB, is there any order or system through which we could approach other philosophers or writers? Should we do it chronologically starting with the Greeks, or geographically starting from the East? Is there any way that you'd recommend?*

Anthony: I would say, plunge into PB immediately and directly and try to go through as much of it as you can. Do not be concerned now with trying to bring together and organize all the various different kinds of philosophies, because we have a limited amount of time. PB has done a great deal of that work. So, in reading him, you'll get acquainted with it—not in a scholarly sense, but in a meaningful way. The wisest thing to do would be to try to get as quickly to the heart of the matter as you can, in the minimal amount of time possible. And the most direct attack that I know of would be to read PB.

There are others, and I could mention some of the people who are worth reading, who would give you a spiritual impulse to get into yourself and find your way. There are quite a few of them and a list of such readings could easily be put together. But it isn't academic philosophy that I would like you to undertake to understand. It's something much more intimate. You could read Emerson, for example. There's the same kind of intimacy that springs up when you read him because he goes to the heart of the matter. I could also recommend a few other people who are very fine spiritual writers.

S: *Do you believe in the additive effect of knowledge, that it can help the world sort out its problems? Can we accumulate knowledge?*

Anthony: I've studied too much history to become optimistic overnight. The amazing thing is that today more than at any other time we have the possibility to make a decent life for ourselves, for humanity. Like a great big orphan, nobody wants to know about humanity. Everybody wants to be a leader, everybody wants to tell everybody else what to do. But everyone has to straighten out his own garden, never mind anyone else's. Each and every one of us has to become a better individual or there cannot be a better society. So I would say, plunge into PB, try to find spiritual literature that you find inspiring, let that impulse take you as far as it can.

That's what I'm doing now—reading PB's notes voraciously. I

read until I can't maintain my concentration any more, and then I back off. I do that every day. Even though I have read very widely, I've pushed all the other things aside. I'm just plunging into these notes, trying to understand. And occasionally I go back and reread some of PB's early books, all the way through.

S: What is the relation of time to the eternal standpoint?

Anthony: Generally the way time is understood is that insofar as the soul is producing or manifesting a world, concomitant with the manifestation of the world is the principle of time. So time is a principle which we correlate with the instantaneous, moment-by-moment production of manifestation which is taking place. But intrinsic in time is also the eternal; the eternal is right here in the now of the so-called present. So in that sense time is in eternity. You could certainly have the experience of eternity in a split second.

S: That sounds rather hopeful.

Anthony: Yes, I think it is hopeful for those of us who have seriously encountered some of the deeper teachings and inwardly have recognized some truth in them. That I consider our greatest hope.

S: So you are an optimist after all.

Anthony: There, yes. I lived through enough of my own agonizing pain to see even that pain and that evil turned to some account, to some good—providing that I tried to work with it, understand it, and meaningfully bring it out so that I didn't have to repeat the mistake anymore. So even in those things I found a spiritual value. The guidance that came through made them worthwhile. From the evil that I know I, like all others, have done, I've learned enough at least to recognize it for what it is, and not be deluded about it anymore.

There are two things that I might point out, because they are what really establishes a person on the path. Number one, he must get a glimpse. Number two, he must recognize what the ego is. When he understands that it is his great adversary, his great enemy, and he has had a glimpse of the soul, now he is on the quest. Prior to that, there may be emotional conviction, there may be intellectual understanding. But only after he goes through these two things—first, the glimpse, regardless of how momentary it is, the experience that there's something beautiful and worth striving for, which may come to him in a momentary flash or prolonged time, and second, the recognition that the beast is here in our hearts—now he is on the quest. Now he is a quester.

S: *It sounds very exciting the way you weave together and organize the different opinions of the various philosophic systems.*

Anthony: That was one of the things I was hopeful of doing when I began to recognize that I could illustrate, in terms of astrological symbolism, the point of view of almost any philosophic school. I could use the symbolism to show, for instance, where a Buddhist might be coming from, or where a Vedantist or a Nyaya logician might be coming from. The project I had in mind was to include and relate all these schools in a schema, because each one is enunciating a certain truth. I mean, you don't have a school of philosophy existing for a thousand years without its having some grain of truth in it.

When I was a young man, I started studying all the various schools of philosophy, whether East or West. At an early age I started reading Eastern literature. I was just as comfortable there as in Western literature. I felt that it was inconceivable that one sage like Shankara and another one like the Buddha could possibly disagree. It wasn't conceivable to me. And yet the fact remains that you have the great Buddhist tradition and you have the Advaitic tradition, and for a couple of thousand years they've been quarreling with each other. I found that very difficult to accept and understand. And within the Hindu tradition the Nyaya logicians are arguing against the Vedantists, within the Buddhist tradition the Yogacara school is arguing with the Madhyamikas, in the Western schools you have the rationalists against the empiricists and the empiricists against the idealists and the idealists against the rationalists, and on and on it goes. And I couldn't accept it. Something in me was saying that somewhere there is a totally comprehensive symbol that will explain the divergences and include everything that is fundamentally true in any one of these schools.

So I got the idea that I might find this in astrological symbolism because it is, in my opinion, the only schema that has initial premises comprehensive enough to include the variety of philosophic traditions. So I went to work on that, and it became really exciting. If I took the Platonic tradition, I could lay out their whole philosophic scheme in terms of the symbolism. If I took the Vedantic or Buddhist tradition, I could do the same thing. And with a school like the

Nyaya logicians in India, or a representative philosopher of the twentieth century, say Santayana, I could show their premises. I could show what parts of their premises are valid and why those parts would have a kind of eternal validity, but also what parts had to be disregarded. So in working with this symbolism I began to get a totally comprehensive view of how they interface with each other, how they interlock, how they interrelate, how they're all different facets of one incomprehensible truth. And the notion that there is any one tradition that could express it became unnecessary.

S: *Is it necessary for people to protect their own beliefs, to believe that theirs are the only valid ones?*

Anthony: A lot of that comes from the fact that individuals are genetically, ontogenetically, and phylogenetically constituted in such a way that the kind of philosophy they're going to believe in is predetermined. In astrology you can see the indefinite plurality of different views. You can see that they can all be subsumed under the astrological symbolism of 360 ideas, which can be combined in a variety of ways to organize or constitute personalities. The astrological chart consists of 360 degrees, each of which is an idea. Each of those ideas can be combined with others in a variety of ways by the ten planets, so the number of possible combinations is practically infinite.

Let me give an example with these three sticks. If I arrange the sticks one way, I get an A. If I arrange them another way, I get an N. As I arrange them in different ways, a new idea is always being produced through the different combinations. So it's not that you have just 360 ideas—it's 360 plus all the possible combinations the ten planets can make of them.

Whatever meanings you find in your life are indicated by these degrees, these ideas. The basic meaning of our lives is in terms of ideas, and when you understand mentalism you can see it *immediately* working in the chart. The higher part of the mind, which is distinct, looks upon those ideas as objects. In one person certain of these ideas are paramount, whereas another person is organized and constituted in such a way that different ideas are of paramount importance to him.

When you begin to see that, then you begin to see the validity in each person's view about reality as he understands it. But you also see the limitations, because no one is comprehensive enough to include the indefinite plurality of ideas which constitutes our mind's functioning. Once you begin to see that, there's a kind of feeling of joy and liberation—liberation because you don't have to believe that this is the only right idea or that's the only right idea. You see that all of them in their totality constitute different facets of the truth and that ultimate truth has to be realized for oneself personally. I saw this in terms of this passage I'll read next.

> . . . All the conflicting doctrines which have appeared in the past were not meaningless and not useless; they have played their part most usefully even where they seemed most contradictory. They were really in collaboration, not in opposition. We need not disdain to illustrate the highest abstract principles by the homeliest concrete anecdotes. . . . A full view of the universe now replaces all the partial views which were alone available before and which embodied merely single phases of the discovery of Truth. Thus the analytic movement which uncovered the various pieces of this world puzzle must now yield to a synthetic process of putting them together in a final united pattern . . . *(V8, 12:2.186 and Perspectives, p. 147)*

Anthony: That's what I had in mind trying to do. To put all these pieces into a pattern and show how to a certain extent they are all valid and also at the same time how they're limited. To show in one way how they're complementary and in another way how they're in opposition.

The nice thing is that it has such a liberating effect. When you see the value in the premises that the Vedantists have and then you see the value in the premises that the Buddhists have, you're free from their conflict. Here's an example. The Vedantists speak about the self-identity, the identity of the knower. They say it must be so, otherwise we couldn't account for the continuity of knowledge and be able to validate it. The Buddhists say no, the world is changing instant by instant, there is no identity of an "I"—there could be a continuity but no identity.

Now if we want to understand another perspective, we could take the point of view of Plotinus, or better still we could use an example from one of the discussions Ramana Maharshi gave. Think of how movies are projected. We have the reel with the film in it, and every instant there's a new still being projected on the screen. Now within each picture that's being projected you could take the position of the

Buddhists. The Buddhists are saying, "Look, here is one picture, then the next picture, then the next picture. Within those discrete pictures, where are you going to find a self-identical 'I'? Still 'A' is different from still 'B,' still 'B' is different from still 'C,' and so on. So where's this 'I' that you are talking about, that is self-identical throughout?" But the Vedantist could come along and say, "Each picture is being illuminated by the light which is in the projector, and it is this light which is always self-identical and the same regardless of which picture is being projected." So one picture can follow after another, and there is constant change; the World-Idea is changing every moment in time. But also, the light that illuminates that remains self-identical. Well, if that's true then both points of view are true. You have to see that if you take the premise of the Buddhist that the World-Idea is in a state of high vibratory oscillation, changing from instant to instant, then from that point of view there is no identity. But if you take the point of view that you are the light in the projection which is always shining regardless of what film is being played out, then there is an "I" which is identical with itself. So then, both points of view are true. Well, then why can't you hold on to the two of them? The two views together perfectly explain everything.

PB and Plotinus both explain it that way. On one hand there is the soul or the mind which is self-identical, always remaining what it is. On the other hand there is the content, the World-Idea which is flashing into the soul from instant to instant. Now the soul tends to identify with the psycho-somatic organism, or a body which the World-Idea contains within itself, and when that soul or mind is identified with that psycho-somatic entity it takes itself to be an "I." But the Buddhists would say, how could you be an "I" because from instant to instant you are not the same, so they will be right in pointing out that *this* has no "I." But the Buddhists will be wrong, however, if they insist that there is change without a consciousness which doesn't change but is aware of change. So the two points of view are not really in opposition, they're complementary.

S: Doesn't the Vedantic position include the Buddhist position?

Anthony: The Advaita Vedantist says that the world is an illusion, so how could his include the Buddhist position? From the Advaita point of view the world doesn't even exist.

S: Don't they use a similar explanation as PB is using and say that the world exists but it is not real?

Anthony: Only the highest level of the Indian philosophers think that way. The majority of the Advaita texts insist that the world is an illusion, doesn't exist, so you don't even have to bother with it. They insist that the only thing that is, is this pure light of consciousness. And they'll hammer on that. But again, from one point of view there is a soul which is self-identical, and from another point of view, there is the World-Idea, which is coming into the soul, oscillating at a vibratory rate that's incredible. We could say that these two together bring about, so to speak, the existence of the soul in the world. The soul can experience the sensible world only by projecting that light that it has into that sensible body, and now it becomes part of that world which is in constant vibratory activity. So if you put these two ideas together, they make perfect sense. If you insist on one or the other as being the ultimate truth, it would be like insisting on telling only half the story.

Plotinus works with both sides. He speaks about the Intellectual Principle as a second hypostasis and the Soul as a third hypostasis and both of these are authentic and real. If you were to ask Plotinus, "Which is real, the world that is appearing—that is, the World-Idea—or the consciousness which is enmeshed in the appearance?" he would say that they are both real. The World-Idea has a reality; it's being projected by the Intellectual Principle and nobody is going to abolish it. But at the same time the soul is also real. It's enmeshed in that process, it's part of what's evolved in that World-Idea, and it's learning from it. So these two principles, the Intellectual Principle and the Soul, come together and you have a manifestation of the World-Idea. The sensible world is an instantiation of the World Idea. And the soul of an individual, the mind of an individual, gets enmeshed in the products of that World-Idea, gets caught up in them, and is now subject to "fate."

So the point I'm getting at is that both these positions are necessary in order to understand philosophy completely. If you take sides, you end up in a lot of trouble. And I found out, over and over again, that any time we find a philosophic school that has endured over a long period of time, there's some truth in it. It can't be all wrong. It can't be all right, but it can't be all wrong. So you have to find out what's worthwhile and bring it out. And do the same with all the others. It's like being a bee—you know, you go around from flower to flower, you take the honey and let the rest go.

S: I'm trying to think about what mentalism means in our daily life. How creative are our thoughts? They seem to have a lot of power to create circumstances. How much of our experience are we ourselves responsible for?

Anthony: I don't know if I could possibly come up with an answer as to how much. I know it's enough. I know that the thoughts that we think are the basic formulators of our destiny. The evil that's in us, in our mind, the thoughts that men hold, have already determined what our future is. The war is already going on in a different realm of existence. It's in the realm of thought, so it has a lot to do with what we think. When you think of one person hating, you don't think it's much. But when five billion people hate one another, it can be really catastrophic.

As far as I understand we are responsible for the thoughts we have, and we are responsible to a very large extent. I think PB says something in *The Wisdom of the Overself* to the effect that once you become self-conscious, reflectively self-conscious, you are responsible for the things that you think. Now, those that are not self-conscious, not reflectively self-conscious, they're not responsible. General karma is taking over and is directing or guiding them. But once you start becoming an individual, from that time on you are responsible. So we as individuals are responsible for our thoughts. If you have a negative thought, you have permitted it to come in, to work its way out, and the permission that you grant it is already acquiescence on your part. So we're responsible. Now, how much? I don't know. But it's more than enough.

S: It can have such power to create external situations, that you can't possibly see that you could have been the cause.

Anthony: But you know, that's a trick. That's a self-deception that sooner or later is not going to work any more. Right now because of our ignorance of epistemology and metaphysics we can say, "I don't see the connection between my thoughts and the environment that I'm living in." You can do that for a while. But after a while, when you start studying these things a little bit and you try to get rid of the ignorance that you always surround yourself with, you begin to see a direct correlation between what you think, the things you think about, and the kind of environment you're living in, the kind of situations that arise, the people and all that. Sooner or later, you begin to see that and it gets harder and harder to say, "It's not my thinking." When you come to the recognition, when reason absolutely shows you that all that you experience is a manifestation of your mind, you cannot so easily say to yourself, "Well I know that I did not produce the world that I am perceiving." You're aware that there's another point of view which says, "No, you have to investigate this, you have to go deeper into what your mind is doing." And the refusal to do so is cowardice on our part, a refusal to be intellectually honest.

So what we think, how we think, the depth of thinking that we engage in, does create our environment, though in the beginning we can't see how it is that our mental processes are doing it. The whole psychological and psychoanalytical movement has shown conclusively that just because you're not consciously aware of something doesn't mean you didn't think it. And they've proven that over and over again. So when a man says, "Look, I can reason to the point where I am utterly aware and reason convinces me that all I experience is my mind," then the next logical step would be to try to understand the deeper layers of the mind that are doing this, rather than denying it. Because that's what the analyst has to do. He has to find out what is this deeper unconscious in us that thinks these things into us so that we have to do them, have to live them. That's what I meant when I said sincerity is the foundation of personality and this shows up especially when you're involved in philosophy. You make one wrong turn and the whole of the rest of the way is going to be wrong. This happens again and again. I know this sounds abstract, but to me it's more concrete than the concrete floor I'm standing on.

S: Would you say that this change of attitude, where you take responsibility for your life, is one of the narrow pathways that you have to get through in order to get an insight into mentalism?

Anthony: Yes, to take responsibility for what you're thinking.

S: Don't we generally know more than we let come up to the surface because we are afraid to take this responsibility?

Anthony: I'm pretty sure that's so. Take, for instance, a man like Freud. He didn't believe in mystical experience, he said, because *he* never had any. But he was a very learned man. He was well versed in many languages, and he had quite an education. Now, am I going to believe that Freud really believed that there is no such thing as mystical experience, that he was being intellectually honest? No, I'm going to suspect that he was willingly practicing self-deception.

S: But isn't that the way most of us are?

Anthony: After a while you'll see that what I mean when I say "intellectual dishonesty" can be brought down to the very primitive level of saying that much of our life is a constant lying to ourselves.

The fundamental and crucial thing about understanding what all of this is about is that really thinking has become quite crucial. The very definition of man, *manas*, is mind, to think. These are things, of course, that you study as you go into and try to understand these doctrines. I think you'll see them for yourself gradually as you go along. You'll get sudden insights and illuminations and you'll let them guide you. They'll take you far. Until people learn to think, they're not worthy of the name of human being.

Another nice thing in PB's writings is the way he points out that you have to experience the vacuum mind but you also have to learn to think, and to think so hard that you could understand. You have to be able to concentrate with thought and you have to be able to concentrate without thought. It's the combination of these two that is going to give you that total global philosophic understanding you need. If you take just one or the other you're going to always end up in this kind of neurotic situation.

You could see how dangerous it would be to tell a person who is at a lower level of evolutionary development to stop thinking. I wouldn't tell such a person to stop thinking. I'd tell him to go on thinking, but I'd tell him, "Take out a little time every day and don't think." But to tell him not to think, or to stop thinking, would be a catastrophe for his development. You tell a person not to think when he's at the level where it's meaningful in terms of the philosophical perspective. In other words, he's at a certain level of development where thought has to destroy itself in order to achieve identity with being. But you don't tell a person that when he's not anywhere near that goal.

S: You have to understand what thinking is all about, what it means to really think.

Anthony: Yes. There is no way around it. You are going to have to use your brains to the utmost. Don't think that they went through all this trouble of creating the brain so that you don't use it! I mean, if you don't walk, for example, then after a couple of months your muscles get atrophied and you can't walk. And if you don't use your head, your brains, after a couple of months that gets atrophied, you can't think. No, it's meant to be used.

S: *Would you say that the creative power of thought comes from a higher level, but the form it takes is from the ego level? What it creates is due to the form . . .*

Anthony: To the way you channelize it, yes. Mind is creative, but you have to watch what you're creating, you have to channel it properly. You can do something about the power. You can increase the power more and more by contemplation. The man who has contemplated a great deal has tremendous power. I'm not talking about evil men. The mind has power and you can tap that power. The deeper your contemplative states go, the more power becomes available to you. A man of knowledge is also a man of power.

Supplementary Reading Material

This list is not intended to be complete or exhaustive, but simply a brief selection of books related to themes in this volume that Anthony Damiani recommended or that his students have found particularly valuable.

Meditation—General Guides and Inspiration

Brunton, Paul

Early writings: 1) *The Secret Path*, 2) *Discover Yourself*, 3) *The Quest of the Overself*

Posthumously published: *The Notebooks of Paul Brunton*, Volume 4 Part 1 (*Meditation*), and Volume 15 Part 1 (*Advanced Contemplation*)

Western Mysticism and Mystics

Brother Lawrence, *The Practice of the Presence of God*

Eckhart, Meister, *Sermons & Treatises*

French, R.M. (trans.), *The Way of the Pilgrim*

Saint Teresa of Avila, *The Interior Castle*

Underhill, Evelyn, *Mysticism*

Oriental Meditation Methods

Dalai Lama, H.H. XIV, *Kindness, Clarity and Insight*. Chapters on "Meditation" and "Aum Mani Padme Hum"

Osborne, Arthur (ed.), *The Collected Works of Ramana Maharshi*. Chapter on "Who Am I?"

Suzuki, Shunryu, *Zen Mind, Beginner's Mind*

Taimni, I.K., 1) *Glimpses into the Psychology of Yoga*, 2) *The Science of Yoga*

On How Knowledge Arises, the Nature of Mind

Berkeley, George, *Three Dialogues between Hylas and Philonous*

Brunton, Paul

Early writings: 1) *The Hidden Teaching Beyond Yoga,* 2) *The Wisdom of the Overself*

Posthumously published: *The Notebooks of Paul Brunton,* Volume 13 Part 3 (*Mentalism*)

Guenther, Herbert, *Mind in Tibetan Buddhism*

Lives of Sages

Brunton, Paul

Early writings: *A Search in Secret India*

Posthumously published: *The Notebooks of Paul Brunton,* Volume 8 and Volume 16 Part 1 (*World-Mind in Individual Mind*)

Maharshi, Ramana, *Talks with Sri Ramana Maharshi*

Nikhilananda, trans., *The Gospel of Sri Ramakrishna*

On the Ego and Vasanas

Brunton, Paul, *The Notebooks of Paul Brunton,* Volume 6 Part 1 (*The Ego*)

Eliade, Mircea, *Yoga: Immortality and Freedom.* Chapter 1, pp. 31–46.

Jung, C.G., *Collected Works,* Volume 8, "On the Nature of the Psyche"

Astrology

Hall, M.P., *The Philosophy of Astrology*

Philosophy, Western Thinkers

Joad, C.E.M., *Guide to Philosophy*

Philosophy, Spiritual and Practical

Brunton, Paul, *The Notebooks of Paul Brunton,* Volume 13 Part 2 (*What Is Philosophy?*)

Deck, John, *Nature, Contemplation and the One*

Emerson, R.W., *Essays,* particularly "Self-Reliance" and "The Oversoul"

Nikhilananda, trans., *Bhagavad Gita*

Plato, *The Republic,* Books 6 and 7

Plotinus, *The Enneads*

Suzuki, D.T., *Zen and Japanese Culture*

Music

Here is a selection of some of the Western musical pieces Anthony played before group meditations or used as sources of inspiration. Some are quiet, others are soaring; some are mysterious or profound.

Bach, J.S.
St. John Passion (especially last part)
St. Matthew Passion (especially last part)
Mass in B minor
Passacaglia and Fugue in C minor for Organ
Toccata and Fugue in D minor for Organ
Cello Suites no. 5 and no. 6
Chromatic Fantasy and Fugue in D minor

Barber, Samuel
Adagio for Strings

Beethoven, Ludwig van
String Quartet no. 15, third movement
String Quartet no. 16, third movement
Grosse Fugue (both the orchestral and the quartet versions)
Piano Sonatas nos. 21, 29, 30, 31, 32
Missa Solemnis
Fantasy in C for Piano, Chorus, and Orchestra

Bruckner, Anton
Symphony no. 8, third and fourth movements

Chopin, Fréderic
Nocturnes

Dvorak, Anton
String Quartet no. 6 in F, third movement

Serenade in E for Strings
Requiem
Symphony no. 8, second and third movements

Elgar, Edward
Serenade in E for Strings
Elegy

Fauré, Gabriel
Requiem

Franck, Cesar (organ music)
Pièce Héroique
Pastorale
Fantasy in A

Gliére, Reinhold
Symphony no. 3, "Ilya Murometz"

Hanson, Howard
Symphony no. 2 ("Romantic"), second and third movements

Hovhaness, Alan
Mysterious Mountain

Holst, Gustav
The Planets

Liszt, Franz
Dante Symphony, last movement
Transcendental Etudes nos. 10, 11, 12
Pilgrimages for piano

Mahler, Gustav
Das Lied von der Erde
Songs from Ruckert
Symphonies nos. 2, 3 (fourth movement, vocal), 4 (third and fourth movements), and 5 (fourth movement)

Messaien, Oliver
Quartet for the End of Time

Mozart, Wolfgang Amadeus
String Quintet in G minor (second, third, fourth movements)
String Quintet in C (third movement)
Requiem
Piano Concerto no. 21 (second movement)

Prokofiev, Sergei
Violin Concertos nos. 1 and 2, last movement of each

Alexander Nevsky, "Field of the Dead"

Rachmaninoff, Sergei
Piano Concerto no. 3, last movement
Vesper Mass
Suite for Two Pianos, opus 5
Rhapsody on a Theme by Paganini

Respighi, Ottorino
Ancient Airs and Dances
The Pines of Rome

Schubert, Franz
String Quintet in C, second movement
String Quartets 13 and 14
Piano Sonata in D, opus 960
Nocturne
Symphony no. 9, first and second movements

Shostakovitch, Dimitri
Symphony no. 11, first movement
Symphony no. 13, first movement
Symphony no. 15, ending
The Gadfly, "Introduction to the Dance," and "Romance"
Piano Concerto no. 2, third movement
Violin Concerto

Sibelius, Jean
The Swan of Tuonela
Pohola's Daughter
Symphony no. 3, second movement
Symphony no. 4, third movement
Symphony no. 5
Violin Concerto

Strauss, Richard
Four Last Songs

Vaughan Williams, Ralph
Variations on a Theme by Thomas Tallis
Mass in G Minor
The Lark Ascending
Symphonies nos. 2 and 6

Verdi, Guiseppe
Requiem

Walton, William
  Balshazzar's Feast

Wagner, Richard
  Parsifal

Index

A

B

C

D

E

F

G

H

I

J

K

L

M

N

O

P

Q

R

Y

Z